The Government and Politics

Aiming to contribute to the reader's greater understanding of Lebanese government and politics, this book provides a comprehensive examination of the origin, development, and institutionalization of sectarian consociationalism in Lebanon.

A recurrent proposition advanced in this book is that Lebanese sectarian consociationalism has been both a cure and a curse in the formulation of political settlements and institution building. On the one hand, and in contrast to many surrounding Arab regimes, consociational arrangements have provided the country with a relative democratic political life. A limited government with a strong confessional division of power and a built-in checks-and-balances mechanism has prevented the emergence of dictatorship or monarchy. On the other hand, a chronically weak state has complicated efforts toward nation building in favor of sectarian fragmentation, external interventions, and strong polarization that periodically brought the country to the verge of total collapse and civil war.

While examining Lebanese sectarian politics of conflict and concession during different historic junctures, many revelations are made that underlie the role of domestic and international forces shaping the country's future. Presenting an implicit description of the power and functions of the various branches of government within the context of sectarian consociationalism, this book is an important introductory text for students of Lebanese politics, and Middle Eastern politics more broadly.

Imad Salamey is an Associate Professor of Political Science and International Affairs at the Lebanese American University. His research interests focus on topics of democratic transition, power sharing, Islamist movements, and governance in Lebanon and the Middle East. His most recent article publications include *The Collapse of Middle Eastern Authoritarianism* and *Democratic Transition and Sectarian Populism: The Case of Lebanon*.

The Government and Politics of Lebanon

Imad Salamey

Routledge
Taylor & Francis Group
LONDON AND NEW YORK

First published 2014
by Routledge
2 Park Square, Milton Park, Abingdon, Oxon OX14 4RN

Simultaneously published in the USA and Canada
by Routledge
711 Third Avenue, New York, NY 10017

Routledge is an imprint of the Taylor & Francis Group, an informa business

British Library Cataloguing in Publication Data
A catalogue record for this book is available from the British Library

Library of Congress Cataloging in Publication Data
A catalog record for this book has been requested

ISBN: 978-0-415-63687-2 (hbk)
ISBN: 978-0-415-63688-9 (pbk)
ISBN: 978-0-203-74642-4 (ebk)

Typeset in Times New Roman
by FiSH Books Ltd, Enfield

MIX
Paper from
responsible sources
FSC
www.fsc.org   FSC® C013056

Printed and bound in Great Britain by
TJ International Ltd, Padstow, Cornwall

To my Wife and Son
Maysoun and Safi
Who dearly love Lebanon

Contents

PART III
Political institutions   **127**

List of illustrations

Figures

Tables

Maps

Boxes

Acknowledgements

The contributions of many students, research assistants, interims, and colleagues are responsible for bringing this book to life. For several years, students of Lebanese politics have helped turn my classes into a forum for debates and discussions. The fact that the classroom often exemplified the greater Lebanese plurality, encompassing students from all regional, sectarian, economic, and political backgrounds, enriched the intellectual deliberation and exchange of ideas. Students often pointed to youth aspirations and visions. They often held common and, at other times, antagonizing aspirations for a responsive and representative government. Their views echo the many topics and issues addressed in this book.

Foreword

Why Lebanese politics and government?

The ancient political question regarding the best form of government continues to puzzle the minds of contemporary political thinkers. The choice has proven increasingly critical to the survival of nations as more countries have begun their political journeys toward democracy. The fact that societies and nations vary by historic, geographic, economic, religious, regional, cultural, and racial peculiarities has required delicate consideration in the formulation of political choices. Indeed, the global diversity of nations and societies has rendered the choice of governance to be among the most critical to make in determining the existence and tranquility of nations.

Political experiences have taught us the grave consequences that await nations when governance choices are made without cultural and political considerations. Many multi-ethnic, post-colonial states in Africa and the Middle East, among others, have suffered the consequences of ill-founded governing institutions. In 1994, the Hutu-dominated Rwandan government provoked a campaign of ethnic cleansing that resulted in the massacre of more than one million Rwandan Tutsis. In South Africa, the system of apartheid led to racial segregation and eventually to racial and ethnic conflicts throughout the post-colonial period. In fact, the governing choice for a plural society has proven to be among the most crucial political decisions to make particularly in divisive, plural, and transitional societies.

Democratic consociationalism, among others, has been proposed as a suitable form of governance for societies that are deeply divided along ethnic, linguistic, religious, cultural, and racial lines. In 1943, Lebanon became one of the earliest states to adopt consociationalism. This resulted in mixed outcomes: on the one hand, and compared with other co-Arab states, consociationalism has provided the country with an exceptional democratic political life. It has resulted in a limited government with a strong confessional division of power and a built-in checks-and-balances mechanism, rendering impossible the emergence of dictatorship or monarchy. On the other hand, the many weaknesses of the state have undermined nation building in favor of sectarian fragmentation and strong polarization that periodically brought the country to the verge of total collapse and civil war. Whether the Lebanese form of democratic consociationalism is an appropriate governing model for a divided society continues to puzzle political scientists and divide them between enthusiasts and critics.

What is evident, however, is that studies of contemporary Lebanese consociationalism have lacked systematic and comprehensive evaluations. This is obviously because of the different interpretations, a fact that has prevented Lebanon from adopting a unified history textbook. This book aims to take on the daunting task of providing the first comprehensive scholarly based examination of contemporary Lebanese politics and government, knowing in advance that this may stir both praise and criticism. But perhaps it is only through this instigated inquisition that research can progress and scholars can magnify their inquiries to improve interpretations.

It shall be noted throughout this book that the study of Lebanese politics and government is unique in various ways, most importantly because of the fact that it continues to evolve around the struggle of state and nation building. A century-old protracted national identity crisis has kept the Lebanese divided over the role and function of the state. The result is the emergence of a dynamic polity contested by a static state institution, rendering the study of Lebanese politics and government in permanent flux. Indeed, a foreign observer could note that Lebanese politics is vibrant, constantly changing, and critically intertwined with global developments. No country as small as Lebanon has persistently attracted world attention and intervention. The country's charming nature, cultural and religious diversity, relative liberalism, strategic location, and global accessibility have captivated foreign imaginations. During its internal strife and many crises, invasions, and wars, the stakes were heightened to implicate other countries, ideological struggles, East–West relations, and worldly religious coexistence. As a consequence, Lebanon has come to strongly implicate and to be implicated in regional and international politics.

Another apparent claim advanced in this book is that the Lebanese government is fundamentally static, standing in defiance of the social, political, and economic developments that have repeatedly stormed the country. The state's robustness is the outcome of a delicate sectarian balance of power that has opposed institutional modification. Fearing the loss of sectarian privileges, sectarian elites have obstructed genuine structural reforms, a reality that has prevented a national census from taking place since last officially recorded in 1932. The rigidity of the state institution has turned any effort for reform or change a conflict-ridden process leading to major outbreaks in communal violence.

To capture the political dynamic and institutional paralysis of the consociational state in Lebanon, this book is divided into several parts. Chapter 1 provides a general typology of political systems that are widely implemented in the world as a way of introducing the Lebanese consociational system and its rationale. Chapters 2–6 provide a general historic overview of Lebanese consociational politics. These chapters provide an examination of the general foundations of sectarian consociationalism as founded by the various pre- and post-independence power-sharing arrangements. They discuss sectarian politics of conflict and concession as well as the underlying domestic and international driving forces at different historic junctures. Chapters 7 to 9 analyze the contemporary politics of Lebanon, including the role played by foreign countries, sectarian groups, political leaders, political parties, and elections. Chapters 10–12 introduce the power-sharing arrangements as institutionalized by the consociational governments of Lebanon. They focus on the contemporary powers and functions of the different branches of government as well as their institutional manifestations of sectarian consociationalism. Chapter 13 concludes with prospects of the sectarian state in light of contemporary political changes and regional upheavals.

Hence, the aim of this book is to contribute to the reader's greater understanding of Lebanese politics and government. It seeks to instigate a dialogue among general readers and students about the nature of consociationalism and its governance suitability for plural and divided societies. Such a dialogue will not only help Lebanon to assert and/or revise its governing structure, but may very well assist similar states in the Middle East and elsewhere to establish an appropriate formulation of governance.

A note on the text

Text in bold indicates the first instance of a term which is explained in the glossary of key terms and concepts at the end of the book. Further references and useful websites are also listed by chapter at the end of the book.

Imad Salamey
Beirut, April 25, 2013

Part I

Political and historic context of Lebanese sectarian consociationalism

1   World democracies and Lebanese consociationalism

This chapter examines different political systems around the world, introducing the particular form of governance established in Lebanon. Different ideological, federal and consociational democracies are examined; in turn, case studies are presented to better inform debate. Lebanon's consociational power-sharing form of government is explored through the social foundations that shape the political institutions of the country.

Politics of democratic systems

Of approximately 200 countries in the world, 82 are considered fully or partially democratic. Most of them share social and political practices and traditions, yet their governments and political systems vary. In general, the variation is distinguished by their social dynamics being framed either by ideological, regional, or communal politics. Ideological politics play a central role in the establishment of representative governments based on **majoritarian** principles. Regional and communal-based politics, on the other hand, give rise to governments which are based on loose decentralized power structures capable of accommodating the diverse interests of social groups in the country. Thus, each particular form of democracy is largely determined by the way in which the government and society are intertwined.

Ideological democracies

In an ideological democracy, the population is typically cohesive in its ethnic, racial, religious, linguistic, historic, and geographic makeup. The main aspects of political quarrels are centered on economic and social policies, the role of private versus public sectors in the economy, security strategies, and freedoms. Politics is played out by different political actors, such as groups and parties that compete to gain the support of the nation's majority and achieve an ideologically driven **policy agenda**. "A majority rule with a minority opposition" characterizes the basic framework of government in ideological democracies.

Mainly ideological democracies are parliamentary with variations in **electoral systems**. Some ideological democracies implement **first-past-the-post** or winner-takes-all, whereas others implement two-ballot or proportionality in their electoral systems. Despite differences, establishing government by a majority-elected party or a coalition of parties is common among all ideological democracies. Owing to majority governance requirements, the number of competing parties is usually reduced to a minimum. Only a few parties are able to obtain sufficient public votes or reach thresholds to win elections. As they gain public confidence through their performances during subsequent elections, parties become fewer, larger, more dominant, and more confined to profound **ideological platforms**. Competing electoral alliances are formed during elections in order to win most popular votes. After elections, a governing majority coalition is formed aiming at implementing an ideological program, usually called government guidelines. Minority coalition(s) or party/ies take on the role of opposing government policies in a struggle to win popular majority and flip the power in subsequent elections in their favor.

It is important to note that in ideological democracies the "minority" refers to the political "losers" in an election who fail to reach the minimum winning thresholds to govern, and does not imply an ethnic, racial, religious, sectarian, or a regional communal constituency. Minority and majority in an ideological democracy are strictly quantified numerically by the count of public votes gained by a political party or a coalition of parties to form a government (majority) or stand in the opposition (minority).

In typical ideological democracies, the path toward **nationhood** has been consolidated through a long historic process of mutually reinforcing experiences between nation building and the development of representative governing institutions resulting in a common **national identity**, the emergence of shared

---

Ideological democracy: Portugal

A good example of an ideological system using two-ballot and proportionality in its electoral system is Portugal. In Portugal, political power is exercised by Portuguese citizens through "universal, equal, direct, secret, and periodic elections". Presidential elections are held by popular vote every five years. Failure by a leading candidate to receive an absolute majority of the vote during the first round of voting will lead to runoff elections (second ballot). The parliamentary or "Assembly of the Republic" elections are held every four years, using the d'Hondt method of **proportional representation**. This form of voting is based on the highest average method, favoring large political parties by awarding them a greater percentage of assembly seats than the percentage of votes that they have actually won. In theory, smaller parties are ensured seats because there is no minimum requirement of votes that a party must win in order to become a member of the assembly. Nevertheless, Portuguese governments are always formed through coalitions, and parties that are not part of any coalition get no parliamentary seats.

political values and practices, and a sense of loyalty towards the state. Thus, majoritarian ideological democracies have been nurtured in **homogeneous societies**, where communally based **cleavages**, such as ethnicity or regionalism, have not been a major determinant of political mobilizations. In most of these countries, such as in Western Europe, ideological diversity is reflected by a moderate political landscape.

Federal democracies

A federal democracy may arise out of practical necessity in countries that stretch over relatively large territorial expanses where regional, linguistic, religious, or cultural groups are instinctively separated by clear geographic demarcations. **Communal solidarism** distinguishes the politics of these countries (e.g. India and Canada). Political division runs along communal lines, with groups competing over federal resources and political power to preserve their own **autonomous rights** and privileges. National identity is formulated loosely in order to accommodate countries' plurality.[1]

In federal democracies, the constitution represents a contractual arrangement binding distinctive groups within the nation. The constitution lays down clear power demarcations that guarantee a balance between the local and federal powers.

Political parties seek to mobilize local support in national politics. In most federal democracies, parties are assembled to encompass the interests of many localities. As a consequence, each party acts as a broad coalition of local interests (political parties in the USA or in Russia). This fact has provided parties with the ability to stretch over vast regions, win elections, and form a **single-party government** (Russia, Germany, USA, and India). Winning elections is determined by the political parties' ability to gain the majority of local support. Party politics is turned **centrifugal** to satisfy the diverse local interests and to gain the widest possible support. Owing to the difficulty associated with the ability of small local parties to win elections in large and diverse constituencies, local groups resort to establishing wide coalitions to support a single party that is viable to win national election. As a consequence, partisan fragmentation is minimized, resulting in the emergence of fewer, larger, and even more dominant parties than those present in ideological democracies.

The federal government is established to manage local affairs through a decentralized power structure. **Autonomy politics** dominates national debates, with significant legislation and decision making occurring at the sub-national level, such as education management, policing, and cultural affairs.

Within a federal order, election winners form government, yet the minority is vested with substantial power to oppose and obstruct unfavorable decisions. The federal government is constrained by a set of constitutional rules that limit its ability to impose laws beyond the consensus of the groups. In strong decentralized states, each region or groups of regions in a province might be granted a **veto power** (Iraq). Veto power over federal decisions might also be granted to local authorities as a means of preserving autonomous rights. In contrast, restricted

Federal democracy: The Russian Federation

The Russian Federation is the largest country on Earth, with a population of over 150 million. Emerging from the collapse of the Soviet Union, Russia became embroiled in a series of political crises as well as military conflicts that erupted due to the ethnic diversity of the northern Caucuses. The adoption of a new constitution in December of 1993 essentially turned the country into a federal presidential republic.

Presidential elections require an outcome of 50% of the popular vote to be won by the leading candidate, while failure to acquire this percentage will lead to a runoff election between the two leading contenders. The president can run for inconsecutive six-year terms. The prime minister is also appointed by the president and is first in line to succeed the president in case of his death or resignation. Powerful Russian President Vladimir Putin assumed office in 2000 and, again, in 2012.

The country's parliament or the Russian Federal Assembly is divided into the lower and upper house. The lower house or the State Duma is the more powerful of the two. Nevertheless, its powers have been severely compromised. Previous privileges, such as the ability to force the resignation of the government, have been revoked. Even though the legislative body can express a vote of non-confidence in the ruling government by a majority vote of all of its 450 deputies, the president has the right to simply disregard the vote. In 2007, all seats became allocated in accordance with "proportional representation (with at least 7% of the vote to qualify for seats)" for a five-year term.

In 2011, the United Russia Party won the elections with 49.32% of the vote, taking 238 seats or 52.88% of the Duma seats. The Communist Party of the Russian Federation was placed second with 19.19% of the vote and 92 seats, while A Just Russia received 13.24% and 64 seats, with the Liberal Democratic Party of Russia getting 56 seats with 11.67% of the vote. Yabloko, Patriots of Russia and Right Cause were unable to secure the 7% election threshold.

The Russian Federation consists of 83 constituent units, which are also referred to as the "subjects of the Federation." There are six different types of constituent units: "Republics, territories, regions, federal cities, autonomous areas, and autonomous regions," the status of which is determined by the federal constitution and the regional charters. The federal system combines both ethnical and territorial components, and even though the units lack sovereign authority they enjoy a great deal of autonomy. The units are all recognized as self-governing, and while the federal law is superior, the local governments can create their own quasi-constitutions or charters and their own political institutions.

Source: Russian Law Online, www.russianlawonline.com/content/political-system-
    russia

decentralized arrangements require collectivity of states or regions to acquire veto power over major decision makings (such as the ramification of the constitution in USA or the inclusion of new states within the union in Iraq). In federal democracies, the power is further decentralized by a process of checks and balances that undermines the ability of the federal government to dominate local authorities.

Bicameralism is a typical legislative arrangement sought to balance the will of the popular and that of the local. The **judiciary** is usually strong and independent since it is not directly appointed by the **legislative branch** or subject to a direct popular election. The independent power of the judiciary is delegated by the constitution to provide the court with the ability to serve as an arbitrator in disputes between the localities. The **executive branch**, on the other hand, rests on the person of the president, the ultimate fusion of popular and local powers, particularly when directly elected (USA, Russia). Thus, federal democracies are typically presidential.

The main political rationality of the federal union is **collective security** and economic benefits. The federal government plays the role of a manager in economic, foreign, and security affairs. On the domestic level, federal authority arbitrates disputes between states and arranges for interstate trade and commerce. The federal institutions are typically supported by federal taxes collected from the general population. On the international level, federal authorities are often delegated the power of raising armies and security forces, managing trade, and establishing international agreements.

In sum, and in contrast to ideological democracies, federal democracies are established over significantly large geographic areas, divided by autonomous groups, and politically decentralized; governments are formed by a loosely qualified majority of localities.

Consociational democracies

Consociational democracies exist in relatively small states where societies are deeply divided among communal groups distinguished by strong linguistic, racial, religious, sectarian or tribal cleavages. National identity in these countries is deeply contested and political allegiance is fragmented along communal lines rather than being embedded in a single centralized national authority (Northern Ireland). One of the main attributes of societies under consociational democracies is the relative demographic and geographic mixing of groups in conjunction with the existence of salient and persisting communal identities. No clear geographic demarcations provide a single group with the ability to claim a distinctive autonomous region. The groups participate in all aspects of national life, yet such encounters are confined by communally established invisible social boundaries and restrictions (such as the prohibition – formal and non-formal – of intersectarian marriage). Despite deep divisions, resentments, and historic grievances the coexistence of groups is essential for mutual advantages and sustained presence.

Consociational democracies are often instituted because they are the most convenient for societies that lack the prerequisite for ideological or federal political arrangements. Most critically, identity politics overwhelm all aspects of social and political lives for groups living within close geographic proximity.

Political scientist Arendt Lijphart attributed to consociationalism the ability of preserving democracies within small, multi-ethnic, and plural societies through governments based on groups' power-sharing between elite cartels. According to Lijphart, four features characterize these power-sharing arrangements: a grand coalition, a mutual veto, proportional representation and segmental autonomy (Table 1.1).[2]

Thus, political parties in consociational democracies are numerous and tend to mirror the specific nature of divisions in society (e.g. ethnic/racial or religious/sectarian). Government requires a wide consensus; otherwise it can easily slip into repression by one communal group against another. Therefore, inclusive national, and sometimes grand winning coalitions, are established between parties in order to govern. A coalition cabinet (usually oversized) emerges out of a proportionally elected parliament, which reflects the different representative sizes of the communal groups. Grand coalitions are necessitated by the fact that each of the communal group is provided with a political veto power of some sort. The coalition establishes group consensus and undermines the use of veto power in the collective decision-making process. The veto power is typically granted to each group in a variety of ways. One possibility can be established by the number

Table 1.1 Characteristics of majoritarian vs. consensus democracy, as defined by Arendt Lijphart

Variable	*Democracy*	
	Majoritarian	*Consensus*
Concentration of executive power	One-party government	Multi-party coalitions
Legislative–executive relationship/dynamics	Dominance of the executive	Balance of power
Fragmentation of party system	Dominant two-party system	Multi-party system
Disproportionality of electoral system	Majoritarian/plurality electoral system	Proportional representation
Interest representation	Pluralism	(Neo-)Corporatism
Federalism	Unitarian state	Federal state
Division of legislative powers (no. of chambers/houses)	One chamber (unicameralism)	Two chambers (bicameralism)
Constitutional rigidity	Weak	Strong
Constitutional court	Weak	Strong
Autonomy of central bank	Not autonomous	Autonomous

Source: Lijphart, A. (1984) *Democracies: Patterns of Majoritarian and Consensus Government in Twenty-One Countries*. New Haven, CT: Yale University Press

Consociational democracy: Bosnia and Herzegovina

Bosnia and Herzegovina, having undergone a brutal civil war during the 1990s, has emerged with a complex political system. As a consociational democracy, the state is still very much divided and governed along ethnic lines. The country's leading political institutions are dissected in accordance to the previously agreed upon ethnic distribution formula outlined in the Dayton Peace Accord.

The Bosnian presidency is a tripartite one, with the president elected by popular vote for a four-year term. This three-member presidency consists of a Serb, a Croat and a Muslim (Bosniak) leader, rotating every eight months. The president is the head of state and his duties revolve mainly around foreign policy issues, such as international treaties.

The legislative branch, or the Parliamentary Assembly, is bicameral. It consists of the House of Representatives with its 42 members elected by proportional representation for four-year terms, and the House of the Peoples made up of 15 members elected by indirect vote to serve four-year terms. The 15 seats are distributed equally between the three main ethnic groups with five assigned to each. In the House of Representatives, 28 seats are allocated from the Federation of Bosnia and Herzegovina (Muslim, Croat), and 14 seats from the Republika Srpska (Serbian Republic).

The executive powers of the state lies in the hands of the Premier, who is nominated by the president and must be approved by the House of Representatives. The Council of Ministers and its chairman oversee all issues related to such matters as foreign, economic, and fiscal policies. The ministers that the Premier appoints are also subject to approval from the House of Representatives, and as the constitutional law indicates, no more than two-thirds of all ministers can be appointed from the same territory in the Federation.

The main political parties include the Party of BiH, Party of Democratic Action, Liberals of BiH, and the Serb Radical Party. For a population of less than four million, Bosnia has over 20 political parties, all of which are representatives only of their own ethnic group. After almost two decades since the war ended, Bosnia remains fragmented, and its ethnic tensions are still considered a serious issue for most of its citizens. With the autonomous Republika Srpska seeking independence from Bosnia and the inability of the Muslims and Croats to find common ground (except having a common enemy), the Serbs, the political, economic and social conditions of the state leave much to be desired. Perhaps these factors can be cited as reasons why the United Nations has created an extremely powerful judiciary in Bosnia, an unusual phenomenon for weak consociational states.

Source: European Forum for Democracy and Solidarity,
    www.europeanforum.net/country/bosnia_herzegovina

of ministerial posts allocated to every group that necessitate particular quorum for decisions to be taken. Another way is through the paralyzing powers granted to the head of key public posts as communally allocated or simply as the constitution declares. These various types of vetoes consolidate communal political powers and set clear legal and extra-legal demarcations between the groups as to preserve their autonomies while undermining the possibility of their respective domination or marginalization.

It should be noted at this point that two particular aspects most characterize consociationalism. First, the communal groups remain politically alarmed by each other and, thus, they enter into an unwavering struggle for power. Each group attempts to strike a coalition and to strengthen its power advantages and remain competitive. This, very often, leads communal groups to seek external support. The result is a vibrant and dynamic politics that touches on all levels of community life. Second, the distribution of power gained by the elite cartel becomes rigid and difficult to change. Any change in the political structure requires consociation and any single objection or veto by one group disrupts the process as a whole. Thus, institutional changes under consociationalism are very difficult if not sometimes impossible to achieve.

As a consequence, governmental institutions are weakened by a permanent process of stalemates over state structural reforms. At best, government institutions are transformed into cliental entities providing employment opportunities and services to the followers of the respective groups. The autonomous institutions of groups, such as schools and hospitals, grow in parallel, to subsidize for state weaknesses and consolidate the communalism of groups.

Lebanese consociationalism

Lebanon is a parliamentary democracy within the framework of consociationalism. The Lebanese sectarian state system is an example of a consociational political arrangement, as defined by Arendt Lijphart. There is no clear geographical demarcation between the country's 18 officially recognized sectarian communities who live side-by-side in a small 10,452 square kilometer region, deeply divided in terms of political orientations and national identity (i.e. fierce sectarian loyalties over and above a single and unifying national identity). A **history of intersectarian grievances** and conflicts has come to consolidate domestic divisions and to assert communal distinctiveness. A deeply divided sense of national identity for a population of four million residing over an extremely small stretch of land has ruled out the possibility of realizing either ideological/majoritarian democracy or federalism. Consociational power sharing has been implemented as the most viable and practical solution.

A major drawback of the consociational system is that it requires collective consensus and it can be easily obstructed by a single veto. Lijphart noted that "decision making that entails accommodation among all subcultures is a difficult process, and consociational democracies are always threatened by a degree of immobilism."[3]

Power sharing is most salient in the division between executive and legislative branches along sectarian lines. The highest offices of government are reserved for representatives from dominant religious communities, which are reflected in other key public positions. The Parliament Speaker's position is reserved to a Shi'ite, the Presidency to a Catholic Maronite, and the Prime Ministerial-ship to a Sunni. All parliamentary seats are distributed along sectarian groups according to a defined quota. The 128 seats are divided in half between Muslims and Christians, and distributed proportionally along the various sects within each confession. Powerful sectarian families serve as **cartels** and play a critical role in mobilizing votes for both local and parliamentary elections. Prominent families such as Jumblatt, Arslan, Al-Khazen, Jemayel, Al-Khalil, Frangieh, Al-Assad, Hamadeh, Slam, and Hariri are some of the few families that have provided political communal leadership. Some of these families are of post-independence and contemporary political relevance, and yet others are drawn from the country's feudal past. A multitude of domestic political parties (some even predating independence), which represent a broad spectrum of sectarian political orientations and ideologies, is considered as evidence of a deeply divided Lebanese national identity and polity. Most governments have been established based on the largest possible participation of main sectarian groups (grand coalition). The exclusion of any sectarian group from power is deemed as a violation of the national covenant and constitution. A sectarian civil status codes system, as expressed in the parallel religious court system with **jurisdictions** over marriage, divorce, custody, and inheritance laws, mark strong but invisible demarcations of communal sectarian autonomies.

Arendt Lijphart observed that "The stability of Lebanon is partly due to its productive economy and the social equilibrium it has maintained so far, but it may not be able to continue its successful consociational politics when the burdens on the system increase."[4] This has been repeatedly proven over the years, where despite social and economic developments in the 1960s, 1970s, and 2000s, sectarian competition over gains and resources led to a complete breakdown of the system. The Lebanese consociational system began to diverge from the type described by Lijphart. The control of sectarian elites over Lebanese society and government dramatically undermined political consociationalism in favor of linking communities within the dynamics of regional conflict and power struggle.

After all, Lebanon has a unique and complex geostrategic position in regional/international politics. On the regional level, foreign-power patronage of the different sects, compounded by a weak central state, has deepened the division of Lebanon's confessional communities; sectarian groups have been placed on opposing sides when confronting regional struggle, such as the Arab–Israeli conflict or the Iranian–Western confrontation.

Thus, the country's political track has been driven by a two-level power struggle: Domestic, which pits sectarian groups vying for political dominance against each other, and regional, which positions sectarian groups in proxy roles played out within the larger context of regional power struggle.[5] Therefore, as geodemographic politics evolve, so does the dynamic of Lebanese sectarianism and its corresponding confessional power-sharing arrangement. This interlocking of domestic and regional politics has been most evident in corresponding shifts in the Lebanese political scenery during three key historic confessional arrangements expressed in the **National Pact** (1943), the Taef Accord (1989), and the Doha Agreement (2008).

In the forthcoming chapters, I discuss the political circumstances that brought out these different national agreements and established the various forms of sectarian consociationalism in Lebanon. It should be noted that each one of these agreements has come to characterize the domestic sectarian power struggle while being strongly shaped by regional and international dynamics. This serves as a prelude to the claim advanced in this book, and demonstrated throughout, that Lebanese consociationalism has been reformulated under three different republics as established by these agreements. The latest stage that characterizes contemporary Lebanese politics and its prospects in light of the contemporary regional political influx and upheavals are described in the later chapters of this book.

Accordingly, four main conclusions can be drawn about Lebanese consociationalism. First, it is a power-sharing formula that is conductive to foreign interventions and, thus, its fate is constantly determined by surrounding regional circumstances. Second, it activates a vibrant and competitive identity politics that quickly mobilizes and polarizes communal groups. Third, it institutionalizes power sharing that renders its reformulation extremely difficult to attain without a major clash. Fourth, it sets in motion a sectarian process of communal checks and balances that rule out dictatorship in favor of a competitive political process.

Summary

This chapter has provided an overview of three forms of democratic rule and described the specific state or societal conditions within which they best operate. In ideological systems, with either proportional or winner-take-all electoral systems, the "majority rule with minority rights" political arrangement reflects the fact that political and social divisions are, for the most part, socioeconomic (class) or ideological in nature, as opposed to ethnic or geographic. Power struggles in these democracies, between relatively homogeneous groups, occur over the control of society's political and economic resources. Conversely, in semi-democratic systems consensus or power-sharing arrangements form the basis of government. In geo-systems, society is physically divided across a large territory into distinctive, self-contained cleavages – be they linguistic or religious. The distribution of power, along geopolitical lines, between the central government and the component states/cantons/provinces ensures that the different groups are able to coexist peacefully by granting each of them a degree of local autonomy. However, in ethno-sectarian systems, which are usually small, deeply divided, multi-ethnic states, no geopolitical borders exist between the different racial, religious, ideological, tribal communities within which a de facto balance of power can be established. Thus, to prevent conflict and to preserve democracy in these complex, highly fragmented societies, the "boundaries" of power sharing are constructed at the institutional level. This is the basis of Lebanese sectarian consociational choice.

References

1   Føllesdalm, A. (2008) Federalism. *The Stanford Encyclopedia of Philosophy*, Available online at http://plato.stanford.edu/archives/fall2008/entries/federalism/
2   Lijphart, A. (1977) *Democracy in Plural Societies: A Comparative Exploration*. New Haven: Yale University Press, p. 25.
3   Lijphart, A. (1969) 'Consociational Democracy' *World Politics*, 21 (2): 218.
4   Lijphart A. (1969) 'Consociational Democracy' *World Politics*, 21 (2): 219.
5   Kerr, M. (2000) *Imposing Power-Sharing: Conflict and Coexistence in Northern Ireland and Lebanon*. Dublin: Irish Academic Press.

2 Origin of Lebanese political sectarianism

This chapter summarizes the modern political origins of Lebanese political sectarianism, dating back to the insurrection of Mount Lebanon in 1841. A chronological account of European involvement and the development of Lebanon being partitioned into two administrative areas between the Maronite Christians and Druze is given. The evolution of the first constitutional arrangement – the Organic Laws of Lebanon (*Règlement Organique du Liban*) – is discussed, illustrating the early political **institutionalization** of sectarian division. Different periods in the development of the region are discussed, with reference to the period of modernization and prosperity (1861–1914), the League of Nations Mandate (1922–1943), and the nature of the Lebanese sectarian demography under the Mandate.

Driving forces for system change

In Lebanon, with its small, densely populated geostrategically significant territory and heterogeneous, communally divided society, consociationalism has been presented as an appropriate form of government. Within such a system, internal sectarian differences can be resolved. Even before the establishment of the Republic of Lebanon in 1943, consociationalism, also referred to as **confessionalism**, has been the preferred political/institutional arrangement within which sectarian competition for socioeconomic and political power was managed. The evolution of geopolitical confessional arrangements in Lebanon throughout its modern history has been driven by internal political demography on one hand, and external events on the other, namely the strategic regional proxy role played out by sectarian groups. Inter and intra-geopolitical changes have exerted tremendous pressure for the rearrangement of power sharing and the reordering of the Lebanese state consociationalism. Such a dynamic began following the early foundation of sectarian-based power-sharing arrangements in Mount Lebanon during the eighteenth century.

Early sectarian struggle and European interventions

Lebanon became part of the Ottoman Empire in the early sixteenth century. Ottoman rule continued for three centuries, while local groups, particularly the

Druze of Mount Lebanon, were granted semi-autonomous rule. Areas outside Mount Lebanon fell under various administrative controls, particularly that of Damascus and local feudal families, who took on tax collection in favor of the Ottoman Sultan.

Under Ottoman rule, Mount Lebanon developed economic and religious ties with Europe. This was largely facilitated by an existing Catholic Maronite population, which sought closer ties with Rome, and protectionism by France. Open to the West, it became a hotbed of political strife between various foreign nations, including France, Russia, and Britain. These powerful colonial countries assumed the protection of certain ethnic religious groups, with France supporting the Christian Maronites. Domestic sectarian tensions and external meddling exacerbated tensions between the various communities in Mount Lebanon. In 1841, insurrection in Mount Lebanon marked the first major, politically significant, sectarian conflict. While several factors contributed to the civic violence that exploded between the Druze and Maronite sects of the mountain, it was mainly the end result of decades of internal social strife.[1] External forces certainly played an important role in catalyzing the conflict, owing to Lebanon's connection with the "**Eastern Question**." However, it would be erroneous to categorize the situation in Mount Lebanon in 1841 as a mere response to imperial **balance-of-power politics**.

Mount Lebanon, which was traditionally a Druze stronghold, was inhabited by close to half a million people.[2] The demographic situation was fluid and it changed over the years as the demand for labor led Druze landowners to recruit Maronite peasant farm workers into the area. As time passed, they grew in number, as did their influence. Thus, the Maronite presence became regarded as a threat to the already waning dominance of the Druze over the mountain and its administration. Hence, their communities often became the targets of vengeful attacks by the Druze. The Maronite and Druze peasantry, in turn, rebelled against the oppression and injustice imposed upon them by the **Ottoman feudal system**, and they often faced severe repression by the local ruling feudalists for doing so.[3] At the same time, both groups of impoverished peasants competed for ever-scarcer territory and resources. The ensuing "tit-for-tat" violence between the sects made the situation in Mount Lebanon extremely volatile and unstable.[4]

Notables from both sects exploited the growing social unrest to garner European patronage against the hated Ottoman administration over Mount Lebanon by inciting violence against "the other". The French seized the opportunity to support their Maronite Catholic co-religionists under the pretext of safeguarding Roman Catholicism in the Levant, while the British, arch rivals of the French in the Middle East, supported the Druze. The encroachment of France on Ottoman domains since the Napoleonic invasion of Egypt in 1798 led the Sultan to also side with the British (and the Druze) against France (and the Maronites), with an aim of weakening Lebanese autonomy.

Contextualizing European involvement in Lebanon

European involvement in Lebanon is largely attributed to the Eastern Question, dealing with the breakdown of the Ottoman empire, and the safeguarding of great power interests/rivalry in the region. Germany, Italy, Britain, France, and Russia all competed for influence in the regions. The religious connection was the most dominant pretext, with French safeguarding the Roman Catholics (Maronites). This led to the British counterbalance in support of the Druze. Russia also stepped in to protect the interests of the Orthodox Christians and to stop the trend of conversion to Protestant and Catholic confessions. Britain was resultantly further motivated to limit Russian influence.

The French means of dominating the region moved beyond religious and political to the economic sphere. The French had already established strong economic interests, with a view of laying claim to the region at the anticipated collapse of the empire. The extent of French investment is well illustrated by the fact that French financiers controlled 62–69% of the Ottoman public debt before the onset of World War I. The Ottoman state bank was owned fully by French and British capital. As a resultant, the European powers retained control over utilities, industries, the railway, and the tobacco monopoly. With the ownership of capital, French influence expanded over coal, silver and copper mines, as well as land and mortgage issues. The basis of most of these economic activities was the establishment of the railroads, widening its economic sphere of influence. Germany began to have a larger share in Ottoman economic spoils through exports tripling between 1900 and 1911. Britain followed in third place in terms of European investment.

Two qaim-maqamats

The climax of the communal violence occurred with a massacre of Christians by the Druze at Deir al Qamar in 1842, while the fleeing survivors were slaughtered by Ottoman regulars.

Thus, with British support to restore peace and order, the Ottoman Sultan finally intervened. On January 1, 1843, Mount Lebanon was partitioned between the warring factions into two jurisdictions, a Maronite area in the north and a Druze area in the south, divided by the Beirut–Damascus road. It was hoped that the partitioning the area into two administrative districts would dampen the rising tension between the two most important religious sects. Both districts were accountable to the Ottoman governor of Saida, residing in Beirut. This marked the first sectarian geopolitical division of Lebanon (see Map 2.1).

However, the so-called "double *qaim-maqamat*" (administrative district) was arguably a recipe for disaster. A major problem with this arrangement in practice was that separating the two belligerent communities from each other proved

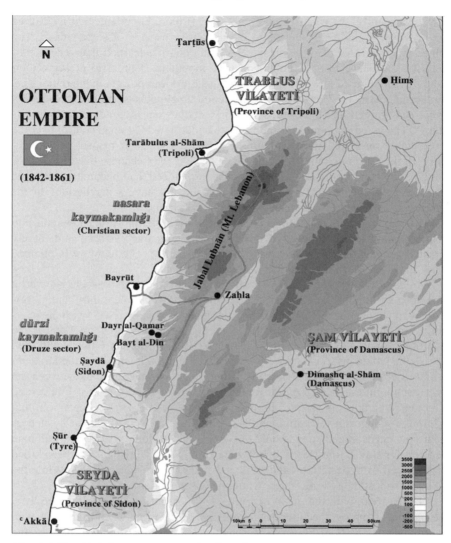

Map 2.1 The Christian *nasara kaymakamligi* (district) and Druze *duzi kaymakamligi*, 1842–1861, with transliterated Arabic place names, and Ottoman administrative units transliterated from modern Turkish.

Source: Garnand, B. (2006) *The Use of Phoenician Human Sacrifice in the Formation of Ethnic Identities*. PhD dissertation, University of Chicago

almost impossible. The numerous mixed villages in each of the *qaim-maqamats* made the prevention of resurfacing violence a practically and politically complicated undertaking. Furthermore, this solution did not take into account the underlying economic and social changes at the root of the tensions.[5]

Consequently, the rivalries of France and Britain, complemented by Russia and Austria, significantly bolstered the disruptive aspects of sectarianism. The elites on both sides of the Lebanese sectarian conflict learned that a degree of unrest would have to be maintained in the mountain in order to preserve their status as the favored local clients of the major European powers in the region (i.e. France and Britain). Thus, the *perioikoi* (communal pockets) within each district were easy targets through which violent sectarian reprisals could be "encouraged". The *qaim-maqamats'* instability also undermined Ottoman control over the area, which furthered European strategic interests via their respective "protection" of the Maronites and Druze in the Levant. As the Lebanese historian Kamal Salibi aptly once said: "The Lebanese question, indeed, had become so involved that scarcely an incident took place which did not have repercussions in the chanceries of Europe, particularly in London and Paris."[6]

The major powers' attempt to create peace by dividing Mount Lebanon into Christian and Druze spheres of influence was temporary at best, and merely created geographic powerbases for the warring parties. The region was plunged back into full-blown civil conflict within just 15 years.

Not only was the 1859–1860 war in Mount Lebanon an inter-sectarian war, it was also an intra-sectarian conflict between the Maronite peasantry and clergy, who revolted against the feudal class. This came to an end in 1858, with the overthrow of the old feudal system of taxes and **levies**. Backed by France, the Maronites openly rebelled against the over-extended Ottoman Empire, and tried to use the Ottomans' relative decline to assert their dominance over the Druze in Mount Lebanon. This exacerbated religious and economic tensions between the two communities. Taking full advantage of British support against France and Ottoman attempts to restore control in Lebanon, the Druze began burning Maronite villages in retaliation and a fearful siege of Deir al Qamar ensued. A Maronite garrison managed to hold out against Druze forces backed by Ottoman soldiers for almost four weeks, but by June 1860, 8,000 Christians had been killed or had died from destitution and another 100,000 were left homeless. While the Druze also lost many lives, their "triumph" was remarkable.

In July 1860, with the threat of European intervention on behalf of the local belligerents looming, the Ottoman government tried to end the conflict. However, it was Napoleon III of France – in sending 7,000 troops to Beirut to back the Maronites – who helped bring an end to the sectarian strife and thus impose a new political power-sharing arrangement in Lebanon.

Mutasarrifiyah of Mount Lebanon

On June 9, 1861, the **Organic Laws for Lebanon** were signed in Istanbul – a constitution that remained in effect until the outbreak of World War I in 1914. This replaced the *qaim-maqamats* and was further revised in 1864. The Mutasarrifiyah of Mount Lebanon referred to the new autonomous territory established by the Organic Laws. Druze de facto control of the territory was recognized, and the Maronites were forced to retreat to a semi-autonomous enclave around Mount Lebanon. The Maronites, in what came to be known as the Province of Lebanon, occupied the ancient territorial jurisdiction of Lebanon, which was reduced in half. It was stripped of the agricultural heartland of the Bekaa and Wadi-Al-Taim, and also isolated from the ports of Beirut and Saida, and major communication routes. Beirut, Saida. and Tripoli were put under direct Ottoman rule (see Map 2.2). This was a deliberate division by the external powers

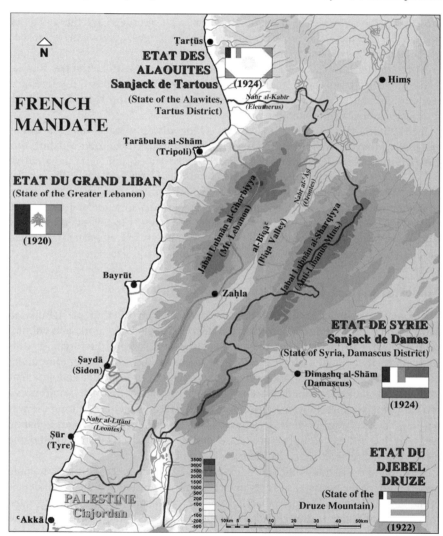

Map 2.2 The Ottoman Empire, *mutaṣarafīya Jabal Lubnān* (Autonomous Province of Mount Lebanon), 1861–1915, with transliterated Arabic place names, and Ottoman administrative units transliterated from modern Turkish

Source: Garnand, B. (2006) *The Use of Phoenician Human Sacrifice in the Formation of Ethnic Identities*. PhD dissertation, University of Chicago

to retain the Christian area and reduce the likelihood of inter-sectarian conflicts.

The Province of Lebanon enjoyed a semi-autonomous status, unique at a time when the Ottoman powers were attempting to centralize the whole Empire. The entire Mutasarrifiyah was, however, placed under direct rule of the governor of Damascus, and carefully watched by the Ottoman Empire. By Ottoman orders, the governor was to be a non-Lebanese, non-partisan, non-Maronite Christian appointed by the sultan and responsible not to the regional Ottoman governors but directly to the sultan. The governorship was also approved by the signatory powers. He had the authority to levy taxes, appoint judges, approve the sentences of the local tribunals, and to maintain security and order.

The Organic Laws were signed by France, Britain, Austria, Prussia, Russia, Turkey, and Italy (in 1867), thus giving Lebanese confessionalism international recognition and legitimacy. However, this also meant careful balancing of both European interests and Ottoman interests.

The Mutasarrifiyah was divided into seven districts, each under a *qaim-maqam*, or mayor. Three districts were Maronite, one Druze, one Muslim, one Greek Orthodox, and one Melkite. There was also a local judiciary and a native police force. The arrangement thus institutionalized the sectarian division of public office and administration, a feature which still characterizes the confessional/consociational Lebanese state today. The period also witnessed large-scale emigration. It is estimated that, between 1860 and 1900, 120,000 people, mostly Christians, left Mount Lebanon to overseas destinations. The emigrants amounted to relatively 25 per cent of the original population.[7]

Modernization and prosperity (1861–1914)

The remainder of the nineteenth century saw a relative period of stability in Mount Lebanon, as the sectarian communities focused on economic and cultural development. During that time, the region saw a flourishing of literary and political activity associated with the attempts to liberalize the Ottoman Empire under the Tanzimat reforms. It is within this context that the first secular and nationalist political ideological trends were sown in the region, and which would prove crucial in the various reformist movements (the Arab Awakening) during the war period.[8] The exchange of new ideas, goods and services between Mount Lebanon and Italy, has left an indelible mark on Lebanese architecture, cuisine and the joie de vivre which characterizes its Mediterranean culture.

The founding of the American University of Beirut in 1886 is one notable undertaking of the period, as events in Lebanon were influenced by global developments in the era of industrialization and modernization. It became the most influential American learning institute outside the United States, offering a secular place for integration for both Lebanese and other Arabs. The establishment of universities and Western printing presses enabled extensive literary and scientific exchanges to follow. Large-scale rural–urban migration to the port cities helped Beirut grow into the cultural and economic hub of the region. Most significant, however, was a marked easing in the sectarian violence that characterized the newfound era of relative peace and stability in Lebanon in the last few decades of the nineteenth century and early 1900s.

The outbreak of World War I brought an abrupt and decisive end to the Mutasarrifiyah era, and Lebanon was to feel the weight of the conflict in the Middle East more heavily than most other regions.

Figure 2.1 Late nineteenth century Lebanese dress: Maronite from Lebanon, inhabitant of Jeïbel, Christian woman from Lebanon

League of Nations Mandate (1922–1943)

Following the collapse of the Ottoman Empire after World War I, the **League of Nations** mandated the five provinces that make up present-day Lebanon to the direct control of France. Initially, the Arab-speaking areas of the Ottoman Empire were to be divided by the **Sykes–Picot Agreement**, into British and French spheres of influence (see Map 2.3). However, the final determinations on the mandates were decided at the **San Remo Conference of 1920**, ratified by the League in 1921 and put into effect in 1922.

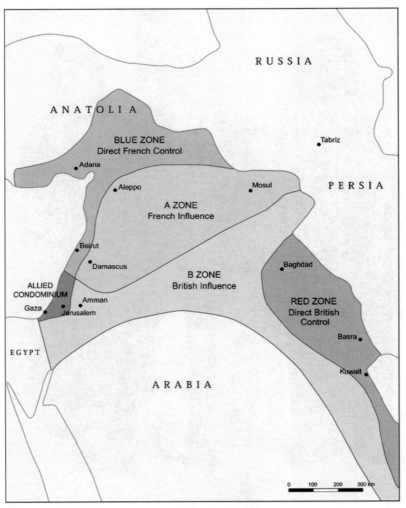

Map 2.3 The division of Lebanon during the Sykes–Picot Agreement
Source: Palestinian Academic Society for the Study of International Affairs

Map 2.4 Regional divisions during the League of Nations mandate

According to the agreements, France also had control over what was termed Syria, in recognition of the capture of Damascus in 1920.[9]

The French exploited local conditions during their Mandate of the Levant by dividing the territories along communitarian lines into geopolitically convenient units to facilitate, and indeed to maximize, their administration and control over the area, through a process called **gerrymandering**. Syria was scheduled to be an independent country, a so-called "class-A mandate", and the rights granted to France over it were far less than over other mandate territories. A class-B mandate granted the right to administer the territories. Thus, the French termed their entire mandate area "Syria", to include the administrative districts along the Mediterranean coast. Wanting to maximize the area under its direct control, containing an Arab Syria centered on Damascus, and ensuring a defensible border, France established the "Anti-Lebanon" mountains, on the far side of the Bekaa Valley, as the Lebanon–Syria border. The territory that had belonged to the province of Damascus for hundreds of years was far more attached to Damascus than to Beirut by culture and influence.

Lebanese sectarian demography under the Mandate

Consequently, the demographics of Lebanon were profoundly altered, as the territory added contained people who were predominantly Muslim. Lebanese Christians, of which the Maronites were the largest subgroup, now constituted barely more than 50 per cent of the population, while Sunni Muslims in Lebanon saw their numbers increase eightfold and Shi'ite Muslims fourfold. By maintaining a Christian majority in the country, France aimed to guarantee the political dominance of its Christian allies. Lebanon was to be governed based on a French-mandated constitution drafted in 1926, and became the essence of a modern secular government. Thus, most resentment was felt by the Sunni, being a part of a majority within the Ottoman Empire, now a minority within a Maronite-favored French Mandate. Hence the focus of inter-sectarian conflict shifted from Maronite–Druze confrontation to a Maronite–Sunni confrontation. The Druze and Shi'ite on the other hand, albeit not pro-French, felt better positioned as a minority within Greater Lebanon than as part of a larger Sunni Arab entity. It is important to note that France did not fragment Greater Lebanon as it did Syria. It merely reinforced existing sectarian cleavages, creating a political entity for the Maronites in the Levant.

French colonialism left a legacy in Lebanon unmatched by any other in the region. This took many forms, such as the imposition of foreign institutions as declared in founding documents, constitutions, and legislative structures. Political calculations or interests underpinning the process of nation building were non-indigenous, as seen by artificially created states and arbitrary borders compounded by "divide and rule" political strategies. Such changes have had a long-lasting effect on the sociopolitical landscape of most post-colonial states, including Lebanon.

With the end of World War I and the collapse of the Ottoman Empire, the League of Nations mandated the five provinces that make up present-day Lebanon and Syria to the direct control of France at the San Remo Conference of 1920. The French exploited local conditions during their mandate of the Levant, by dividing the territories along communitarian lines into geopolitically convenient administrative units to facilitate, and indeed to maximize, their control over the area. The French included the administrative districts along the Mediterranean coast. Also, wanting to contain the surging Arab nationalism centered on Damascus. The Bekaa Valley, which had previously belonged to the province of Damascus for hundreds of years, as well as the former Ottoman provinces of Tyre, Sidon, Beirut and Tripoli, were joined to the traditional Maronite and Druze enclave of the Mutasarrifiyah of Mount Lebanon.

As a result, the demographics of Lebanon were profoundly altered. The newly founded mandated region established a slight Christian population majority, while Sunnis were detached from their Syrian brethren and turned into a minority in the mandated Lebanon. Both the Druze and the Shia remained minorities, though they felt relative advantages in the new distribution (Table 2.1).

Thus, through French gerrymandering, the State of Greater Lebanon was established on September 1, 1920, by a decree published by the French High Commissioner, General Henri Gouraud. These geopolitical boundaries laid the foundations for the form of government and political organization of contemporary state of Lebanon. For the following six years, Greater Lebanon was to be administered by four consecutive governors of French origin, appointed by the High Commissioner, who also nominated the 17 members of the local Advisory

Table 2.1 Results of the 1932 census in Lebanon

Community	Population (n)	Population (% approx.)
Maronites	226,378	29
Greek Orthodox	76,552	10
Greek Catholic	45,999	6
Armenians	3⁻,156	4
Other Christian groupings	22,308	3
Total Christian population		52
Sunni Muslims	175,925	22
Shi'ite Muslims	154,208	19
Druze	53,047	7
Total Muslim population		48

Source: McDowall, D. (1983) *Lebanon: A Conflict of Minorities*, Report No. 61. London: Minority
  Rights Group, p. 11

Council, representing the various sects in the country to assist the Governor. On March 8, 1922, the administrative arrangement was eclipsed by the institution of a Representative Council for Greater Lebanon. Seats in the Representative Council were distributed proportionally along confessional lines between the six administrative districts into which Lebanon was divided at the time, and its three consecutive elected Presidents were all Maronites. The Representative Council ushered in the Lebanese Republic and became its first Council of Deputies.

Summary

The chapter introduced the first significant sectarian-driven conflict in Lebanon, between the Druze and Maronites in 1841. This conflict took place in Mount Lebanon and was the result of long-standing internal social strife. However, the European community took interest in seizing control in the then unstable and unfavorably Ottoman-controlled area. The French sided with Maronites while the Sultan and the British supported the Druze. The Sultan, with British support, intervened and partitioned Mount Lebanon into two politically autonomous districts known as *qaim-maqamats*, with Maronite jurisdiction in the north and Druze in the south, divided by the Beirut–Damascus Road. This was the first geopolitical sectarian division in Lebanon. With disastrous consequences, the separation ignored the root causes of the problem and exacerbated conflict in mixed villages within the divisions.

The new arrangements failed to provide a genuine solution to sectarian tensions and, in 1860, the Maronite–Druze war erupted, where more than 8,000 Christians and Druze were killed, while more than 100,000 were left homeless. It was ultimately French military intervention, in support of the Christians, that helped end the war. In 1861, The Organic Laws of Lebanon, a constitution further dividing the country by sectarian lines, was signed in Istanbul and recognized by several European countries. Between 1861 and 1914, the Mutasarrifiyah of Lebanon experienced a period of relative stability marked by economic and cultural modernization and growing European influence.

After the end of World War I and the collapse of the Ottoman Empire, the five districts that make up present-day Lebanon were mandated to France by the League of Nations. France was also given control of Syria. Syria was scheduled to become an independent country, but France termed their entire mandated area "Syria" and divided it along communitarian lines to create geopolitical units that were easier to control. This greatly altered the demographics of Lebanon, creating a large influx of Muslims while maintaining slight Christian demographic advantages. The French continued to favor the Maronites, causing resentment among the Sunni population, who were accustomed to being an Ottoman majority. The Maronite–Druze conflict shifted to become a Maronite–Sunni one. The Druze and Shi'ite felt more comfortable being minorities in Greater Lebanon than they did as a part of a larger Sunni Arab entity. Colonialism would continue to influence politics in Lebanon and shape its twentieth century politics.

References

1   Abraham, A. J. (1981) *Lebanon at Mid-century: Maronite-Druze Relations in Lebanon, 1840–1860: A Prelude to Arab Nationalism*. Washington DC: University Press of America.
2   Weiss, M. (2009) 'The Historiography of Sectarianism in Lebanon', *History Compass*, 7 (1): 141–54.
3   Traboulsi, F. (2007) *A History of Modern Lebanon*. London: Pluto Press.
4   Hourani, A. (1966) 'Lebanon from Feudalism to Modern State', *Middle Eastern Studies*, 3 (2): 256–63.
5   Churchill, C. (1994) *The Druzes and the Maronites Under the Turkish rule From 1840 to 1860*. London: Bernard Quaritch.
6   Salibi, K. (1965) *A Modern History of Lebanon*. New York: Frederick A. Praeger, p 77.
7   Khalifah, B. (2001) *The Rise and Fall of Christian Lebanon*. Toronto: York Press.
8   El-Solh, R. K. (2008) 'Lebanese Arab Nationalists and Consociational Democracy During the French Mandate Period' in *Liberal Thought in the Eastern Mediterranean: Late 19th Century Until the 1960s*. C. Schumann, ed. Leiden: Brill, pp. 217–35.
9   Shorrock, W. (1970) 'The Origin of the French Mandate in Syria and Lebanon: The Railroad Question, 1901–1914', *International Journal of Middle East Studies*, 1 (2): 133–53.

3 Lebanon under the French Mandate, independence, and the National Pact Republic

This chapter explores the nature of the state under the **French Mandate** outlining the first Lebanese Constitution of 1926 and the role of the 18 officially-recognized sects. It discusses the struggle for independence and the resultant National Pact of 1943. The Pact is discussed in detail to illustrate Lebanon's unique power-sharing formula. The result of demographic changes and Palestinian issues on the sectarian relations are examined, demonstrating the recurring sectarian crisis within the Lebanese consociational model.

The Lebanese constitution

On May 23, 1926, the first Lebanese constitution was promulgated. **Greater Lebanon** was transformed into a republic modeled after the French **Third Republic**. The original constitution established a bicameral Parliament composed of a **Chamber of Deputies** (parliament) and a **Senate** – which was later dropped – a President with strong legislative and executive powers, and a Council of Ministers (cabinet). The President was elected by the Chamber of Deputies for one six-year term, while deputies were popularly elected to sectarian-allocated seats. While confessionalism was the political order of the day, the first Lebanese constitution was a secular document *par excellence* and did not refer to Lebanon as a confessional state. The determination of political posts along sectarian lines became the output of various agreements and, consequently, a politically recognized custom agreed upon by influential sectarian elites and recognized by the French authorities. Eighteen religious sects were recognized (Box 3.1).

The Lebanese Constitution was the first of its kind among Middle Eastern and North African post-World War I countries to lay down the foundation of a democratic republic. It thus marked a principal departure from traditional Ottoman feudal rules. The constitution recognized Lebanese as equal citizens before the law whose liberty, property, and access to education was constitutionally guaranteed. Three branches of government (executive, legislative, and judicial) were introduced. An elected **unicameral assembly** called the Chamber of Deputies was established, with power to legislate and elect the President of the Republic. The presidential term of office was limited to six years. All Lebanese citizens of

Box 3.1 Lebanon's 18 officially recognized sects

- Maronite (Maronite Catholic)
- Greek Orthodox
- Greek Catholic
- Armenian Orthodox (Gregorian)
- Armenian Catholic
- Syrian Orthodox (Jacobite)
- Syrian Catholic
- Roman Catholic (Latins)
- Copts
- Evangelical Christian (including Protestant groups such as Baptists and Seventh-Day Adventists)
- Chaldean Catholic
- Nestorian Assyrian
- Twelvers Shi'a
- Sunni
- Isma'ili (Sevener Shi'a)
- Druze
- Alawite
- Jewish (very few Jews remain in Lebanon today)

Source: Bureau of Democracy, Human Rights, and Labor (2012) *International Religious Freedom Report for 2011*. Washington, DC: US Department of State. Available online at www.state.gov/j/drl/rls/irf/2011/nea/192895.htm

21 years of age and above, regardless of their religion, gender, or economic affiliations, were granted rights to vote.

During its various political transitions, the constitution was modified and amended to correspond to emerging developments. Major amendments introduced were in 1927, 1929, 1943, 1947, 1948, 1976, and 1990. Reference to sectarian division of power emerged only in its latest revision under Article 24, which allocated parliamentary seats evenly among Muslims and Christians and proportionally along sectarian affiliations. The latest revised constitution of 1990, also known as the Taef Constitution, considered this sectarian allocation to be temporary in nature and establishes in its preamble the aim to abolish confessionalism altogether. At the same time, the constitution left it up to Parliament to decide on electoral law, which has consistently distributed, under various electoral rules, parliamentary seats on sectarian basis. Efforts to implement the constitutional provisions, particularly Article 95, which calls for devising a transitional plan for the abolition of confessionalism, have been aborted by self-perpetuated sectarian elites (see Appendix A).

The Constitution originally established a strong presidential power structure of governance. This allowed the Maronite President to play a central role in the formation of every cabinet, the appointments of key public officers including that of the judiciary, the determination of the legislative agenda along with a veto power, and the ability to dissolve Parliament and the Council of Ministers. These combined powers were restrained by a constitutional term limit, whose extension was often confronted by a strong public and political opposition – particularly by non-Maronite sectarian groups. The presidential term limit has helped Lebanon to avoid authoritarianism and family succession of power such as practiced by the surrounding Arab states. Still, the Taef Constitution of 1990 not only redistributed sectarian power but further undermined the power of the President, stripping from him key privileges, in favor of the Sunni Prime Minister and Shia Parliament Speaker.

The struggle for independence

At the height of World War II, France, under the Vichy government that assumed power in 1940, was occupied by Germany. General Henri-Fernand Dentz was appointed as the new High Commissioner of Lebanon. During the War, the Vichy authorities allowed Germany to move aircraft and supplies through its mandated territories to Iraq for use against British forces. Thus, fearing that Nazi Germany would gain control of the Levant by pressuring the weak Vichy government, Britain sent troops into Syria and Lebanon to confront German advances. Hostilities ended only after an armistice was signed in Acre on July 14, 1941.

Under political pressures from both within the country and outside, on November 26, 1941, Lebanon's independence was recognized under the authority of the new Free French government led by General Charles de Gaulle. The United States, Britain, the Soviet Union, the Arab states, and certain Asian countries recognized this independence, and some of them exchanged ambassadors with Beirut. However, even though the French recognized Lebanon's independence in theory, they continued to exercise authority over the country.

Elections were held on November 8, 1943, and the first government of independent Lebanon amended the Constitution, abolishing the articles that referred to the Mandate and modified those that specified the powers of the high commissioner, thus unilaterally ending the Mandate. The French authorities retaliated by arresting the Christian president, the Muslim prime minister, and other cabinet members and exiled them to the Rashayya Castle located along the country's southern coast. This action united both Christian and Muslim leaders in their determination to oust the French. Their calls for self-determination were also supported by international pressure from Britain, the United States and the Arab countries. The French finally accepted Lebanon's independence and released the prisoners on November 22, 1943; since then, this day has been celebrated as Lebanon's Independence Day. The Allies kept the region under control until the end of World War II, and the last French troops withdrew from Lebanon in 1946.

The National Pact Republic

The foundations of the independent Lebanese Republic were established in the summer of 1943 by an unwritten gentlemen's agreement, the National Pact (*al Mithaq al Watani*), as a result of numerous consultations between the country's sectarian/political elite. The Pact recognized the various sectarian elements of the country and laid the foundations of a sectarian power-sharing system, or confessionalism, as the basis of government in the Lebanese state. At the heart of the National Pact negotiations was the Lebanese attempt to find an expedient solution to the mutual fears and philosophical disagreements over the national character of the newly independent state. Christians feared being overwhelmed by the Muslim communities in Lebanon and the surrounding Arab countries, while the Muslims feared encroaching Western **hegemony**. Thus, Lebanon's absolute sovereign independence was to be mutually guaranteed by the two sides. The Christians promised not to seek foreign (i.e. French) protectionism against their fellow citizens and to accept Lebanon's "Arab face". In turn, the Muslims agreed to recognize the independence of Lebanon according to its 1920 boundaries and to renounce aspirations for a merger with Syria.[1]

More notably, the Pact reinforced the sectarian system of governance, which began under the French Mandate, by formalizing the confessional distribution of the highest public offices and top administrative ranks according to the proportional distribution of the dominant sects within the population. This was based on the (last) official national census conducted by the French in 1932, which revealed a slight Christian demographic dominance over Muslims (Table 2.1). Thus, seats in the Chamber of Deputies (parliament) were distributed by a six-to-five ratio favoring Christians over Muslims. This proportional share was to be applied to all highest level public and administrative offices, such as ministers and directors. It was agreed that the President of the Republic would be a Maronite Christian, the first of whom was Bechara al-Khoury; the Premier of the Council of Ministers would be a Sunni Muslim – the first was Riad al-Solh, the President of the National Assembly a Shi'a Muslim – the first was Sabri Hmede; and the Deputy Speaker of Parliament a Greek Orthodox Christian.[2]

The National Constitution, which did not codify the gentlemen's agreement made under the National Pact, in later amendments noted in its Preamble that the mutuality of existence of all Lebanese groups is a requirement for the constitutional legitimacy of any authority. This has been presented as a constitutional essence of Lebanese sectarian consociationalism alongside the Pact.

Although the original constitution was a secular code and did not refer to the proportional division of legislative seats and public offices along sectarian lines, it provided flexibility for the Assembly of Deputies to revise appropriate laws, including sectarian electoral law. The Pact further established a covenant rooted in traditional practices of sectarian consociationalism and formed the de facto governing agreement in Lebanon for the post-independence period. While the National Pact represented an elite consensus over the terms of Lebanon's national identity and governance after independence, there was large disagreement over the Pact. This was voiced by liberal "constitutionalists" who denied its legality as a binding agreement and suggested alternatively that the Pact was only a temporary ministerial agreement established during the term of first President Khoury. However, proponents of the Pact, the "consociationalists," defended inclusive confessional power sharing as essential to ensuring effective government within Lebanon's fragmented polity. The early consociationalist thinker, constitution writer, and former Depute, Michel Chiha, established the fact that Lebanon is uniquely founded on the consensus of its various sectarian minorities.[3]

Still, the deep rift among Muslims and Christians was rooted in a disagreement over the country's national identity and international affiliation.[4] While the Christians sought to establish closer ties with Christianity in Europe, and particularly France, the Muslims were haunted by the specter of Western colonialism. The National Pact offered an accommodative arrangement by acknowledging the country's Arab orientation while asserting its independence and international openness, including that of economic and friendly relations with Europe.

The political power-sharing formula established in Lebanon through the National Pact was perceived as a workable, albeit contentious, arrangement that formed the foundation of the first independent sectarian Lebanese Republic. It provided a modicum of stability, for at least the first decade after independence, within which the country flourished economically, socially and culturally. Nevertheless, the shortcomings of consociationalism would resurface in later years as the pressures of a changing demographic balance and regional geostrategic shifts converged on Lebanon.

Demographic changes in Lebanon since 1943

Lebanon underwent major socioeconomic and cultural transformations throughout the post-independence era. Shifts in the demographic balance triggered major internal political grievances, compounded by external ideological pressures that have come to challenge the essence of power-sharing formulations and the National Pact.[5] Three major demographic trends characterized the post-independence era, which brought pressure against the Christian-favored power structure in Lebanon: urbanization, a shift in the demographic balance, and Palestinian refugees.

Urbanization

In response to the modernization and commercialization of the economy, large-scale migration to the coastal cities occurred, particularly to the metropole of Beirut, as the Lebanese left their traditional sectarian enclaves in search of business and educational opportunities in the cities. Not only did this increase inter-sectarian contact, it also raised the stakes of communal conflict as the new city dwellers competed for access to jobs, services and, inevitably, power. Demands for labor and consumer markets represented a serious challenge to confessionalism as a whole, and to the Maronite power-base in particular. Throughout the 1950s, 1960s, and 1970s, mass liberal education produced a highly politicized inter-sectarian young generation that rejected political confessionalism and demanded an egalitarian citizen-based society. Arab, Syrian, and Lebanese nationalist parties, as well as various versions of social democratic and left-wing groups, attracted most young people.

In 1960, Greater Beirut's population stood at 450,000 residents; by 1975, that figure had increased threefold to 1,250,000.[6] This population boom turned Beirut into the most populous city in Lebanon by a vast margin. It came at the cost of confessionally, especially Christian, segregated neighborhoods. The Shia, for instance, were drawn in massive numbers to the traditionally Christian and Druze southern suburbs of Beirut (*Dahye*) as well as the areas in East Beirut known as Al-Naba neighborhood, and later denoted as the suburban "belt of misery". By 1975, deepening socioeconomic spatial stratification between the primarily affluent Maronite eastern suburbs of Beirut and the adjacent poorer Shia southern suburbs led to deep confessional resentment between the groups. As a result, it was no coincidence that the first front of the 1975 Civil War (the Green Line) stretched between these neighborhoods: Shia Shayah versus Christian Ayn Al-Rummanah, which, by the 1980s, had expanded to separate the largely Christian East Beirut from Muslim West Beirut.[7]

Shift in the demographic balance

Urbanization coincided with a high rate of Christian (relative to Muslim) emigration, especially to the American and European continents. This migration, which began in the mid-nineteenth century after eruptions of civil strife in 1860 in Mount Lebanon, continued during World War I (1914–1918), and accelerated after World War II.[8] Christian migration was confronted by lower rate of Muslim migration, which soon tipped the demographic balance. By the 1960s and 1970s, and in the absence of a population census, Lebanese Muslims began to claim the majority presence to step up demands for the redistribution of power to reflect demographic reality.

Palestinian refugees

In 1948, the State of Israel claimed independence in Palestine, following massive waves of European Jewish immigration and a long struggle with the existing Palestinian Arab population. The declaration of the state of Israel in 1948 signaled the beginning of the Arab–Israeli conflict over Jewish versus Arab claims to Palestine. One of the most tragic outcomes, however, was the displacement of over 700,000 Palestinians into surrounding countries.[9] In Lebanon, Palestinian refugee camps were erected throughout the country, to house the predominantly Sunni Muslim and minority Orthodox Christian Palestinian refugees. Original estimations placed the number of refugees in 1950 at 127,000.[10] The so-called "Palestinian question" became a highly politicized and sensitive issue, which further complicated the Lebanon's delicate inter-confessional balance and struggle for power. Overwhelming Lebanese sympathy toward Palestinians soon became a decisive sectarian issue. While many Lebanese youth joined the rank of Palestinian armed groups and considered the struggle against Israel as part of fighting Western colonialism, most Christians stood hesitant. The Christians' cautiousness emerged out of fear that the possible "naturalization", settlement, and power growth of Muslim Palestinians in Lebanon, would soon jeopardize the Christian majority in the country. This concern became a major driving factor in the outburst of the 1975 Civil War in Lebanon, which is further discussed in Chapter 4.

Thus, at least three demographic factors emerged challenging the Christian-favoring distribution of power. Urbanization was attracting various sectarian groups to suburbs and districts traditionally populated by Christian groups, such as the Southern District and many neighborhoods of Beirut. Migration of Christians to the West was also a factor undermining their population advantage. And last, but not least, is the growth of Palestinian power in the country, which contributed to the advantage of the Lebanese Muslim population. The consequences were growing Christian grievances against a widening demographic gap confronted by Muslim demands for a greater share of political power (see Map 3.1).

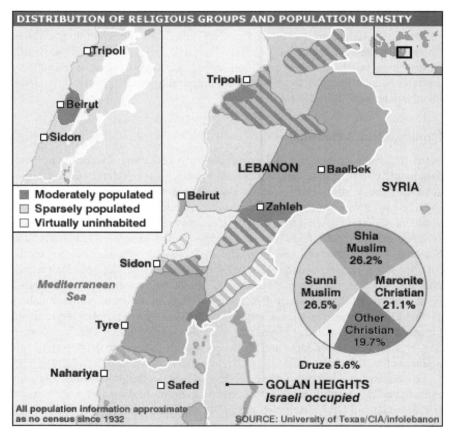

Map 3.1 Lebanese sectarian distributions

The first sectarian republic in crisis

The new demographic and social reality in Lebanon, coupled with clashing regional and international powers, further pitted the local sectarian communities against one another. The ideological and political polarization of the international system (US versus Soviet spheres of influence) juxtaposed with the anti-colonial movement sweeping across much of the developing world; converged on the Middle East in the form of a resurgent **Pan-Arabism** – embodied by Jamal Abdel Nasser's Egypt – fueled by anti-Western and Anti-Zionist sentiment.[11] Several prominent Lebanese Muslim elites and citizens voiced their support of the reassertion of the "Arab cause" and the defeat of the state of Israel, which was viewed as the resurgence plan of Western colonialism against Arab national independence. However, the mainly Christian Lebanese nationalists, who had strong ties to the capitals of Europe and the United States, advocated a more moderate policy of Lebanese neutrality. They grew weary of the growing Muslim influence, both ideologically and demographically, on the predominant "Maronism" that had characterized the Lebanese state. On the other hand, the largely Muslim pro-Arabism coalition demanded that the predominantly Christian pro-Western front submit to a redistribution of power that suited the demographic realities. Christians rejected calls for power redistribution and were confronted by Muslim radicals that sought the total abolition of political sectarianism. Contradictory aspirations soon plunged the first sectarian republic into a full-blown constitutional, social and political crisis.

Failure of consociationalism

Many nationalists perceived that post-independence Lebanon would experience democratic consolidation, national cohesion, consensus building, and the consequential decline of political confessionalism. This perception, however, was shattered by growing sectarian fears over communal destiny in the light of a turbulent regional and antagonizing sectarian environment. Instead of its demise, confessionalism proliferated as the safeguard for group co-existence. The National Pact guaranteed the *"partage de pouvoir"* (sharing of the spoils) between Lebanese sectarian groups. Most importantly, the National Pact turned into an ingredient for the perpetuation of power by sectarian elites through a system of **clientelism** (*zuama*), which further fortified political confessionalism as the ultimate realism of Lebanese nationalism. Hence, post-independence Lebanese confessionalism, originating from the sects' mutual fears of domination, was further consolidated and grew less accommodating to demographic and political changes.

The contradiction between state rigidity and demographic changes was soon exacerbated by external factors, most notably the mobilization and power growth of Palestinians in Lebanon. In the late 1950s, the Lebanese population was politically polarized along confessional lines between Muslim supporters of Arab–Palestine cause and Christian Lebanese nationalism. In 1958, division ran deep among the sects and the outburst of violence spread across Beirut following the declared intention of pro-Western Maronite President Camille Chamoun to extend his term in office by an extra-constitutional amendment. Violence ended only after approximately 2,000 people were killed and the US Marines intervened in support of the President.[12]

After the 1967 Arab–Israeli war, the activism of Palestinian armed groups grew in direct challenge to United Nations-sponsored 1949 Arab–Israeli General Armistice Agreements, which held states responsible for withholding of ceasefire across borders. Frequent clashes between Palestinian groups and the Lebanese Army ended following the 1969 Cairo Agreement, which legitimized Palestinians rights in Lebanon to arms, training, and recruitment of fighters against Israel.[13] In 1970, King Hussein of Jordan waged a major operation against Palestinian armed activities in Jordan. Palestinians refer to these events as "Black September" as thousands were killed.[14] Following these events, the **Palestinian Liberation Organization** (PLO) decided to move its central command and fighters from Jordan and establish its main base in Lebanon.

The Lebanese confessional state was soon confronted with a dual power structure emerging between its regular uniformed army and that of the PLO, which had already been attracting Lebanese radical youth to its ranks. During the early 1970s, clashes between the Lebanese army and armed Palestinian groups were common. The outcome was the growth of confessional rift among the Lebanese, with state institutions emerging weak and divided. By 1975, all reasons for a civil war had ripened.

Michael Hudson, who spent many years studying Lebanese politics, attributed to the failure of Lebanese confessionalism social, economic, and historic fabrics characterized by three broad traits:

- A fragmented political culture within a deeply divided society, marked by strong vertical cleavages, resulting in a disunited nation state or conglomeration of primordial communities each having strong, particular self-identities based on sectarian and kinship bonds living uneasily side by side.
- Socioeconomic inequality as a direct result of the **corporatist** nature of the independent liberal state and its subsequent inability to rectify the discriminatory and inequitable wealth distribution in society. This was most evident in the rapid urbanization and modernization that occurred in the mid-twentieth century and which favored Beirut at the expense of the surrounding suburbs. The corporatist sectarian make-up of the country also meant that socioeconomic advantages were centered around Beirut, which was favored by the dominant Christian and Sunni elites, over the impoverished predominantly Shi'ite slum belt in the southern suburbs and the Bekaa Valley.
- A history of external intervention in its internal affairs has complicated government in Lebanon. Since the Ottoman Empire, domestic politics have been deeply influenced by disaggregated foreign influences and interests, which, in combination with a fragmented political culture and a weak central state, has prompted local elites to seek the patronage of foreign powers (in

the form of both diplomatic and material support), often to improve their relative leverage over their peers. In the absence of a unified and strong central Lebanese state, the precarious geostrategic location of Lebanon has made it especially vulnerable to becoming a proxy for regional/international political upheavals and competition.[15]

Hudson's characterization of Lebanese politics sheds light on the fragile state of the nation and society. Division among Lebanese grew to unprecedented levels so that, by 1975, it proved impossible for the confessional regime to withstand domestic and external pressures. A total breakdown of state and society resulted in a devastating 15-year-long civil war that followed.

Summary

At the end of World War I, France was given control to both Lebanon and Syria, marking the end of Ottoman rule in the region. The French divided their new territories into manageable, controlled, geopolitical administrative districts. This redistribution of territory dramatically changed the demographics of Lebanon. A Christian majority emerged, and the Sunni Muslims, now separated from their Syrian brethren, became a minority. Through French gerrymandering, the State of Greater Lebanon was established on September 1, 1920. The geopolitical boundaries laid the foundations for the contemporary government and state of Lebanon.

On May 23, 1926, a Lebanese constitution was drafted. Greater Lebanon was transformed into a Republic modeled after the French Third Republic. The constitution established a bicameral parliament composed of a Chamber of Deputies (parliament), an executive branch headed by a President with strong legislative and executive powers, a Council of Ministers (cabinet), and a judiciary.

The Constitution represented a departure from traditional Ottoman feudal rules, as it introduced a modern republican form of government. Although the constitution was a secular document, the country recognized 18 religious sectarian groups and politics proceeded in various informal confessional arrangements. Lebanon's independence was formally gained in 1943. Elections were held and the constitution was revised to exclude provisions of the French Mandate. The last French troops withdrew from Lebanon in 1946.

Official manifestation of sectarianism in the political structure of government was institutionalized following independence and was expressed in the unwritten National Pact of 1943. The Pact reinforced the sectarian system of governance by formalizing the confessional distribution of the highest public offices and top administrative ranks along sectarian lines. This political power-sharing formula was a workable, albeit contentious, arrangement. It provided a short period of stability during which the country enjoyed social, economic, and cultural growth.

However, the combination of demographic changes, internal political disputes, and external ideological pressures did not allow for continued stability. Lebanon's largely Muslim Arabist coalition demanded from the predominantly Christian pro-Western front to submit to a redistribution of power to suit new demographic realities, thus plunging the first sectarian Republic into a full-blown crisis. Consociationalism was based on the sects' mutual fears of domination and neglected the dynamic nature of the social and political realities of Lebanon. In 1958 and 1975, political tension over domestic and external factors, such as the issue of the Palestinian refugees and armed struggles against Israel, erupted into civil strife.

References

1   Chaitani, Y. (2007) *Post-Colonial Syria and Lebanon*. London and New York: Tauris.
2   Binder, L. (1966) *Politics in Lebanon*. New York: John Wiley.
3   Hartman, M. and Olsaretti, A. (2003) '"The First Boat and the First Oar": Inventions of Lebanon in the Writings of Michel Chiha', *Radical History Review*, (86): 36–65.
4   Salibi, K. (1993) *The Modern History of Lebanon*. New York: Caravan Books.
5   Faour, M. (2007) 'Religion, Demography and Politics in Lebanon' *Middle Eastern Studies*, 43 (6): 909–21.
6   Collelo, T. (ed.) (1987) *Lebanon: A Country Study*. Washington, DC: GPO for the Library of Congress.
7   Collelo, T. (ed.) (1987) *Lebanon: A Country Study*. Washington, DC: GPO for the Library of Congress.
8   Issawi, C. (1992) 'The Historical background of Lebanese Emigration: 1800–1914' in A. Hourani and N. Shehadi, eds, *The Lebanese in the World: A Century of Emigration*. London: Centre for Lebanese Studies and Tauris, pp. 13–31.
9   Gabbay, R. (1959) *A Political Study of the Arab–Jewish Conflict: The Arab Refugee Problem, A Case Study*. Geneva: Librairie E. Droz, pp. 167–8.
10 UN System Lebanon (2011) United Nations Relief and Works Agency for Palestine Refugees in the Near East (UNRWA). Available online at www.un.org.lb/Subpage.aspx?pageid=65
11 Ayoubi, N. (1995) *Over-stating the Arab State: Politics and Society in the Middle East*. London: Tauris, pp. 135–58.
12 Collelo, T. (ed.) (1987) *Lebanon: A Country Study*. Washington, DC: GPO for the Library of Congress.
13 El Khazen, F. (2000) *The Breakdown of the State in Lebanon: 1967–1976*. London: Tauris, pp. 164–7.
14 Nevo, J. (2008) 'September 1970 in Jordan: A Civil War?', *Civil Wars*, 10 (3): 217–30.
15 Hudson, M. (1976) 'The Lebanese Crisis: The Limits of Consociational Democracy', *Journal of Palestine Studies*, 5 (3/4): 109–22.

4   The Lebanese Civil War 1975–1990

The context of Lebanese sectarian contentions and the consequential governance crisis throughout the National Pact Republic are examined in this chapter. The 1958 civil strife is analyzed in detail. Regional power shifts in the post-colonial order, demographic changes and the rise of Palestinian power are included among the main causes of the 1975 Lebanese Civil War. The parties that played major roles in the war are identified and described. A timeline is provided at the end of the chapter outlining the various developments during the war.

The 1958 Crisis

The establishment of the state of Israel in 1948 radically changed the environment in which Lebanon was situated, both geographically and politically. Arab opposition to Israel, and by extension the former colonial European powers, was bolstered by significant diplomatic and materiel support from the Union of Soviet Socialist Republic (USSR) as a part of its Cold War strategy to establish a geostrategic zone of influence in the Middle East. The ideological and political backlash against the West and its ally Israel was coupled with the rise of Arab nationalism, purported by such leaders as **Jamal Abdel Nasser**, who seized power in Egypt in 1952. Riding a wave of anti-Western sentiment that fanned Arab resistance to Israel, Nasser became the champion of the Arab nationalist cause, which espoused Arab unity, calling for the liberation of Palestine and the eradication of **political Zionism**.

In Lebanon, as elsewhere in the region, Arab nationalism resonated with the young, increasingly urbanized and politically mobile population, and hence, Nasserism quickly gained widespread popularity within Lebanon's Muslim polity. The majority of Lebanese Christians who had established historical ties with France and the West stood hesitant.

Relations between Lebanon and Egypt deteriorated as pro-Western Maronite President **Camille Chamoun** (1952–1958) did not break diplomatic relations with the Western powers that had attacked Egypt during the **Suez War** of 1956, also known as the Tripartite Aggression. This angered Egyptian President Jamal Abdel Nasser and alienated many of the Muslim Nasserite supporters at home, led by Prime Minister **Rashid Karami**. Egyptian–Lebanese relations were already strained by the fact that Chamoun showed closeness to the pro-Western **Baghdad Pact** of 1955. The Pact was a Cold War alliance known as the Central Treaty Organization, formed by Iran, Iraq, Pakistan, Turkey, the United Kingdom, and United States for the purposes of mutual military and economic aid. The Nasserites viewed the Baghdad Pact as a threat against Arab nationalism; to counter it, Egypt and Syria united to form the **United Arab Republic** (UAR). The new Republic threatened Lebanon's precarious sovereignty, and further polarized the two dominant sectarian communities. Lebanese Muslims pushed the government to join the UAR, while Christians wanted to keep Lebanon independent and aligned with Western powers. The pressures of ideological competition and regional rivalries evoked already volatile sectarian contradictions. In July 1958, Lebanon was on the verge of a civil war between Lebanese nationalists (mostly Maronite Christians) and Arabists (mostly Muslims who supported the Egyptian regime under Nasser). Armed violence erupted between the two camps.

Tensions between the UAR and the Lebanese government came to a head when the UAR was allegedly accused of arming the Muslim insurgency. President Chamoun appealed to the United Nations Security Council against UAR interference in Lebanese affairs. Moreover, the toppling of a pro-Western government in Iraq on July 14, 1958, through a military coup, placed the Arab nationalist **Ba'ath party** in power and increased pressure on the Chamoun government. Finally, after the spread of violence throughout various parts of the country, President Chamoun called for United States military assistance. Dwight Eisenhower, the US President at the time, responded by authorizing **Operation Blue Bat** on July 15, 1958. This marked the first application of what came to be known as the "Eisenhower Doctrine", giving the US a self-proclaimed right to intervene in countries threatened by communism.[1] The goal of the operation was to bolster the pro-Western Lebanese government of President Chamoun against internal Nasserite opposition and threats from Syria and Egypt. The presence of approximately 14,000 US troops successfully quelled the opposition and the US withdrew its forces on October 25, 1958.[2]

The 1958 crisis only came to an end after an inter-elite bargain was struck between the opposing pro-Nasser and Lebanese nationalist factions. Chamoun resigned as President of Lebanon and was succeeded by **Fuad Chehab**. The latter was regarded as a consensus candidate supported by both the Lebanese nationalist and Arabist blocs. Chehab adopted a centrist and moderate stance on internal and regional politics. Tensions between the Muslims and Christians were eased and Lebanon's sovereign independence was secured under a new national reconciliation government formed by Prime Minister Rashid Karami in 1959.

An uneasy peace was held intact for a few more years, but was threatened by the political turbulence gripping the region. The Black September of 1970, sometimes referred to as the "era of regrettable events", was a month during which King Hussein of Jordan waged a campaign aimed at crushing militant armed Palestinian organizations in Jordan.[3] King Hussein meant to restore his monarchy's rule and contain the growing Palestinian military presence in the kingdom. The armed conflict between Jordanian forces and various Palestinian militant groups lasted until July 1971, resulting in the death of several thousand people, mostly Palestinians, and the expulsion of the PLO, together with scores of Palestinian fighters to Lebanon.[4] As a result of the September fighting, the PLO lost its main base for operations in Jordan and was driven to Lebanon and its Southern areas, regrouping and resuming cross-border attacks against Israel. The enlarged PLO presence in Lebanon and the intensification of fighting on the Israeli–Lebanese border stirred up internal unrest in Lebanon. These developments helped precipitate the Lebanese Civil War, in which the PLO was heavily involved from 1975 until the mid-1980s.

Prelude to the 1975 civil war

As evidenced, the collapse of the Lebanese sectarian state in 1975 can be attributed to various interrelated domestic and external contributing factors. Ideological polarization was exacerbated by significant demographic shifts in favor of the Muslims. This was reflected by the urbanization of the Muslim population and the large-scale Christian migration to the West. Urbanization occurred, with the expansion of Beirut and its suburbs. In 1959, 27.7 per cent of all Lebanese lived in Beirut and suburbs, but this figure ballooned to more than 50 per cent in 1975.[5] The growth of the capital, which occurred at the expense of the rest of the country, intensified sectarian interactions and exasperated sectarian competition for public access to services, resources, housing, jobs, and ultimately power. Lebanon's service-based economy acted as an agent for Western industries and Arab markets alike, leading to the centralization of firms and resources in Beirut to serve as a transit point for trade between the east and west and as an entertainment hot-spot for wealthy Arab tourists. Social grievances intensified as economic disparity between the rich and poor widened. This was also directly fed by consecutive governments' negligence of rural development in favor of the metropolis. The so-called "mountain and village people" (i.e. the Druze, Shi'a, Sunni, and less fortunate Christians) grew increasingly resentful of the amassed wealth, prestige and privilege of those "city dwellers" who held access to capital and power in Beirut. The environment was ripe for ideological radicalization.[6]

The mobilizing force of Arab nationalist ideology and demographic changes occurring in Lebanon soon tipped the sectarian balance of power in favor of the Muslims. The relative decline of political Maronism, which had dominated the Lebanese state system since independence, as well as the rise of Arab nationalism as the major political force in the Middle East – with its leftist, quasi-socialist ideology – proved difficult for the rigid Lebanese convocational state system to bear. Political sectarianism, surviving upon a tacit **gentlemen's agreement** since 1943, began to erode. The Maronite resistance to the redistribution of power amid a growing, largely disfranchised Muslim population was a major catalyst in the breakdown.

The Palestinian presence in Lebanon was not helpful in curtailing domestic sectarian and political polarizations. After the creation of the state of Israel and the displacement of over 700,000 mostly Sunni Palestinians, 127,000 of them were dispersed among different refugee camps in Lebanon.[7] The so-called "Palestinian question" had an unsettling effect on the country's delicate inter-confessional balance of power. In the aftermath of the 1967 **Six-day War**, Palestinians began to play a fundamental role in Lebanese domestic affairs. Palestinian fighters, infiltrating from neighboring Syria and refugee camps, began launching raids across the Lebanon–Israel border. The 1969 Cairo Agreement condoned such behavior and further undermined the state's monopoly over the country's security and border control.

The Lebanese Army's attempts to regulate the Palestinian armed movement in the country were widely opposed by pro-Palestinian Lebanese Muslim and leftist leadership. It was natural for the Palestinians, following their eviction from Jordan in 1970, to find a new sympathizing host in Lebanon. The new influx of Palestinian fighters to Lebanon established a duality of power or a "state within a state". The Lebanese state's immobility in responding to the increasing Palestinian power was a cause for fear amongst Christians. The Maronites reacted by establishing and training their own militias to counter the Palestinians'.

The 1975 Lebanese civil war

The spark that ignited the Lebanese civil war occurred in Beirut on April 13, 1975, when an attempt on Christian party leader **Pierre Gemayel**'s life by masked gunmen killed two Phalangists. Believing the assassins to be Palestinian, the Phalangists retaliated later the same day against a bus carrying Palestinian passengers across a Christian neighborhood, killing approximately 26 of the occupants.[8] The next day, fighting erupted, with Christian Phalangists against Palestinian militiamen. The confessional layout of Beirut facilitated random sectarian killings, and, while most Lebanese stayed inside their homes during these early days of battle, few imagined that the street fighting they were witness-ing was the beginning of a war that would devastate and divide their country for the next 15 years.

The war was multifaceted and resulted in a protracted 15-year conflict which caused an estimated 130,000 civilian deaths. An additional one million people (about one-quarter of the population) were wounded, and half of those were left with lifetime disabilities. Some 900,000 people, representing one-fifth of the pre-war population, were displaced from their homes. Hundreds of thousands migrated out of the country.[9]

The involvement of Syria, Israel, Russia, the United States, and the PLO, among other external powers, exacerbated the civilian strife in Lebanon. The **Arab League** mediation and Syrian intervention provided a short break in the fighting in 1976. However, the Palestinian–Lebanese and Muslim–Christian conflicts continued to rage on, predominantly in the country's southern region and in Greater Beirut. During the course of the fighting, alliances between the different factions shifted rapidly and unpredictably. The 1980s were especially bleak. A large part of Beirut lay in ruins as a result of the 1976 Karantina massacre carried out by Lebanese Christian militias, the destruction of Palestinian refugee camps by the Syrian troops, the Syrian Army shelling of Christian neighborhoods in 1978 and 1981, the fighting between Left-wing groups and the Shia **Amal Movement**, and the Israeli invasion that evicted the PLO from the country in 1982. The clashes not only destroyed most civilian infrastructure of Beirut but also divided it along Muslim and Christian cleansed sectors, separated by the so-called "Green Line". Later years witnessed intra-sectarian fighting between Sunnis and Shias, Shias and Palestinians, and Christian–Christian militias trying to establish turf in various streets and neighborhoods.

It is widely agreed that several factors triggered the Lebanese civil war. The seeds of civic strife and unrest in the country can be traced as far back as the Ottoman Empire's administration of Lebanon into *qaimaqameya* and *mutasarri-fiyah*. The end of the age of European colonialism over the region at the end of World War II, the rise of the Cold War and regional political developments, the establishment of the state of Israel and Palestinian displacement into Lebanon, the rise of Arab nationalism and armed struggle against Israel, the growth of economic and regional disparity between the Lebanese, and the demographic sectarian shifts all had powerful disintegrative effects on the political landscape of Lebanon's First Pact Republic. Regional conflicts and ideological struggles spilled over and disrupted Lebanon's confessional balance, exacerbating its contradictions. Most salient among these were the Arab–Israeli conflict and the rise of Arab nationalism.

Regional polarization had a visible and direct effect on Lebanon's political and social landscape. Divergent ideological loyalties split the country's two dominant sectarian communities and opposing blocs at both popular (horizontally) and elite levels (vertically). On one hand, Lebanon's Arab nationalist supporters sought greater solidarity between Lebanon and the other Arab nationalist states in their common "Arab Struggle" to liberate Palestine and defeat the state of Israel. In contrast, the conservative **state-centric** Lebanese nationalists, who were represented by former President Camille Chamoun and the President at that time, Suleiman Frangieh, had strong ties to the West and were fearful of the growing influence of Arab and Palestinian nationalism, advocated a policy of neutrality for Lebanon within the conundrum of regional politics.[10]

Throughout the war, most or all militias operated with little regard for human rights and furthermore, the sectarian character of some battles made civilians frequent targets. As the war progressed, the militias degenerated into mafia-style organizations.[11]

Finances to sustain their wartime operations were obtained from foreign support, usually from one of the rival Arab governments, Israel, or one of the superpowers (i.e. the United States or USSR), and often with conditionality.[12] Alliances shifted frequently during the course of the war. Alternatively, the militias turned to crime as a source of income, which soon became their main occupation. Extortion, theft, bank robberies and random checkpoints at which "customs duties" would be collected, were common offenses committed by groups on all sides of the conflict. Moreover, smuggling operations, largely in narcotics, arms, and all kinds of stolen goods, turned Lebanon during the civil war into one of the world's largest narcotics (hashish) producers, with much of the production centered in the Bekaa Valley.[13] As a result, many militia battles were fought over control of Lebanon's ports, which gave smugglers access to the sea routes. Ironically, in both times of peace and war, Lebanon served as the middle-man in European–Arab business.

Parties to war

The Lebanese State

Despite the urgent need to control the fighting, the political machinery of the Lebanese government became paralyzed when the war broke out. Deeply divided between the predominantly Maronite and the Muslim Arab nationalist supporters, the government was unable to agree on whether or not to use the army to stop the bloodshed. Army officers themselves were divided by sectarian and political affil-iations. Serious concerns existed over the split of the army along confessional lines. In fact, the army witnessed various defections and splits throughout the war. Different battalions were established under the Lebanese Arab Army, which supported the Muslim–Left–Palestinian alliance, while the South Lebanon Army was backed by a Christian–Israeli alliance.[14]

Jumblatt and his leftist supporters in the Lebanese National Movement (LNM) tried to isolate the Phalangists politically. Other Christian sects rallied to Gemayel's camp, creating a further rift in the government. As a consequence, Prime Minister Rashid al Solh and his cabinet resigned in May 1975, and a new government was formed under Rashid Karami. Although there were many calls for his resignation, President Frangieh steadfastly retained his office.

The Lebanese Front

The Lebanese Front was a right-wing coalition of mainly Christian parties formed in 1976, presided by former President of Lebanon and head of the National Liberal Party, Camille Chamoun. Noumour Al Ahrar (Tigers of the Liberals) was the military wing of the NLP during the Lebanese Civil War, led by Chamoun's son, Danny Chamoun. The Lebanese Front's main participants also included the Kataab (or Phalange) Party – the largest political party in Lebanon at the time – founded and led by Pierre Jemayel and the Marada Brigade, the private militia to the family of president Suleiman Frangieh, who had just finished his presidential term. Besides prominent political and government officials, the Lebanese Front also included first-class intellectuals in its membership, such as Fuad Frem al-Boustani, the President of the Lebanese University, as well as the distinguished professor of philosophy Charles Malik, who received 63 honorary doctoral degrees and headed the United Nations General Assembly. For a brief period, the poet Said Aql was a member of the Lebanese Front. The Front also had religious figures within its ranks, such as Charbel Qassis, the head of the permanent congress of the Lebanese monastic orders, who was later replaced by Bulous Naaman.

Christian militias under the Lebanese Front controlled East Beirut and suburbs, as well as the Northern Part of Mount Lebanon and several Christian populated pockets in the Bekaa Valley, South Lebanon, and the Chouf. The unity of the Christian parties, however, proved to be fragile. Intra-Christian struggle for power and control of territories soon proved bloody. Not only did this struggle divide the Front among its main components, but also divided the Kataab party itself between the Lebanese Forces, led by field militia leader Samir Geagea, and the traditional Jemayel family leadership. A major blow to the Lebanese Front came after the split of the Marada Party, which was a close ally to the Syrian president **Hafez Al-Assad**. This led to direct confrontation between the Lebanese Front and the Syrian Army, leading eventually to closer ties between Christian parties and Israel, to confront both Syrian and Palestinian forces. In 1982, following the invasion of Israel and the pullout of the PLO from the South and Beirut, the Phalangist party leader Bashir Jemayel was elected President, only to be assassinated a few weeks later. His brother Amin Jemayel succeeded him as President and tried in vain to contain Syrian-backed Lebanese Muslim militias.

Lebanese National Movement

The LNM was a leftist and Arab nationalist gathering of parties and organizations opposing the Maronite-dominated sectarian order in Lebanon. As a self-proclaimed "democratic, progressive and non-sectarian" front, the LNM was the main opposition against the Lebanese Front in the early years of the Civil War. The LNM was led by Kamal Jumblatt, the Druze leader of the Progressive Socialist Party, which served as an effective Druze militia, supported by its excellent ties with the Soviet Union. Mohsen Ibrahim, leader of the Communist Action Organization in Lebanon, was the general secretary of the LNM. Other prominent political parties within the LNF included the Lebanese Communist Party, the Syrian Social Nationalist Party, both the pro-Syrian and the pro-Iraqi Lebanese Ba'ath factions, Nasserite groups including al-Mourabitoun and several other minor parties. Numerous Palestinian organizations established a close link with the LNM, notably those from the **Rejectionist Front**. Both the **Popular Front for the Liberation of Palestine** (PFLP) and the Democratic Front for the Liberation of Palestine (DFLP) were active affiliates with whom the LNM later established the United Forces.

The LNM was also associated with an array of smaller less-known parties which, despite their limited support base, were quite active between the 1960s and early 1970s. They shared the same objectives as the leading LNM parties (i.e. the recognition of Lebanon as an Arab country and unwavering support for the PLO). Most of these organizations adopted revolutionary or populist ideologies, such as Arab nationalism, libertarianism, anarchism, radical socialism and Marxism. They were united in their common opposition against the status quo and strived for social revolution that would transform Lebanese society toward the anti-imperialism camp.[15]

Some of these parties include the Revolutionary Communist Group, the Front of Patriotic Christians, the Democratic Lebanese Movement, the Movement of Arab Lebanon, the Arab Revolutionary Movement, the Partisans of the Revolution, the Vanguards of Popular Action, the Organization of Arab Youth, the Units of the Arab Call, the Movement of Arab Revolution, the Sixth of February Movement, the 24 October Movement, the Lebanese Movement in Support of Fatah, the Knights of Ali, and the Black Panthers.[16]

At the beginning of the war in 1975, the different militias were estimated at roughly 25,000 LNM militiamen (not including allied Palestinian factions) against 18,000 right-wing Lebanese Front militiamen. The total number of fighters from the two different factions was relatively large, given that the total population in Lebanon was close to three million at the time.[17]

After the 1979 Iranian Revolution, militant Shia groups began to emerge, such as the Amal Movement, and later, **Hezbollah**. Both groups, while at odds with the Christian groups, were not part of the LNM and presented a direct challenge to both the Left and the PLO. Shia groups were backed by Syria and Iran and presented themselves as more capable and organized to confront Israeli aggressions. Fighting by the Syrian-backed Amal Movement against the LNM spread throughout the early 1980s and against the PLO factions during the mid-1980s. Intra-Shia struggle proved deadly after the establishment of the Iranian-backed Hezbollah, who challenged the Amal Movement over Shia leadership and control. Hezbollah emerged as the most effective and organized military group.

Palestinian Liberation Organization

The PLO was undoubtedly Lebanon's most potent fighting force after relocating to the country from Jordan in 1970, after the events of Black September. The PLO was armed, financed, trained, and supported by the Soviet Union and various Arab countries. The PLO was a loose confederation of militant groups under the leadership of **Yasser Arafat**, who was unable during later years of the war to control the fierce intra-factional rivalry that undermined both the PLO's operative strength and Lebanese sympathy for its presence in the country. With time, the organization's image in Lebanon was marred by radical factions, who turned out to be nothing more than **protection rackets**. The most important PLO combatants were Arafat's powerful Fatah, which adhered to a nationalist doctrine and waged guerrilla warfare, the PFLP and its splinter the DFLP; the latter groups adopted a version of Maoism in their struggle, but remained close to the Soviet Union. Lesser roles were played by the fractious Palestinian Liberation Front and another splinter group from the PFLP, the Syrian-aligned Popular Front for the Liberation of Palestine – General Command (PFLP-GC). To complicate matters, the Ba'athist governments in Syria and Iraq both set up Palestinian puppet organizations within the PLO.[18]

The PLO–LNM military alliance, known as the Common Forces, achieved major military victories throughout the first two years of the war. The Lebanese Front lost most of the areas that it controlled and the Common Forces advanced rapidly. By the end of 1976, it appeared imminent that the Palestinian–Lebanese

Left alliance was sure of victory. This alarmed not only Israel, but Syria and most Arab states as well, who were fearful of a growing radical left-wing influence and a Palestinian power base in Lebanon. Syria soon intervened against the PLO and the Arab League convened to mandate to Syria the **Arab Deterrent Force**, with the mission of ending the Lebanese Civil War. The ADF succeeded in halting the fighting in 1977, but soon became part of the war, as its forces were reduced only to those of the Syrian Army. The power of the PLO was significantly reduced.

Syria

By June 1976, fighting raged throughout Lebanon and the Lebanese Front were on the verge of defeat. Christian fears had also been greatly exacerbated by the **Damour massacre**, where many Christians were either killed or evicted from the coastal town of Damour after being overrun by Palestinian and allied forces. Many felt that the stakes had been raised above mere political power and became existential. Thus, President Suleiman Frangieh called for Syrian intervention in Lebanon to aid in ending the civil war. Moreover, Syria's own political and territorial interests in Lebanon were at stake, such as Lebanon harboring opposition parties to the Ba'ath government of Hafez al Assad, including cells of the Islamist **Muslim Brotherhood** and various factions of the PLO. Syria responded by ending its prior affiliation with the Palestinian Rejectionist Front and began supporting the Maronite-dominated government. In theory, this put Syria on the same side as Israel, which had already begun to supply Maronite forces with arms, tanks, and military advisers in May 1976.[19]

At the President's request, Syrian troops entered Lebanon, occupying Tripoli and the Bekaa Valley, easily defeating the LNM and Palestinian defenses. A ceasefire was imposed, but it ultimately failed to stop the conflict. Damascus began to increase the pressure, and paved the way for Lebanon's Christian militias to break through the defenses of the Tel al-Zaatar Palestinian refugee camp in East Beirut, which had long been under siege. A massacre of about 3,000 Palestinians followed, which unleashed heavy criticism against Syria from the rest of the Arab world.[20] In October 1976, Syria accepted the proposal of the Arab League summit in Riyadh. This gave Syria a mandate to keep originally 27,000 troops in Lebanon, expanded during later years, to serve as the bulk of an Arab Deterrent Force invested in restoring calm.[21] Other Arab nations were also part of the Arab Deterrent Force, but lost interest relatively soon, and Syria was again left in sole control of keeping the peace in Lebanon, except now with the Arab Deterrent Force as a diplomatic shield against international criticism. The civil war officially ended at this point, and an uneasy quiet settled over Beirut and most of Lebanon. In the south, however, the climate began to deteriorate as a consequence of the gradual return of PLO combatants, who had been required to vacate central Lebanon under the terms of the Riyadh Accords.

Syria pursued a strategy of controlling both Lebanese and the Palestinian factional politics. On the Lebanese front, it supported sectarian and intra-sectarian factionalism in order to gain the upper hand and emerge as a mediator and peace keeper. Syrian efforts succeeded in undermining both the Lebanese Front and the LNM, and alternatively empowered its proxy groups such as the Shia Amal Movement and Christian Marada, as well as splinter groups of the Lebanese Forces headed by Houbeyka. On the Palestinian fronts, it backed its own groups such as the PFLP-GC and instigated various splits and division among its rival Fatah group. It also backed the Amal Movement in waging wars against Palestinian refugee camps.[22]

Israel

The continual violence near the Lebanese border between Israel and the PLO, which started in 1968, made Israel a major player in Lebanese politics. Israel began assisting Lebanese Christian militias in their fight against the PLO as early as 1976. Israel's main Lebanese partner was the Phalange party, led by Bashir Jemayel. The border conflicts peaked with Operation Litany in 1978, which resulted in the creation of the **United Nations Interim Force in Lebanon** (UNIFIL), following the adoption of Security Council Resolution 425 in March 1978. Although the resolution stipulated an Israeli withdrawal from Southern Lebanon, Israel established a security zone in southern Lebanon, with mostly Christian inhabitants, in which they began to supply training and arms to Christian militias, which would later form the South Lebanese Army. Hundreds of Lebanese militiamen began to train in Israel at the Israel Defense Forces Staff and Command College. The relationship between Israel and the Phalange grew into a political and strategic alliance. The Israeli government began to conceive a plan to install a pro-Israel Christian government in Lebanon.[23]

With the completion of Israeli withdrawal from Sinai in March 1982, under the terms of the **Egyptian–Israeli Peace Treaty** (Camp David Agreement), the **Likud**-led government of Israel became more aggressive with its operations in Lebanon. The Israeli invasion of 1982 caused a staggering blow to the Palestinians and the LNM, and dramatically strengthened the Lebanese Front, bringing Bashir Jemayel to presidency. However, within days of assuming office, Bashir Jemayel was assassinated, and his brother, Amin, was hastily elected in his place. Growing American involvement in Lebanon post-Israeli invasion was aimed at brokering a withdrawal agreement between Lebanon and Israel. The agreement was hoped to be a precursor for a more comprehensive peace treaty between the two countries. However, by 1984, the Israeli "new order" in Lebanon had all but collapsed. The May 17, 1984, **Lebanese–Israeli agreement**, which faced strong opposition from Syria, was not ratified and was soon abrogated by the Lebanese government. Thus, Israel began withdrawal from most Lebanese territories, except for a border strip in South Lebanon under the control of the surrogate South Lebanon Army. The Lebanese government turned away from Israel and the United States and opened dialogue with Syria to find a way out of the impasse. By 1985, Syria had regained most of the power over Lebanese affairs that it lost to the Israelis and Americans in 1982.

Lebanon during the 1980s

The Tripartite Agreement

In 1983, the first major attempt at securing a peace agreement was undertaken by representatives from the major Lebanese factions, who met in Geneva for a national dialogue conference. It achieved little progress, and they were only able to agree on the issue of Lebanon's Arab identity. When the representatives met again in Lausanne the following year, they were still incapable of making any further progress. In December of 1985, with the encouragement of the Syrians, representatives of the dominant sectarian militias (the Christian Lebanese Forces, the Shia Amal Movement, and the predominantly Druze Progressive Socialist Party) met in Damascus and reached an agreement designed to end the Lebanese conflict, and to implement political reforms and special relations with Syria. This agreement is known as the Tripartite Agreement. It provided for an immediate ceasefire and official proclamation of the end of the state of war within one year. The militias would be disarmed and then disbanded. Sole responsibility for security would be relegated to the reconstituted and religiously integrated Lebanese army, supported by Syrian forces. Moreover, the accord envisaged a "strategic integration" of the two countries in spheres of military affairs, national security, and foreign relations. The accord also mandated fundamental political reform, including the establishment of a bicameral legislature and the domination of the old confessional formula, which was to be replaced by majority rule and minority representation.[24] However, in early 1986, President Amin Jemayel and Samir Geagea (then intelligence chief of the Lebanese Forces) organized a coup against the Lebanese Forces leader, Elie Hobeika, who was ousted from his position. Thus, the Tripartite Agreement was rendered null and void.

Intensification of intra-confessional clashes

A state of political paralysis settled over Lebanon, as Prime Minister Rashid Karami and the cabinet boycotted every one of President Gemayel's decisions. Karami resigned the following year, but was assassinated shortly afterward on June 1, 1987. Nevertheless, the cabinet continued to function, with **Salim al-Hoss** as acting Prime Minister. At the end of Gemayel's term, on September 23, 1988, the failure to elect a new president led to a political vacuum. Jemayel appointed an interim cabinet headed by Army commander **Michel Aoun**, but the cabinet's authority was only accepted in predominantly Christian areas. The three Muslim officers of the six-man interim government boycotted the decision because the National Pact of 1943 reserved the position of Prime Minister for a Sunni Muslim. In West Beirut and other regions of the country, the original cabinet headed by Salim al-Hoss was regarded as the legitimate cabinet. Executive authority was thus split between the military government of Aoun and the civilian government of Hoss. The two governments each claimed exclusive legitimacy and opposed each other. The legislative authority also experienced a vacuum because the parliament failed to renew the one-year term of the speaker or to elect a new one. The crisis intensified with the fragmentation of the military establishment, led by General Aoun. On March 14, 1989, Aoun and the Lebanese army troops under his command began a self-declared "War of Liberation" against the Syrians. Conflict in this period was also exacerbated by increasing Iraqi involvement, as **Saddam Hussein** searched for proxy battlefields for the Iran–Iraq war. Saddam Hussein supported Aoun and supplied him with arms to counter Iran's influence through Amal and Hezbollah. The areas under General Aoun's authority were besieged and devastated by the battles, resulting in a massive emigration of the inhabitants. Moreover, instead of curtailing the Syrian presence in Lebanon, it increased their numbers from around 30,000 to 40,000 troops.[25]

Intra-confessional battles during the 1980s (in the Mountain and Chouf area during 1983, Beirut in 1984 and East Sidon in 1985) highlighted the increasingly sectarian character of the Lebanese conflict. The War of the Camps was one of the wars between members of the same camp. On May 1985, heavy fighting erupted between Amal and Palestinians for the control of Sabra, Shatila and Burj el Brajne camps. Tensions were also present in the South. The presence of Palestinians in the predominantly Shia area led to frequent clashes in different camps in Tyre and Sidon. The Maronites and the Shia were the most intensely affected by the series of intra-confessional clashes that raged in Lebanon amongst rival groups battling for power over the two sects. Confessionally based militia rule prevailed over the various enclaves of the country. In the "Christian areas", the militias spread slogans of a "Christian republic," claiming that "Christian security" would be promoted through federalism and partition. In the "Muslim areas", emerging radical Shia Islamic movements raised the slogans of a just Islamic republic.[26]

Aoun exploited the popular mood, which deeply resented the militia order and the traditional political establishment, which was considered largely responsible for the disintegration of Lebanon, and placed heavy emphasis on the issues of reasserting the independence and sovereignty of Lebanon. On January 30, 1990, another war broke out between Aoun's troops and the Lebanese Forces militia, now led by Samir Geagea. This intra-Maronite war was militarily indecisive, yet politically divisive because it eroded the capacities of both forces to effectively or legitimately act on behalf the Christians in Lebanon. Similarly, an intra-Shia war took place in South Lebanon and the southern suburbs of Beirut where destructive battles raged between the two major Shia forces: Amal and Hezbollah. The Shias were split both ideologically and in terms of outside support. Syria supported Amal, who fought for territory and political position with the Iranian supported Hezbollah. Intra-sectarian power struggles, between opposing Shia and Maronite parties left the communities divided. In the absence of effective leadership and international support, the power struggles undermined the negotiating positions of the Christian groups during the Taef negotiations; resulting in their relative marginalization from the post-war political order.

Chronology of major events

1975:   April 13   An attempt on Phalangist party leader, Pierre
                        Jemayel, outside a church in a Beirut suburb kills
                        two Phalangist fighters. The militia retaliates by
                        firing against a bus carrying Palestinians in East
                        Beirut. This was the spark setting off fighting all
                        over the country which, in its first stage, would last
                        for over a year.

1976:   January   Intense fighting all over the country destroys the
                        most important state institutions and public build-
                        ings.

        April: The CF alliance of LNM and PLO manages to take
                        control of nearly 70 per cent of Lebanon.

        June: Syrian troops invade Lebanon and soon become the
                        strongest party to the war, controlling many of the
                        most important strategic positions in the country.

        September: Following a Libya-brokered ceasefire, Elias Sarkis
                        wins a Syrian backed presidential election.

        November: A truce takes hold across the country, except in the
                        south where the PLO faces a Christian militia
                        supported by Israel.

1977:   Syria intervenes under the Arab League Mandate
                        (Arab Forces then Deterrent Forces). Kamal
                        Jumblatt is assassinated.

1978:   Israel intervenes in South, occupying most areas
                        south of the Litany River and establishes a Security
                        Zone under the Israeli-backed South Lebanese
                        Army. The UNSC passes Resolution 425 demand-
                        ing full Israeli withdrawal from Lebanese
                        territories. UNIFIL is established to observe the
                        ceasing of hostilities.

1982:   Israel invades Lebanon and occupies the capital city
                        Beirut. The PLO is forced to withdraw its fighters
                        and Syria pulls out from most Israeli-occupied
                        areas. Bashir Jemayel is elected President and assas-
                        sinated a few days later; he is then succeeded by his
                        brother, Amin. Palestinians are massacred in Beirut
                        refugee camps. Lebanon and Israel establish a secu-
                        rity agreement in May, 1984. US Marines, Italian
                        and French forces that intervened to preserve the
                        peace are attacked by suicide bombers.

1985:		Lebanese resistance to Israeli occupation escalates. Hezbollah is formally established. Israel is forced to withdraw from most occupied areas. Druze–Christian fighting in the Chouf Mountain leads to massacres.
1987:		The PLO recognizes Israel (Algerian Conference – two-state solution).
1988:	September 22:	The outgoing President, Amine Jemayel, dismisses the civilian administration of Prime Minister Selim al-Hoss, and appoints a six-member interim military government headed by Maronite Army Chief, Michel Aoun (as prescribed by the Lebanese Constitution should there be no election of a President as was the case at the time), composed of three Christians and three Muslims, although the Muslims refused to serve. Aoun becomes Acting Prime Minister.
1988–89:		Aoun wages two wars: liberation against the Syrians, and elimination against rival Christian group, the Lebanese Forces.
1989:		Iraq invades Kuwait; Syria and the Kingdom of Saudi Arabia side with the USA.
1989:		The Taef Agreement calls for the end of the war and the restructuring of the Lebanese state; Aoun opposes the agreement and is backed by Iraq.
1990:		Syria invades Christian areas controlled by Aoun; Lebanon is placed under Syrian protectionism; Taef is incorporated into the constitution (Ratified by Parliament). Aoun is exiled.

Summary

The chapter began by examining the 1958 crisis, which gave an introduction to the international struggle over Lebanon's geopolitically strategic territory that contributed to civil conflict among the Lebanese. The creation of Israel and the following Arab–Israeli war marked the height of ideological and political polarization of the international system. The support of Arab nationalist regimes by the USSR would encourage anti-Western sentiments in the MENA region, straining relationships between the region and the West. The USSR influence accompanied by declining colonialism encouraged the rise of the left-wing movement, seen in the rise of Communist parties, the ascendance of socialist-leaning Nasserism, and the establishment of the Ba'ath regimes in Syria and Iraq.

Lebanon's then conservative government, led by Maronite President Chamoun, was closely allied with the West and thus fearful of the rising power of Arab nationalism. The Lebanese government grew resistant to USSR influence. Relations between Lebanon and governments in Egypt, Iraq, and Syria were strained. Domestic politics were also divided. Horizontal polarization of society (at the popular level) between supporters of Arab nationalism versus Lebanese nationalism was echoed by a vertical division among Christian and Muslim elites. The civil war in Lebanon would last from 1975 to 1990. An estimated 130,000 civilians were killed in the course of the 15-year conflict, while one million (nearly one-quarter of the population) were wounded; there was also a mass migration from the country during this time.[27] The Lebanese Civil War, in addition to its many atrocities, was also marked by regular shifts in alliances between the fighting factions.

Following a detailed description of the conflict itself, the chapter went on to introduce the major parties to the Lebanese Civil War: The Lebanese State, the Lebanese Front, the Lebanese National Movement, the PLO, Syria and Israel. Each party's role in the war, together with its strategic alliances, has been described in detail. The chapter ends by describing the Tripartite Agreement, which was the first agreement that entailed ending the civil war, and finally the Taef Accord, which would effectively end the war and call for the restructuring of the Lebanese State.

References

1　Yaqub, S. (2004) *Containing Arab Nationalism: The Eisenhower Doctrine and the Middle East*. Chapel Hill and London: University of North Carolina Press.
2　Gerges, F. (1993) 'The Lebanese Crisis of 1958: The Risks of Inflated Self-Importance', *Beirut Review*, (5): 83–113.
3　Nevo, J. (2008) 'September 1970 in Jordan: A Civil War?', *Civil Wars*, 10 (3): 217–30.
4　Zakariah, M. (2010) 'The Uprising of the Fedayeen Against the Government of Jordan, 1970–1971: Declassified Documents from The British Archive', *International Journal of West Asian Studies*, 2 (2): 47–64.
5　Collelo, T., ed. (1987) *Lebanon: A Country Study*. Washington: GPO for the Library of Congress.
6　Salamey, I. (2013) 'The Crisis of Consociational Democracy in Beirut: Conflict Transformation and Sustainability through Electoral Reform' in *Urban Sustainability: A Global Perspective*. East Lansing: Michigan State University Press, pp. 177–98.
7　UN System Lebanon (2011) United Nations Relief and Works Agency for Palestine Refugees in the Near East (UNRWA). Available online at www.un.org.lb/Subpage.aspx?pageid=65.
8　Chamie, J. (1976/77) 'The Lebanese Civil War: An Investigation into the Causes', *Political Science Quarterly*, 139 (3): 171–88.
9　Khalaf, S. (2002) *Civil and Uncivil Violence in Lebanon: A History of the Internationalization of Communal Conflict*. New York: Columbia University Press.
10　Seaver, B. (2000) 'The Regional Sources of Power-Sharing Failure: The Case of Lebanon', *Political Science Quarterly*, 115 (2): 247–71.

11   Corm, G. (2004) *Modern Lebanon: History and Society*. Beirut: Al-Maktabh Al-Sharkeyah [Arabic].

12   Seaver, B. (2000) 'The Regional Sources of Power-Sharing Failure: The Case of Lebanon', *Political Science Quarterly*, 115 (2): 247–71.

13   Picard, E. (2000) 'The Political Economy of Civil War in Lebanon' in S. Heydemann (ed.) *War, Institutions, and Social Change in the Middle East*. Berkeley: University of California Press, pp. 292–322.

14   Seaver, B. (2000) 'The Regional Sources of Power-Sharing Failure: The Case of Lebanon', *Political Science Quarterly*, 115 (2): 247–71.

15   El Khazen, F. (2000) *The Breakdown of the State in Lebanon: 1967–1976*. London: Tauris, pp. 164–7.

16   Badran, T. (2008) The Lebanese Civil War. *Middle East Review of International Affairs*, 12 (2), Article 7. Available online at www.gloria-center.org/2008/06/badran-2008-06-07/

17   Badran, T. (2008) The Lebanese Civil War. *Middle East Review of International Affairs*, 12 (2), Article 7. Available online at www.gloria-center.org/2008/06/badran-2008-06-07/

18   Hudson, M. (1978) 'The Palestinian Factor in the Lebanese Civil War', *Middle East Journal*, 32 (3): 261–78.

19   Hudson, M. (1978) 'The Palestinian Factor in the Lebanese Civil War', *Middle East Journal*, 32 (3): 261–78.

20   Harris, W. (1996) *Faces of Lebanon. Sects, Wars, and Global Extensions*. Princeton: Markus Wiener Publishers, p. 165.

21   Makdisi, S. and Sadaka, R. (2003) *The Lebanese Civil War: 1975–1990*. Lecture and Working Paper Series (2003 No. 3). Beirut: American University of Beirut, Institute of Financial and Economics. Available online at www.aub.edu.lb/fas/ife/Documents/downloads/series3_2003.pdf

22   O'Ballance, E. (1998) *Civil War in Lebanon, 1975–92*. London: Palgrave Macmillan.

23   Zisser, E. (1995) 'The Maronites, Lebanon and the State of Israel: Early Contacts', *Middle Eastern Studies*, 31 (4): 889–918.

24   See Taef Agreement, paragraph 7, Political Reforms. Available online at www.mideastinfo.com/documents/taif.htm

25   Abdelnour, Z. and Gambill, G. (2003) 'Syria's Fourth Redeployment from Lebanon', *Middle East Intelligence Bulletin*, 5 (7). Available online at www.meforum.org/meib/articles/0307_11.htm

26   Salamey, I. and Pearson, F. (2007) 'Hezbollah: A Proletarian Party with an Islamic Manifesto – A Sociopolitical Analysis of Islamist Populism in Lebanon and the Middle East', *Journal of Small Wars and Insurgencies*, 18 (3): 416–38.

27   Khalaf, S. (2002) *Civil and Uncivil Violence in Lebanon: A History of the Internationalization of Communal Conflict*. New York: Columbia University Press.

5 Consociationalism reformed I

The Taef Republic (1989–2008)

This chapter examines the factors that led to a decline in domestic support for belligerents. The external factors facilitating a settlement are examined in terms of the waning Palestinian–Israeli conflict, the growing Syrian influence, and the end of the Cold War. The Taef Agreement, electoral reform and remaining political, economic and security contentions are analyzed. The chapter looks in detail at the United Nations Security Council (UNSC) Resolutions concerning Lebanon and examines more contemporary events, such as the 2006 war and the crisis of 2008 leading up to the **Doha Agreement**.

Prelude to the Taef Agreement

Declining domestic support for the belligerents

Public's opposition to the war and support for a quick settlement grew rapidly, as intra-sectarian conflicts degenerated into a series of ever-bloodier retaliations. The majority of ordinary Lebanese citizens, as well as many social, cultural, and popular organizations, rejected the separation of citizens, regions and cities along confessional lines. They expressed their desire for unity and openly opposed the militias, as demonstrated by a massive labor-organized joint Christian–Muslim protest in 1987 along the **Green Line**.[1] Moreover, it was generally accepted that none of the warring factions could decisively win the war, and the only alternative was the formation of a political compromise, ensuring the continuity of Lebanon as an entity with a united central political system. Thus, the rebuilding of the Lebanese state was viewed as the only rational way out of the civil war system.

External factors facilitating a settlement

The changes in public opinion internally coincided with both regional and international developments that favored a political settlement to the war in Lebanon. The ideological and political polarization between Lebanese factions, and their subsequent efforts to defend or promote their interests invited external intervention. However, just as it was necessary to settle internal disputes to minimize the influence of external forces, it was also necessary to have their tacit acceptance, at least, to minimize their capacity to oppose such a settlement in order for it to succeed.

Decline of Palestinian–Israeli conflict

Within the context of the Arab–Israeli conflict, various Lebanese factions repeatedly attempted to exploit their associations with opposing regional players, to promote their own agendas. Israel lost interest in Lebanon after 1984–85 and was preoccupied with the rising **Palestinian Intifada**, which erupted in December 1987 in the occupied territories of the West Bank and Gaza Strip. In addition, the Palestine Liberation Organization's (PLO) power in Lebanon, guaranteed in the Cairo Agreement, was diminished with the exile of PLO leadership to Tunis and the disbanding of its heavily armed forces in Lebanon in 1982. Later developments between 1983 and 1988 (i.e., the battles between Syrian and Palestinian troops in the north) battles between Amal and the Palestinians in Beirut, and various intra-Palestinian fights further contributed to the weakening of the Palestinian military force in Lebanon, and most armed Palestinians forces were isolated within a few refugee camps of South Lebanon.

The 1987 Algiers Conference presented a formal acceptance of the PLO for a two-state solution according to UNSC Resolution 242, which implied recognition of the State of Israel. The PLO's new stance was not only a reflection of the declining power of the PLO, but also of its intention to enter into a direct peace negotiation with Israel for a final settlement. Thus, the Algiers Conference represented an end to the PLO's long-held position that considered armed struggle as the only means to liberate Palestine.[2]

Syrian influence

In contrast to the Israeli and Palestinian presence, Syrian influence in Lebanon increased as the war progressed. The Syrian military intervention in Lebanon took place on June 1, 1976, upon invitation from the President and the Lebanese Front against the Lebanese National Movement (NLM) and their Palestinian allies. It provided the Ba'ath regime with solid diplomatic and material footing in Lebanese affairs. In October 1976, two Arab summits held in Cairo and Riyadh endorsed the Syrian intervention, and deployed an Arab Deterrent Force (mainly composed of Syrian troops) to impose a ceasefire over Lebanon. In 1978, the Lebanese Front forced the Syrian troops to evacuate the areas they had occupied (East Beirut and adjoining regions to the north) only after a military confrontation. In 1982, Syrian troops, together with the Palestinian troops, were forced by the Israelis to evacuate West Beirut. However, within a few years, Syria was able to regain its footing in Lebanon. In 1987, Syrian troops reentered West Beirut, various regions of the Mountain, the Chouf and the southern suburbs of Beirut. In 1990, Syrian troops reentered East Beirut and other predominantly Christian areas, enclaves which they had occupied in the past.

The consolidation of Syrian influence in Lebanon occurred with Arab and Western acquiescence. This was particularly the case after Syria joined the Western–Arab alliance against Iraqi president Saddam Hussein's invasion of Kuwait. Syrian support to the US-led first Gulf War alliance was supplemented by international support for a Syrian–Saudi guardianship over Lebanon. This culminated in a green light for Syrian forces to terminate Aoun's opposition to the Taef Accord, and, ultimately, to the military takeover of Christian controlled areas. Aoun was thus removed from Lebanese polity, at least for a period of time. The alternative political rise of the Lebanese–Saudi businessman **Rafik al-Hariri** to power in 1992 was a sign of a growing Saudi–Syrian rapprochement over Lebanon.

End of the Cold War

The end of the Cold War and the breakup of the Soviet Union brought to a close the flow of material and diplomatic support from the Communist bloc to the array of leftist groups embroiled in the Lebanese conflict. As a result, these groups saw their support and power bases dwindle. As the only remaining superpower, America's influence strengthened in the region with fewer obstacles. The United States was primarily interested in bringing an end to the crisis in Lebanon as to gain influence and to advance the Arab–Israeli peace process. After the development of the Gulf Crisis in 1990, the United States was concerned with containing Iraq and gaining Syrian support for the Gulf war coalition. Thus, the United States supported the Taef negotiations.

The Taef Agreement

The cause of the Lebanese Civil War was neither exclusively internal nor external, nor was its settlement. During the three decades after independence, various internal tensions inherent to the Lebanese system and multiple regional developments collectively contributed to the breakdown of governmental authority and the outbreak of civil strife in 1975. The Lebanese Civil War came to an end at a specific historical juncture, at a time when movement toward internal reconciliation coincided with favorable regional and international developments.

After 22 days of discussion and consultation in the Saudi city of Al-Taef, the 62 surviving members of the 1972 parliament reached an agreement to end the Lebanese Civil War once and for all on October 22, 1989. The agreement was based on a document that had already largely been prepared by the Arab Tripartite Committee (comprising Algeria, Morocco, and Saudi Arabia) after much consultation with Syria, the United States and various Lebanese leaders. On October 31, the UNSC declared its support to the Taef Agreement.[3] The signing of the Taef Agreement (officially named the Document of National Accord) by the belligerent Lebanese factions on October 22, 1989, and its ratification on November 4, 1989, under the auspices of Syria and the Saudi monarchy, provided the basis for the ending of the civil war and the return to political normalcy in Lebanon.

Upon their return to Lebanon, Parliamentarians ratified the agreement on November 4, and elected **Rene Moawad** as President the following day. Moawad's presidency was short-lived as he was assassinated in a car bomb seventeen days after his inauguration. Elias Hrawi was consequently elected and remained in office until 1998.

The Taef Agreement reconfigured the political power-sharing formula that formed the basis of government in Lebanon (first established by the National Covenant of 1943) and provided the foundation of the "Second Sectarian Republic" in the following ways:

- It introduced into the preamble of the ratified constitution a clause asserting Lebanon as the final homeland of all its inhabitants, being an Arab, parliamentary, and democratic country based on the separation of powers and the declarations of human rights.
- It relocated most presidential powers in favor of Parliament and the Council of Ministers. The Maronite Christian President lost most of his executive powers and retained symbolic roles (See Articles 49–53, 55, 64 and 65 of the ratified Taef Constitution in Appendix A).
- It redistributed important public offices, including those of Parliament, Council of Ministers, general directors, and grade-one posts evenly between Muslims and Christians. This upset the traditional ratio of six to five that favored Christians established by the National Covenant of 1943.
- It recognized the chronic instability of confessionalism and called for devising a national strategy for its political demise. It required the formation of a national committee to examine ways to achieve deconfessionalization and the formation of a non-confessional Parliament (Article 95). To date, this provision has not yet been implemented.
- It established unique relations of mutuality with Syria, legitimized its guardianship, and called for the gradual withdrawal of its troops. Even though Taef set a schedule for Syrian withdrawal within two years, Syria remained a major player in Lebanese affairs for decades to come.
- It required the disarmament of all Lebanese militias. Only Hezbollah was allowed to remain armed as a "resistance force" in recognition to its fight against Israel in the South.

The result of various power reconfigurations, the Taef Agreement marked the birth of the second Lebanese Republic (1990–2008).

The end of the war

Acting Prime Minister and military General, Michel Aoun, refused to accept the Taef Agreement and denounced the election of Rene Moawad as the President of the Lebanese Republic. Moawad was assassinated in a car bomb in Beirut on November 22, 1989. He was succeeded by Elias Hrawi (who remained in office until 1998). Aoun again refused to accept the election, ordering the dissolution of Parliament. However, the MPs refused his instructions.

On January 16, 1990, General Aoun ordered all Lebanese media to cease using terms like "President" or "Minister" to describe Hrawi and other participants in the Taef government. The Lebanese Forces, which had grown into a rival power broker in the Christian parts of the capital, protested by suspending all its broadcasts. Fearing that the Lebanese Forces were planning to link up with the Hrawi administration, on January 31, 1990, Aoun ordered the Lebanese Army forces to attack the Lebanese Forces. This brought fierce fighting to East Beirut between the opposing Christian factions.[4]

As Saddam Hussein focused his attention on Kuwait, Iraqi supplies and support to Aoun dwindled. On October 13, Syria seized the opportunity to launch a major operation involving its army and air force against Aoun's stronghold around the presidential palace, where hundreds of Aoun supporters were executed. The Syrian operation could not have taken place without the agreement of the United States. In exchange for its support to the US-sponsored international campaign waged against the Iraqi regime of Saddam Hussein, the United States convinced Israel to refrain from attacking Syrian aircraft approaching Beirut, implicitly giving Syria a green light to bring a decisive end to Aoun's defiance. General Aoun was obliged to go into exile, leaving behind his family and supporters. The Syrian-backed government of President Hrawi was now in control over all Lebanese territories. In practice, the Lebanese Civil War came to an end.

Lebanese election and reform

On March 1991, Parliament passed an **amnesty law** that pardoned all political crimes prior to its enactment. The amnesty was not extended to crimes perpetrated against foreign diplomats or certain crimes referred by the cabinet to the Higher Judicial Council. In May 1991, the militias were dissolved, with the important exception of Hezbollah, and the Lebanese Armed Forces began to slowly rebuild themselves as Lebanon's only major non-sectarian institution.

Although the Taef Agreement stated that the abolition of confessionalism was a national goal, no specific deadline or timetable was provided for its actualization. The Chamber of Deputies was increased to 128 members, shared equally between Christians and Muslims. A cabinet was established similarly divided equally between Christians and Muslims. Lack of balanced internal representation in Parliament because of the Christians' decision to boycott the 1992 parliamentary election led some of those who had initially participated and supported the agreement to join the opposition.

Post-war social and political instability, fueled by economic uncertainty and the collapse of the Lebanese currency, led to the resignation of the first post-Taef Prime Minister **Omar Karami**, in May 1992, after less than two years in office. He was replaced by former Prime Minister Rashid al Solh, who was widely viewed as a caretaker, to oversee the election of the first Chamber of Deputies since 1972. By early November 1992, a new Parliament had been elected, and the Saudi-backed Prime Minister Rafik Hariri was appointed to form a cabinet.

The formation of a government headed by a successful billionaire businessman was widely seen as a sign that Lebanon would make a priority of rebuilding the country and reviving the economy. Solidere, a private real-estate company set up to rebuild downtown Beirut, was a symbol of Hariri's strategy to link economic recovery to private sector and foreign investment, also known as Horizon 2000. The Hariri government relied on borrowing money from domestic and international lending institutions for the rebuilding of the country, which amounted to 18 billion dollars in the early years.[5] During the Hariri premiership, major undertakings succeeded in rebuilding most of the country's destroyed infrastructure, including its airport, downtown, government buildings, seaports, roads, power stations, and telecommunication systems.

Hariri, however, was soon ousted from office after the election of his rival commander of the Lebanese Armed Forces and strong Syrian loyalist Émile Lahoud as President in 1998. Another opponent of Hariri and a former Prime Minister, Salim Al Hoss, replaced him in the post. The Syria–Hariri rift widened as a result of his growing power. Syria's Alawi-dominated regime was fearful from the emergence of a strong Saudi-backed Sunni leadership in Lebanon. Yet, the Hariri bloc's overwhelming victory in the 2000 parliamentary election forced his return to office as the Prime Minister despite the reluctance of the President and the Syrian regime. He was again dismissed as Premier in 2004 and replaced by Syrian loyalist and former Prime Minister Omar Karami. Hariri was finally assassinated in February 2005. His assassination marked a major turning point in the contemporary history of Lebanon, signaling the coming collapse of the Second Sectarian Republic.[6]

The Second Sectarian Republic witnessed major achievements. A power-sharing agreement was reached by the Taef Agreement, the war ended, parliamentary and municipal elections were held, and Lebanese civil society was on the mend, enjoying significantly more freedoms than elsewhere in the Arab world (Box 5.1). Yet, despite the various aspects of recovery from the catastrophic damage to infrastructure that incurred during its long civil war, the social and political divisions that gave rise to the conflict remained largely unresolved. Lingering sectarian power struggles and uneasiness about Syrian and other external influences remained.

Persisting contentions

Political divisions

Opposition from Lebanon's Christian parties (organized under the **Quornat Shehwan Gathering**, Free Patriotic Movement and Lebanese Forces), who were marginalized from power under the post-Taef system, opposed the Syrian presence in Lebanon. General Aoun and many Maronite Christians either opposed Taef outright or reluctantly accepted its terms. They also opposed and boycotted new parliamentary elections in 1992. The Maronite patriarch emerged as a staunch critic of Syrian activities in the country.

The post-Taef era produced a three-man show or a "troika' consisting of three

Box 5.1 Lebanon: Basic political statistics, 2012

Population[1]	4,131,583
GDP per capita (PPP)[2]	US$15,900
Human Development Index Rank[3]	72 (of 187 countries with comparable data)
Freedom House Rating[4]	Status: partly free
Political rights	5
Civil liberties	4
Freedom of the Press Rank[5]	101 (of 179 countries)
Corruption Index Rank (2011)[6]	128 (of 176 countries)

Notes:
GDP = gross domestic product; PPP = purchasing power parity.

1 Estimate, as at April 18, 2013. Central Intelligence Agency (2013) *The World Factbook*. Washington, DC: Office of Public Affairs. Available online at www.cia.gov/library/publications/the-world-factbook/geos/le.html (accessed March 28, 2013).
2 Estimate, as at April 18, 2013. Central Intelligence Agency (2013) *The World Factbook*. Washington, DC: Office of Public Affairs.
3 United Nations Development Programme (2013) *International Human Development Indicators, National Human Development Reports for Lebanon 2013 Report*. Available online at http://hdrstats.undp.org/en/countries/profiles/LBN.html (accessed March 28, 2013).
4 Freedom House (2012) *Freedom in the World 2012: Lebanon*. Washington, DC: Freedom House. Available online at www.freedomhouse.org/report/freedom-world/2012/lebanon (accessed March 28, 2013).
5 Reporters Without Borders (2013) *World Press Freedom Index 2013*. Paris: Reporters Without Borders. http://en.rsf.org/press-freedom-index-2013,1054.html (accessed March 28, 2013).
6 Transparency International, *Corruption Perceptions Index 2012*. http://cpi.transparency.org/cpi2012/results/ (accessed March 28, 2013).

figureheads: a Sunni prime minister, a Maronite president, and a Shia speaker, each referred to as President. Although the three "Presidents" paid their allegiance to the Syrian guardianship, sectarian strife infuriated their competition for power. Christians, however, were weakened and divided by contradictory agendas. The elections of August–September 1996 revealed the marginalization of the Maronites, as reflected in the subordination of the Maronite allocated office of the President to the influence of the Sunni prime minister and the Shia speaker. Worse, Christian opposition was split, with a group of notables in exile (General Aoun, Raymond Eddy, and former president Amin Jemayel) calling for the boycott of the election while others seeking participation.

Hariri rebuilding strategies and opposition

To finance the country's considerable reconstruction, the Lebanese government borrowed massive sums of money from the local and international lending institutions. This left Lebanon with one of the largest debt-to-GDP ratios in the world. The controversial economic platform adopted by the government, promising reform and privatization, and rising debt levels became major points of criticism against the Hariri government. In 2001, Prime Minister Hariri reached out for international backing and succeeded in convening a donor meeting known as the Paris I Conference. He succeeded in attracting 500 million euros to support development projects in return for wide-reaching government reforms, promises of modernization and privatization, and the improvement of revenues and collections. Another meeting, known as Paris II, convened the following year, and this time participants pledged over four billion dollars in international aid and investments. Hariri's domestic opponents, whether Christian, Shia, or pro-Syrians, were alarmed by the growing economic and political power of the Prime Minister and his Sunni sect. Their opposition to his policies also increased under different pretexts. Staunch criticism rose against his privatization policy. His critics claimed that privatization caused increased public economic vulnerability, debts, and international dependency.[7] Sectarian elites, however, feared most that privatization would undermine their system of sectarian patronage, nurtured within the public sector.

Hezbollah and the struggle for liberation

The situation in South Lebanon, after the Taef Agreement, remained extremely tense and prone to violence. As Israel maintained occupation forces in the area along with its Lebanese ally, the South Lebanon Army (SLA); the resistance, dominated by Shia Hezbollah, launched frequent operations against **Israeli Defense Forces** (IDF) targets in Lebanon. In 1993, hostilities between Israel and Hezbollah came to a head when Israel launched "Operation Accountability" a seven-day offensive designed to put an end to Hezbollah's shelling and attacks on IDF soldiers. An agreement by both parties to cease attacks on civilian targets was mediated by the United States to end the conflict. Nevertheless, tensions in the South remained. A devastating air campaign by Israel against Hezbollah, called "Operation Grapes of Wrath" was launched in April 1996 and caused the deaths of over 150 civilians.[8] This time, France mediated an agreement to establish rules of military engagement, barring attacks against civilian populated centers.

Hezbollah's guerilla-style warfare, backed by both Iran and Syria, mounted increasing pressure on Israeli troops and infrastructure. Hezbollah's incessant harassment of Israeli military outposts in occupied Lebanese territory was incredibly unpopular in Israeli public opinion and even prompted some Israeli forces to abandon their positions or refuse military service all together. Israeli Prime Minister Ehud Barak, who was elected in 1999, faced with considerable pressure, announced his intention to withdraw all troops from southern Lebanon. Israel's actual withdrawal from South Lebanon in 2000 resulted in the collapse of the SLA and the rapid advance of Hezbollah forces into the freed area. Thousands of Lebanese rushed back to the South to reclaim their villages and properties. The end of Israeli occupation of Lebanese territories marked a decisive victory for Hezbollah and its backers, namely Iran and Syria.

Hezbollah took control over the reconstruction and rehabilitation of the South and remained heavily armed despite Israel's withdrawal. As a staunch Iranian ally and supporter of the Syrian regime, whose influence over Lebanese affairs grew greater with time, the question of Shia Hezbollah's military activities and future role within domestic political life became a major source of controversy and contention within the Lebanese domestic sectarian landscape.

Emerging crises in the Second Republic

Western–Islamic contentions after 9/11

After the bombing of the Twin Towers in New York by Al Qaeda, the United States launched an ambitious and aggressive new security strategy in the Middle East. It called for preemptive military operations with claimed rights to strike against perceived threats to the United States. It also sought an agenda for democracy promotion in the region (by force if necessary) to counter rising Islamic fundamentalism and to eliminate so-called "**rogue states**", which perceived to pose threats to the United States and its allies.[9] A distinct Western–Islamic rift seemed to settle over the international community, dividing regimes between supporters and opponents of the United States. The US Administration, under George W. Bush, launched a "war on terror" in 2001 and invaded Afghanistan on the suspicion that Osama Bin Laden, blamed for the 9/11 attacks, was in hiding there. The United States then moved on to occupy Iraq in 2003, allegedly for possessing weapons of mass destruction. The most vehement oppositions to the imposition of US designs in Iraq and elsewhere in the region were shown by Syria and Iran who feared for their own regimes. Accordingly, Iran and Syria joined forces to undermine the US campaign in Iraq. While publicly and diplomatically denouncing the US invasions, they also provided substantial material support to armed groups in the region who fought to undermine US efforts and sponsored visions of a proclaimed democratic "**Greater Middle East**".[10]

Lebanon, Syria and the international system

Within this context, Lebanon, whose political leadership was split between pro and anti-Syrian supporters turned into a battleground. The issue of Syria's increasing dominance in Lebanon and continuous military guardianship, after the 2000 withdrawal of Israeli forces from the country, became the center of a diplomatic showdown. The Syrian deployment in Lebanon, legitimized by the Lebanese Parliament in the Taef Agreement and supported by the Arab League, was no longer accepted. After all, Syria had failed to comply with the Taef

Agreement that stipulated its gradual withdrawal from the country. Thus, demands for Syrian withdrawal from Lebanon became a rallying cry for the Christian opposition. Damascus and its loyal government in Beirut replied by justifying its continued military presence with the fragility of the Lebanese Armed Forces in the face of internal and looming external security threats, particularly from Israel. International critics of the Syrian regime, notably France and the United States, denounced Syria's claim. Rejection to Syrian presence in Lebanon grew dramatically following the extra-constitutional extension of the tenure of Syrian loyalist President Lahoud. This came after Syria pressured the Lebanese Parliament, through a series of parliamentary consultations in Damascus with President Bashar Al-Assad, to extend President Lahoud's term in office for an additional three years.

Amid Syrian opposition to the US invasion of Iraq and a growing rift between both countries, the US Congress passed the Syria Accountability and Lebanese Sovereignty Restoration Act in 2003, stating its aims for regime change in Lebanon. Tension escalated following the reinstatement of President Lahoud in office in 2004. The United States and France responded with UNSC Resolution 1559, which demanded the withdrawal of all foreign troops from Lebanon and the disarmament of non-government militias (see Appendix B).

UNSC Resolution 1559

In the spring and summer of 2004 the United States and France intensified their pressure on Syria, but their repeated pleas for respecting the independence and sovereignty of Lebanon fell on deaf ears in Damascus. Chirac and Bush discussed the situation in Lebanon during Bush's June visit to France to commemorate the 60th anniversary of the Allied landing at Normandy. According to Lebanese commentator Nicolas Nassif, it was Chirac who requested that Lebanon be placed on the summit agenda.[11] The two leaders expressed nearly identical positions regarding Lebanon. Chirac stressed that "Lebanon has to be assured that its independence and sovereignty are guaranteed." President Bush noted that "the people of Lebanon should be free to determine their own future, without foreign interference or domination."[12] It is against this background of concerted action over Lebanon and mounting tension with Syria that the two capitals introduced and lobbied for the passage of Resolution 1559 (2004), which the UNSC adopted on September 2, with nine votes in favor and six abstentions. Resolution 1559 called on Lebanon to establish its sovereignty over all of its land and for "foreign forces" (referring to, but not limited to, Syria) to withdraw from the country and to cease intervening in the internal politics of Lebanon. The resolution also called on all Lebanese and non-Lebanese militias (i.e. Hezbollah and various Palestinian groups) to disarm and disband. The resolution also declared support for having a "free and fair electoral process", in a tacit rejection to the extension of President Lahoud's term. The Resolution, however, was not passed under Chapter 7 of the UN Charter and lacked enforcement and the full backing of all members of the UNSC. Ousted Prime Minister Rafik Hariri, a close friend of the French

President, was suspected by Syria and its Lebanese allies of having a hand in guiding French efforts in drafting UNSC Resolution 1559.[13]

Reactions to UNSC Resolution 1559

The political landscape in Lebanon, since the conciliatory years after the end of the civil war, was coming to the verge of a collapse over Syria's presence in the country. UNSC Resolution 1559 separated the country into two main camps. The so-called Bristol Camp, composed of Christian groups (including the Lebanese Forces and Phalanges) and Druze Progressive Socialist Party, together with the tacit support of former Prime Minister Hariri and the Sunni elites, protested against Syrian intervention in Lebanon and urged the implementation of UNSC Resolution 1559. Conversely, the Ain el Tineh Camp, made up of Syrian loyalists, notably the Shia Hezbollah and Amal alongside other Druze and Maronite figures, denounced the Resolution as Western imperialism. Inter-elite relations in the government became increasingly tense and institutions were basically held hostage by the standoff, which reached a climax on October 1, 2004, with the attempted assassination of Marwan Hamade, a Druze member of parliament within the Bristol Camp.

On October 20, 2004, Prime Minister Rafik Hariri, named to form a new cabinet, resigned his appointment, having failed to obtain the consent of Syrian loyalists. Hariri criticized President Lahoud's intervention in the cabinet formation, which undermined the Sunni prime minister's prerogative to assign portfolios and to form a cabinet. The day after his withdrawal, the former prime minister and loyal supporter of Syria Omar Karami was appointed with the task to form a new government, which he succeeded in forming. The Karami government excluded Hariri and the Bristol Camp parties. To make matters worse, Hariri was assassinated on February 14, 2005, with 21 others in a massive car bomb which rocked central Beirut. The political standoff reached a deadlock, as members of the Bristol Camp, supported by the United States and France, in particular, openly accused Syria for having carried out the assassination. On March 8, 2005, tens of thousands of supporters of the Ain el Tineh Camp gathered in a large public demonstration to show their support for the Syrian regime. The Bristol Camp responded a week later, on March 14, with another massive public rally, demarking what many describe as the beginning of the **Cedar Revolution**. The March 14 public gathering demanded the withdrawal of Syrian troops from Lebanon, the formation of a new government through free and fair elections, and the full implementation on UNSC Resolution 1559. Protesters began an open sit-in in the downtown area until demands were met. Lebanon was sharply divided between March 8 and 14 supporters.

UNSC Resolution 1595

On February 28, 2005, faced with massive opposition and suspicions, the Prime Minister Omar Karami resigned his pro-Syrian government. UNSC Resolution

1595 adopted by unanimous vote on April 7, 2005, established an Independent International Investigation Commission (UNIIIC) to assist the Lebanese authorities in their investigation into the Hariri assassination (see Appendix C). The Resolution also reiterated calls for the strict respect of the sovereignty, territorial integrity, unity and political independence of Lebanon under the sole and exclusive authority of the government. Under considerable international pressure, Syrian troops withdrew from Lebanon on April 26, 2005.

Reactions to UNSC Resolution 1595

With a precarious and fragile political and security landscape prevailing in Lebanon, in line with the traditional norms of consociationalism, the major Lebanese political and sectarian leaders decided to convene a national dialogue conference in an attempt to find a common position to the many issues confronting post-Syrian Lebanon. Participants agreed to support the international investigation of the Hariri assassination. However, they failed to reach additional consensus and postponed the discussion of other vitally important security and political issues to a later date. Chief amongst these security concerns was the presence of non-state weapons. Later conferences in 2006 achieved agreements on a range of issues, including the formalization of Lebanese–Syrian relations and the demarcation of borders, the disarmament of Palestinian groups outside the refugee camps, and a defense strategy to be discussed at later dates. Only the exchange of Ambassadors between Syria and Lebanon was implemented, three years after.

A coalition of anti-Syrian politicians and sectarian leaders composed mainly of the parties to the Bristol bloc, together with the Maronite patriarch, rallied around Saad al-Hariri, the son and political successor of Rafik al-Hariri, in his bid to follow his father's footsteps. What became known as the **"March 14" Alliance** won a decisive electoral victory in May 2005 and formed a government under the Premiership of Fuad Saniora. Thus, the Lebanese political milieu was once again divided between the anti-Syrian government and the pro-Syrian **"March 8" Alliance** led by Hezbollah and Amal. Former General Michael Aoun, returned from exile and initially joined March 14 Alliance, but soon withdrew after rejecting a secondary share of Christian leadership within the coalition. His **Free Patriotic Movement** (FPM) stood as an independent for a short period before fully merging with the pro-Syrian March 8 Alliance.

2006 Israeli war on Lebanon

A reign of terror targeting mostly Christian civilians and March 14 leadership characterized the months following the withdrawal of the Syrian troops from Lebanon in April 2005. A rocky security situation and assassinations continued throughout the following years, accompanied by deep political polarizations. Throughout 2006, the fragile government of Saniora was confronted by disagreement between pro and anti-Syrian Ministers over the role of the UN-sponsored

Summary of 2004–2005 major events

2004

26 August: Rafik Hariri meets with Syrian President Bashar El-Assad in Damascus to discuss the extension of the term of President Lahoud. Hariri expresses his opposition to the extension of Emile Lahoud's presidential term. Syrian President Bashar Al Assad orders Hariri to submit to Syrian instructions and support the extension.

2 September: The United Nations Security Council adopts Resolution 1559 concerning the situation in the Middle East, calling for the withdrawal of all foreign forces from Lebanon and disarming of all non-state armed groups.

3 September: The Rafik Hariri bloc is forced to approve constitutional amendment to extend President Lahoud's term in office for an additional three years.

7 September: Economy Minister Marwan Hamade, Culture Minister Ghazi Aridi, Minister of Refugee Affairs Abdullah Farhat and Environment Minister Fares Boueiz, resign from the Cabinet in protest against the constitutional amendment.

1 October: Resigned member of parliament Marwan Hamade survives a car bomb attack, but is severely injured.

4 October: Rafik Hariri resigns.

11 October: Syrian President Bashar El-Assad delivers a speech condemning his critics within Lebanon and the United Nations.

19 October: United Nations Security Council expresses concern that Resolution 1559 has not been implemented.

20 October: President Lahoud accepts Hariri's resignation and names Omar Karami to form the new government.

2005

14 February: Rafik Hariri and 22 other individuals are assassinated in a massive blast.

25 February: The United Nations Fact-Finding Mission into the assassination of Rafik Hariri arrives in Lebanon.

28 February: The government of Prime Minister Omar Karami resigns.

8 March: Hezbollah organizes a "pro-Syrian" public march in Downtown Beirut.

14 March: A counter demonstration demands the withdrawal of Syrian troops and the arrest of the chiefs of the security and

intelligence services, believed responsible for the assassination of Hariri.

19 March:	A bomb explodes in Jdeideh, a northern Christian suburb of Beirut, wounding 11 people.
23 March:	Three people are killed and three others wounded in an explosion in the Kaslik shopping center, in the northern Christian suburbs of Beirut.
25 March:	The United Nations Fact-Finding Mission issues its report in New York.
26 March:	A suitcase bomb explodes in an industrial zone in northeast Christian suburbs of Beirut, injuring six.
1 April:	Nine people are injured in an underground garage in an empty commercial and residential building in the Christian town of Broumana.
7 April:	The Security Council forms the United Nations International Independent Investigation Commission into the assassination of Rafik Hariri.
19 April:	Transitional government's Prime Minister Najib Mikati announces that parliamentary elections will be held on 30 May.
26 April:	The last Syrian troops leave Lebanon ending a 29-year military presence.
6 May:	A bomb explodes in Jounieh, a Christian area north of Beirut, injuring 29 people.
30 May:	The first round of the elections is held. The Rafik Hariri Martyr List, a coalition of Saad Hariri's Future Movement, the Progressive Socialist Party and the Qornet Shehwan Gathering, win the majority of the seats in Parliament.
2 June:	Christian journalist and Syrian critic Samir Kassir is assassinated when his car explodes in east Beirut.
21 June:	Former Lebanese Communist Party leader and Syrian critic George Hawi is assassinated when his car explodes close to his home in Wata Musaytbeh.
30 June:	Fuad Saniora, former finance minister under Rafik Hariri, forms a new government composed of 23 ministers, and joined by pro-Syrian groups including Hezbollah and Amal. Aoun's Free Patriotic Movement takes on the opposition.
12 July:	Syrian critic Defense Minister and Christian figure Elias El Murr is injured after an assassination attempt against his life through a car bomb.

22 July:	At least three people are wounded near rue Monot when a bomb explodes in Ashrafieh, a Christian quarter of East Beirut.
22 August:	Three people are injured in an explosion in a garage near the Promenade Hotel in Al-Zalqa, a Christian area north of Beirut.
16 September:	One person is killed and ten others wounded by a bomb near a bank in Ashrafieh.
25 September:	A car bomb injures prominent news Christian anchor and Syrian critic, May Chidiac, in north Beirut.
19 October:	The Mehlis United Nations report is released, implicating Syria as party to the assassination of Rafik Hariri.
28 December:	March 14 Christian leader and journalist Gibran Tueni is assassinated through a massive car bomb.

Source: Tistam, P. *Timeline: Events Surrounding Lebanon's Rafik Hariri's Assassination.* About.com Middle East Issues. Available online art http://middleeast.about.com/od/lebanon/a/me090203a.htm (accessed March 28, 2013).

investigation into the Hariri assassination. March 14 ministers demanded the inclusion of all assassinations within the UN-sponsored investigation. March 8 objected to expanding such a role and claimed the politicization of the UN investigation and reports. A deadlock was finally reached and the March 8 ministers walked out of the Council of Ministers, suspending their participation in its meetings.

In July 2006, a military conflict broke out between Israel and Hezbollah, which lasted for 34 days. Lebanon's civilian infrastructure, including the Beirut Rafik Hariri International Airport, suffered heavy damages. The southern region of the country was devastated by Israeli air strikes, heavy artillery fire, and a ground invasion. The conflict was triggered by the July 12, 2006 kidnapping of two Israeli soldiers by Hezbollah paramilitary and continued until a UN end of hostility agreement under UNSC Resolution 1701 (Appendix E) was brokered on August 14, 2006. More than 1,000 people were killed during the conflict – most of whom were Lebanese civilians – and some one million others were displaced.[14]

The fighting resulted in a huge financial setback for Lebanon, with an official estimate of a fall in growth from +6 per cent to –5 per cent and the loss of five billion dollars (or 22 per cent) of GDP in direct and indirect costs.[15] Nevertheless, the main casualty of war was arguably the fragile unity between Lebanon's sectarian and political groups. Inter-sectarian tensions resurfaced between the mainly Shia pro-Syrian forces and the FPM, on one hand, and the predominantly Sunni March 14 bloc supported by the Maronites opposing Aoun, namely the Lebanese Forces and Phalangists, on the other hand.

Throughout and in the aftermath of the 2006 conflict, Lebanese politics were deeply polarized. March 8 supporters condoned the military action taken by Hezbollah against Israel, and which aimed to abduct Israeli soldiers to swap them with three long-held Lebanese prisoners. Despite the heavy toll of the 2006 war, Hezbollah supporters and the FPM considered the action as legitimate and justified. March 14 supporters, on the other hand, considered Hezbollah's act to be illegal, being initiated without the prior approved of the government. Others went as far as accusing the party of purposely invoking Israeli retaliation against Lebanon to divert attention from the Hariri investigation and the issues of its arms being discussed at the National Dialogue Conference. Thus, the right of Shia Hezbollah to arms and, subsequently, to initiate military conflict without state consent became the major divisive aspect of Lebanese politics for the years to come.

UNSC Resolution 1701

End to hostilities

On 11 August 2006, an end to hostilities was brokered by the UNSC, which unanimously adopted Resolution 1701. Both the Lebanese and Israeli governments agreed on the resolution. The Resolution also called for the disarmament of non-state armed groups, the withdrawal of Israel from South Lebanon, and the deployment of an enlarged United Nations Interim Force (UNIFIL) alongside the Lebanese Army within a 15-kilometer range of Lebanon's southern border. The resolution provided UNIFIL with an expanded mandate, to use force to prevent their area of operations from being used for hostile activities, and/or to resist forceful attempts to prevent them from doing their duties.

Reactions to UNSC Resolution 1701

The enactment of UNSC Resolution 1701 deepened the divide between the "two Marches" in the Lebanese government, which eventually reached a deadlock when key Shia members of parliament from Amal and Hezbollah resigned their cabinet portfolios, halting the proper functioning of institutions in the country. Moreover, severe political violence clearly targeting the March 14 supporters between 2005 and 2008 engendered further international criticism and public outcry against the pro-Syrian camp in Lebanon. At the end of President Lahoud's tenure on November 23, 2007, the Lebanese Parliament failed to reach a consensus on the nomination and election of a new President, leaving a vacuum of power in the executive and plunging the country into a volatile constitutional and political crisis.

2008 conflict

In November 2007, the Lebanese Parliament failed to reach an agreement to elect a new president. A domestic crisis began to rise, because of deepening disputes and the power vacuum. On May 5, after a 12-hour deliberation, Saniora's government passed two **decrees**: one to establish an inquiry into Hezbollah's private communication network and the other to transfer Beirut airport's head of security, Wafik Shkair, who is said to have close links to the Hezbollah. After 17 long months, political tensions in Lebanon turned hostile and finally spilled on to the streets. On May 8, 2008, Hezbollah's General Secretary Hassan Nassrallah described the government's May 5 decision a "declaration of war" against the resistance. Minutes after his declaration, heavy street battles in mixed Shia–Sunni neighborhoods of Beirut broke out, and soon spread to other parts of the country. The Lebanese Army withdrew from areas of fighting, fearing its own split along the fighting parties. Within hours, Hezbollah fighters overran Sunni held areas of West Beirut and surrounded the prime minister's palace, into which Saniora and his March 14 Ministers had barricaded themselves. Intensive mediation efforts by the Arab League and the Qatari delegation succeeded in halting military drives by Hezbollah and its allies and stopped the fighting. This was followed by a meeting of leaders called for by the Qatari government and held in Doha, with the purpose to end the disputes and achieve political settlements. On May 21, 2008, after intensive negotiations and consultations with regional powers, such as Iran, Turkey, and Syria, the Doha Agreement was concluded between the rival groups, paving the way for the reversal of the May 5 government decision, the end of fighting, the formation of a new national unity government, the election of a new consensus President, and the conduct of the 2009 parliamentary election under a new electoral law. The agreement and its deprecations will be discussed in greater details in the next chapter.

Summary

This chapter has given a detailed analysis of the political climate in Lebanon, from the decline of the Lebanese civil war in 1989, to the 2008 crisis and resulting Doha Agreement. The conditions leading to the Taef Agreement, both internal and external, are explained as follows: domestic support for belligerents was on the decline, as the Lebanese public demanded unity and an end to inter-sectarian conflict. The decline of the Palestinian–Israeli conflict, an increased Syrian presence in Lebanon, and the lessened Soviet support and increased American influence (both results of the end of the Cold War) meant that declining regional and international conditions called for external intervention in the Lebanese conflict.

The signing of the Taef Agreement by the belligerent factions ended the Lebanese civil war and gave birth to the "Second Sectarian Republic." Prime Minister and military General Michel Aoun denounced the agreement and the Presidency of Rene Moawad, who was assassinated 16 days after being elected to office. Against the wishes of General Aoun, Moawad was replaced by Elias Hrawi. Aoun's discontentment would lead to further violence in 1990, until he was ousted from Lebanon by Syrian forces with tacit support from the United States.

An amnesty law was passed in 1991, pardoning all political crimes prior to its enactment, with the exception of those committed against foreign dignitaries. In the following years, political reforms were intended, with the futile intentions of ending confessionalism. Prime Minister and businessman Rafik Hariri would rebuild much of the war-torn state, although his efforts would be continually interrupted by sectarian tensions. Hariri was ousted from office to be replaced by his rival, Salim Al Hoss, in 1998 only to be reelected in 2000, replaced again in 2004, and assassinated in 2005.

The chapter then described the ongoing political tensions within Lebanon, including the division of the country between pro-Syrian "March 8" and anti-Syrian "March 14" alliances and the escalating violence in 2004 and 2005. A detailed account was given of the 2006 Hezbollah–Israeli conflict and UNSC Resolution 1701 that called for an end to the hostilities between both parties and introduced a strong UNIFIL and Lebanese Army into the southern region of the Litany River. Lastly, the 2008 crisis that arose from discontentment between the "two Marches" was examined. The crisis culminated when an attempt by the Saniora government to monitor Hezbollah communications and limit their control of the Rafik Hariri Airport in Beirut was considered as an act of war by Hezbollah leader Hassan Nassrallah. Heavy battles ensued and only ended with regional powers intervening to negotiate a settlement in Doha, Qatar – which would come to be called the Doha Agreement, and would eventually lead to the election of a new president and prepare the ground for a parliamentary election in 2009 under a new electoral law.

References

1   Massara, A. (1988) *The Prospects for Lebanon: Challenge for Coexistence*. Oxford: Centre for Lebanese Studies, p. 17.
2   Boyle, F. (1991) 'Forum: The Algiers Declaration on Palestine: The Creation of the State of Palestine', *European Journal of International Law*, 1 (1): 301–6.
3   Abdel-Kader, N. (2010) 'Multiculturalism and Democracy: Lebanon as a Case Study', *Defense Magazine*, 331. Available online at www.lebarmy.gov.lb/ article.asp?ln=en&id=24777 (accessed March 28, 2013).
4   O'Ballance, E. (1998) *Civil War in Lebanon, 1975–92*. London: Palgrave Macmillan.
5   Gebara, K. (2007) *Reconstruction Survey: The Political Economy of Corruption in Post-War Lebanon*. Beirut: Lebanese Transparency International; London: Tiri. Available online at www.integrityaction.org/sites/www.integrityaction.org/files/ documents/files/Reconstruction%20Survey%20Lebanon.pdf (accessed March 28, 2013).
6   Safa, O. (2006) 'Lebanon Springs Forward', *Journal of Democracy*, 17 (1): 22–37.
7   Corm, G. (2004) *Modern Lebanon: History and Society*. Beirut: Al-Maktabh Al-Sharkeyah [Arabic].
8   Sherry, V. (1997) 'Israel/Lebanon: "Operation Grapes of Wrath" The Civilian Victims', *Human Rights Watch*, 9 (8): 4.
9   Anghie, A. (2005) 'The War on Terror and Iraq in Historical Perspective', *Osgoode Hall Law Journal*, 43 (1): 45–66.
10 Salamey, I. and Pearson, F. (2007) 'Hezbollah: A Proletarian Party with an Islamic Manifesto: A Sociopolitical Analysis of Islamist Populism in Lebanon and the Middle East', *Journal of Small Wars and Insurgencies*, 18 (3): 416–38.

11   Nassif, N. (2004) 'Chirac Yatlub Idraj Lubnan Banda fi Ijtima bi-Bush' [Chirac Asks that Lebanon be on the Agenda in the Summit with Bush], *Al-Nahar*, June 1, 2004: 3.
12   President Bush, President Chirac Mark 60th Anniversary of D-Day, Remarks by President Bush and President Chirac on Marking the 60th Anniversary of D-Day, The White House, June 6, 2004. Available online at http://georgewbush-white-house.archives.gov/news/releases/2004/06/20040606.html (accessed March 28, 2013).
13   Baroudi, S., and Salamey, I. (2011) 'US-French collaboration on Lebanon: How Syria's role in Lebanon and the Middle East contributed to a US-French Convergence', *Middle East Journal*, 65 (3): 398–425.
14   Hutson, R., Kolbe, A., Haines, T., Stringer, B., Shannon, H., and Salamey, I. (2009) 'Testing Received Wisdom: Perceptions of Security in Southern Lebanon' in Small Arms Survey (eds) *Small Arms Survey 2009: Shadows of War*, Cambridge: Cambridge University Press, pp. 317–35.
15   United Nations Development Programme. About Lebanon. http://www.undp.org.lb/about/AboutLebanon.cfm (accessed March 28, 2013).

6 Consociationalism reformed II

The Doha Republic (2008–2011)

This chapter offers a close examination of the Doha Agreement, giving illustrative abstracts of its clauses. The effect of the agreement on the power-sharing arrangement within Lebanon is analyzed in terms of the appointment of the president, formation of a national unity government, and the new electoral law. The collapse of the Doha Agreement in 2011 and the subsequent collapse of consociationalism are also examined in this chapter.

The Lebanese National Dialogue Conference

On May 5, 2008, the Lebanese government issued two decisions to shut down Hezbollah's telecommunication networks and relieve General Wafik Shkair of his post as security chief at the Rafik Hariri International Airport because of alleged ties to Hezbollah. The decisions were deemed by Hezbollah and the National Opposition as acts of hostility against the Resistance, causing massive riots that would eventually turn into an outright civil strife and armed clashes between factions.[1] On May 13, 2008, the army intervened to defuse tensions and prevent further fighting. The intervention failed and the army withdrew fearing splits within its own rank.[2] An Arab diplomatic delegation traveled to Lebanon to arbitrate an end to the conflict and a deal was reached between the reluctant pro-government factions and the opposition to negotiate and reverse the decisions that sparked the conflict. This was associated with an invitation to Qatar, by its prince Sheikh Hamad bin Khalifa Al Thani, for all Lebanese sectarian and political leaders to meet in Doha. On May 15, 2008, a delegation of pro-government and opposition parties traveled to Qatar to negotiate an agreement that would end Lebanon's 18-month political stalemate.

The negotiators of the Doha Agreement were members of the Lebanese National Dialogue Conference (NDC), which consisted of key and prominent political and sectarian leaders. The Doha Conference itself witnessed a series of bilateral and collective meetings and consultations between the different parties and involved countries represented in Arab Ministerial Committee, as well as observers from both Iran and Turkey, and culminated in such an agreement to end the conflict. After rigorous negotiations and regional consultations, the Doha Agreement was finally reached and signed by all sides on May 21, 2008. The settlement ended the standoff and altered, in various aspects, tenants of the Taef Agreement.

The Doha Agreement

The settlement consisted of five major elements and was announced the morning of May 21 in the presence of the President and members of the Arab Ministerial Committee. The Arab Ministerial Committee decided to register this agreement before the Arab League General Secretariat as soon as it was signed.[3] Among the Agreement resolutions and its repercussions are the following issues.

First, as agreed upon by both parties, the Doha Agreement primarily called for Parliament's Speaker Nabih Berri to convene the Parliament within 24 hours to elect General Michel Suleiman as Lebanon's President by consensus, knowing that this would be the best constitutional method to elect the president under the exceptional circumstances. Suleiman was the only person among various candidates who was agreed upon by all parties. Thus, the March 14 Alliance, which held majority membership in Parliament, was denied the ability to elect a president from its own rank in favor of consensual figure. The agreement established the practice of appointing the **president by consensus** instead of election. Many critics of the Doha Agreement have argued that the practice has endangered democratic institutionalism and undermined the ability of the parliamentary majority to translate its will in the election to a representative president. This practice has contributed further to the already existing tension between consociationalism and democracy, whereby selection by consensus provided political and sectarian minorities with excessive power relative to the existing majority. Majoritarian politics, which is essential for democratic practice, was rendered irrelevant.

Second, the Agreement stipulated the formation of an interim "**national unity cabinet**" – composed of 30 ministers – that would serve until the holding of June 2009's parliamentary elections. The 30-seat interim cabinet or Council of Ministers would reserve 16 seats for the parliamentary majority (the March 14 Alliance), 11 seats for the minority (the March 8 Coalition) and three seats for the President. This decision guaranteed the opposition with a so-called "**obstructional" or "guaranteeing" third** in the Council of Ministers, meaning its members were able to block any ministerial quorum needed over matters of vital national issues, and also had the ability to dismiss the entire Council of Ministers upon its resignation. In principle, though, all parties agreed not to resign or dismiss government until elections were held. The new formation of the Council of Ministers, as well as the new consensual approach of electing the president, presented a new foundation for consociationalism. Parliamentary majoritarianism was further restrained in favor of a strict political and sectarian agreement in any vital practice or share of power.

Third, the attendees agreed to hold the 2009 parliamentary elections on the basis of the **1960 Electoral Law**. In accordance, smaller voting constituencies – the *Qada* – were institutionalized in electoral redistricting. Beirut would be divided into three electoral districts:

- The first district including Ashrafieh, Rmeil and Saifi, where Christian majority constituency is granted.
- The second district comprising Bachoura, Medawar and the Port is of mixed sectarian constituency with a slight advantage given to the Armenian community.
- The third district incorporating Minet al-Hosn, Ain al-Mreisseh, Al-Mazraa, Mousseitbeh, Ras Beirut, Zoqaq al-Blat, is predominantly Sunni.

The redistricting of the country achieved several objectives. It relieved the Christians from the dominance of Sunni or Shia majority in electoral large districts such as Beirut, Bekaa, Nabatiyeh, and North. Sunnis were no longer in full electoral control over the North or Beirut. Shia and Druze maintained most of their monopoly over their electoral districts in the South, the Bekaa, and the Chouf Mountain. The 1960 Electoral Law, which replaced large electoral districts by smaller ones, was the electoral regime demanded by most Christian groups. The purpose was to preserve sectarian representation in Parliament against excessive inter-sectarian concessions that were necessitated by coalition building in larger and sectarian mixed districts. The outcome of such a law, however, was the growth of sectarian appeal in vote getting. Deepening sectarianism, as a consequence, was the call of the day, and consolidated sectarianism in the electoral practice of Lebanese politics.[4]

Fourth, both March 14 and March 8 Alliances agreed to refrain from using treason rhetoric or any other type of derogatory dialogue that could instigate sectarian strife in Lebanon. They also agreed on resorting to a national dialogue instead of violence as a means to resolving political conflicts. The NDC was to be resumed under the aegis of the president as soon as he is elected and a national unity government is formed, and with the participation of the Arab League in such a way as to boost confidence among the Lebanese. The NDC was to formulate agreements over unresolved issues, particularly those pertaining to a National Defense Strategy and non-state weapons. Once again, the Doha Agreement delegated significant power to sectarian elites, charging them with the task of agreeing over vital national issues. The role of the elected parliament was significantly marginalized. It turned into a superficial rubberstamping institution dedicated to approving elite arranged agreements over almost every aspect of its political jurisdictions: drafting electoral laws, electing the president, and approving the formation of the Council of Ministers.

Finally, all parties agreed to resort to the earlier agreement reached in Beirut, especially Paragraphs 4 and 5 that stated the following:

- Paragraph 4: The parties commit to abstain from having recourse or resuming the use of weapons and violence in order to record political gains.
- Paragraph 5: Initiate a dialogue for promoting the Lebanese state's authority over all Lebanese territory and their relationship with the various groups on the Lebanese stage in order to ensure the state's and the citizens' security.

Hence, the dialogue was initiated in Doha on promoting the state's authority according to Paragraph 5 of the Beirut Agreement, and a settlement was reached on the following:

*   Prohibiting the use of weapons or violence or taking refuge in them in any dispute whatsoever and under any circumstances, in order to ensure respect for the national partnership contract, based on the Lebanese people's commitment to live with one another within the framework of the Lebanese system, and to restrict the security and military authority over Lebanese nationals and residents to the state alone so as to ensure the continuity of the coexistence formula and civil peace among all the Lebanese; and the parties pledge to all of the above.
*   Implementing the law and upholding the sovereignty of the state throughout Lebanon so as not to have regions that serve as safe havens for outlaws, out of respect for the supremacy of the law, and referring all those who commit crimes and contraventions to the Lebanese judiciary.

Although the agreement prohibited the use of weapons, it provided no practical plan for the state to control neither their use nor their processions.

Predicament of the Doha Agreement

The Doha Agreement altered the Taef stipulated power sharing arrangement within the Lebanese State, plunging deeper into sectarian consociationalism. First and foremost, the new arrangement introduced the concept of appointing the country's president by consensus. As stipulated, President Michel Suleiman was chosen and agreed upon after Doha by sectarian leaders without resorting to the parliamentary election process. This arrangement not only undermined the role of parliament, but also stripped the national election from any majoritarian or popular meaning. Furthermore, the Doha Agreement allowed sectarian elites to assert themselves above any political institutional process and above the popular majority. A sectarian veto power over any presidential election was in full swing.

Additionally, the Agreement stipulated the formation of a grand governing coalition with the political minority securing an "obstructional" or "guaranteeing" third share of ministerial portfolios. The 16-11-3 cabinet formula would be an interim solution for a consensual government until the June 2009 elections. But this arrangement was replicated in the formation of post-election government. This spelled another constraint against any meaningful majoritarian rule by government in favor of comprehensive consociationalism. The share of the minority in government rendered it impossible for any significant national decision to be taken without the full consensus of all parties. However, the President was provided with three ministerial seats to insure him a swing and balancing power; his appointments guaranteed his neutrality and passive role in the overall political process. More critically, ruling through a grand coalition cabinet, largely appointed by sectarian elites, allowed for the suppression of the elected parliament in terms of applying its legislative or oversight roles. This arrangement provided sectarian elites with additional political powers not subject to any form of serious public and institutional accountability.

Furthermore, the new electoral redistricting – moving from mid-sized "Muhafaza" to a small-sized *Qada* electoral district – further consolidated sectarianism and elites' grip on the electoral patronage. Within smaller districts, voters were more likely to be of single sectarian constituencies. For instance, unlike previous elections in which Muslims would vote for Christian deputies, the new electoral law limited Christians to voting only for their own representatives. Therefore, electoral campaigns and coalition formation became purely sectarian in nature and were manipulated by dominant sectarian political groups. Moderating sectarian rhetoric, reaching out to mixed sectarian constituencies, trading sectarian votes, or forming a cross-sectarian coalition were no longer as essential or required in order to win Parliamentary seats. The resulting outcome was a total manipulation of the electoral process by sectarian elites in favor of their absolute dominance over the electorates. Subsequently, Lebanon emerged as sectarian as ever and sectarian consociationalism was entrenching deeper within the country's political fabric.

Finally, the mere fact that an agreement between the different Lebanese parties could only be achieved outside of Lebanon further signaled the country's dependence on outside intervention to maintain its unity and civil peace. It is common knowledge that during negotiations between the different factions in Doha, external pressures, negotiations, and rewards were exacted before the agreement was reached. The consequences were further sectarian factions' indebtedness to foreign countries and dependence on their interests in the overall regional struggle. This fact further complicated domestic disputes, particularly those associated with the arms of Hezbollah and that of the Syrian backed parties in Lebanon, rendering their resolutions linked to the dynamic of regional struggles and their resolutions.

The collapse of the Doha Agreement

The confessional predetermination of state power among multiple sects, each having veto power over public decisions, undermined the realization of a functional and strong government system. Instead, a deeply divided and weak confessional state was established. The immediate result was a spread of social and political insecurity among its citizens, forcing sectarian groups to rely on their own social and security networks, and to look for support beyond Lebanon's borders. The state, acting as a trustee, became notorious for its immobility and its inability to implement policies that promoted progress and prevented deterioration.

Consequently, the sectarian conflict dynamic heightened and violent conflict followed, causing the state to fail repeatedly. The Doha Accord of 2008 brought to a halt a short period of sectarian civil strife, but this recent episode was only the latest in a series of foreign-sponsored initiatives that have attempted, in vain, to undermine the splintering nature of sectarian consociationalism and its conflicting orientations.

The chronically weak nature of state consociationalism in Lebanon and the continuous failure of international efforts to provide a sustainable governing system are attributed to short-term agreements that have neither helped accommodate nor minimize political sectarianism in the country. In fact, the Doha Agreement did not fare any better than its predecessors. The agreement managed to place a president in power, establish a national unity government, and lay preparations for elections. The parliamentary election was held on time in June 2009. Yet, the election provided no serious breakthrough in the power balance among major sectarian and political groups. The March 14 coalition continued to control a slight majority with 71 parliamentary seats and was, thus, bound by the Doha-stipulated agreement to form a government that would abide by consociational power sharing.

This was first reflected in the newly formed March 14 parliamentary majority reelecting alongside the March 8 minority the Shi'ite and March 8 leader Nabih Berri as a speaker. This concession was the price for the minority accepting the nomination of majority leader Saad Hariri to form the new government. Soon after, the March 14 majority reluctantly conceded to the Doha Agreement's distribution formula of ministerial portfolios. The same arrangement was maintained of 16-11-3, although it was falsely claimed that the President's share was four and the minority share was ten. This fact was later demonstrated in the resignation of one of the President's four claimed ministers along the minority leading to the government's collapse.

In November 2009, the Hariri national unity government was formed after a stormy five months of negotiations. Qatar and Turkey played a leading role in providing assurances and sponsorship to the various parties. Immediately after its formation, it was evident that rifts between the different sides of the national unity government were too wide to bridge. The Hariri government was plunged into a series of disputes and disagreements over almost every detail of its conduct. The Hariri rapprochement toward Syria, with Saudi encouragement, infuriated domestic opposition and especially that of Hezbollah who was alarmed by the possible establishment of Saudi–Syrian–Hariri alliance that would undermine that of Hezbollah and Iranian influence in the region. Saudi King Abdullah accompanied Syrian President Bashar El-Assad to Lebanon in his royal airplane in a push to rebuild ties between Assad and Hariri. Saudi efforts also aimed at establishing a new agreement between Syria, Hariri, and Hezbollah, where the latter's weapons would be traded for political power and the dismissal of any international charges against the party. Hezbollah's fears grew as the international investigation into the killing of former Prime Minister Hariri began to point fingers at its leaders. The day after, Hariri publicly reversed his former accusations against the Syrian regime, of having orchestrated the assassination of his father. Hezbollah responded viciously and accused Hariri supporters of having formulated false testimonies against Syria for political gains. Hezbollah and its March 8 allies demanded that the Higher Judicial Council take instant action and bring to trial the accused. Hariri and the March 14 Alliance rejected the charges. Hezbollah responded by withdrawing its approval of the Hariri Special

International Court and its investigation, labeling it as a mere Zionist ploy against the party. March 14, in turn, rejected Hezbollah's views and supported the Court. By the end of 2010, it was evident that the government was on the verge of collapse. In January 2011, Hariri traveled to Washington seeking support for his government. But during the same day, and while meeting with President Obama, March 8 ministers announced their resignations, bringing down the government.

The resignation of March 8 ministers signaled a major breach in the stipulated clause of the Doha Agreement. Most importantly, it shed doubts on the ability of Qatar and the various regional powers, including Turkey and Saudi Arabia, to influence either the Syrian supported groups or Iranian-backed Hezbollah in establishing a consensus agreement.

Parliamentary consultation to name a prime minister, which was accompanied by active Turkish and Qatari mediation, failed to select Hariri. The sudden defection of Druze leader Walid Jumblatt to the side of the March 8 camp finally diminished any remaining chances for Hariri's return to power. Alternatively, March 8's newly claimed majority named Najib Mikati to the post of prime minister. He was able, after a few weeks, to form a new government that excluded March 14 parties, thus, officially ending the era of the Doha Agreement and Lebanon's Third Sectarian Republic.

It is widely believed that the failure of the Qatari-mediated solution for the Lebanese crisis and the rejection of Iran and Syria, through their Lebanese allies, from yielding to an accommodating solution enraged and alarmed Qatar and the regional powers. Both Qatar and Turkey, as well as Saudi Arabia, have since begun a new anti-Iranian, anti-Syrian campaign with the aim of undermining the influence of Iran in Lebanon and overthrowing the Syrian regime altogether. This is not to claim that Lebanon was the cause behind this regional confrontation, but most certainly represented a catalyst that sparked this battle.

Summary

This chapter has given a close examination of the 2008 Doha Agreement and its impact on the state of affairs in Lebanon for the following three years. The Doha Agreement reached by opposing Lebanese factions in Qatar on May 21, 2008, marked the end of an 18-month long political impasse. The agreement called for the selection of a president by consensus, the formulation of an interim "national unity cabinet" to serve until elections, the holding of elections in accordance with the 1960 Electoral Law – which institutionalized smaller voting districts – and an agreement between March 14 and March 8 to abstain from inciting sectarian strife, instead using national dialogue to solve disputes. The agreement redistributed the power-sharing structure of the Taef era in terms of electoral districts and pre-conditional consensus in presidential elections, which effectively stripped the power from the parliamentary majority. The different parties further relied on international support to promote and protect their respective interests in the agreement. The Doha Agreement paved the way for the election of a new president, as well as a new national unity government that succeeded in administering the 2009 parliamentary election. Under the Doha stipulated power sharing distribution a new post-election national unity government was also formed. However, sectarian power struggle and increasing regional intervention proved too difficult to sustain the Doha Agreement. In January 2011, the "Doha national unity government" collapsed to be replaced by a March 8 government, with the March 14 Alliance becoming the new opposition.

References

1   Rabil, R. G. (2008) 'Hezbollah: Lebanon's Power Broker', *Journal of International Security Affairs*. Fall (15). Available online at www.securityaffairs.org/issues/2008/15/rabil.php (accessed March 28, 2013).
2   Quilty, J. (2008) Lebanon's Brush with Civil War, *Middle East Research and Information Project*, May 20. Available online at www.merip.org/mero/mero052008 (accessed March 28, 2013).
3   The Doha Agreement, trans. by NOW staff. *NOW*, May 21, 2008. Available online at https://now.mmedia.me/lb/en/nowspecials/the_doha_agreement (accessed March 28, 2013).
4   Katrib, J. (2008) *Ending (or Deepening) the Political Crisis in Lebanon: The Role of Electoral Reform*. Policy Watch 1378. Washington DC: Washington Institute for Near East Policy. Available online at www.washingtoninstitute.org/policy-analysis/view/ending-or-deepening-the-crisis-in-lebanon-the-role-of-electoral-reform (accessed March 28, 2013).

Part II
The Lebanese political system

7 From politics to government

The chapter introduces the second part of the book: Lebanese government. It outlines political developments since 1943. It also highlights the institutionalization of sectarianism in Lebanese political life, discussing the function of the President of the Republic, parliament and the make-up of political parties. An update on political developments and difficulties since the withdrawal of Syria from Lebanon is also provided.

The manifestation of politics in government

In the ideal democratic society, government is formed by the people to express the popular will (Figure 7.1). However, in reality, politics reveals an interactive dynamic between the people and their governments in the decision-making and enforcement process. It is difficult to specify the exact political meaning and the measurement of popular will. Yet, most interpretations have defined it as a numeric majority in support of government. This interpretation has driven

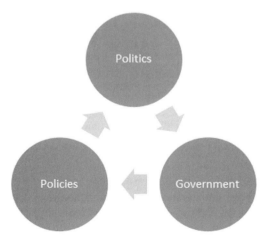

Figure 7.1 The political process

government opposition groups to often contest the size of government's support. At other times, social scientists have debated whether the popular will is shaped independently of government and corporate interests. Prior to the Second Gulf War, and in order to seek public support, the US administration under President George Bush falsely led the American public to believe that Iraq's President Saddam Hussein possessed nuclear and chemical weapons that placed the United States in imminent danger. Soon after, President Bush received overwhelming public approval and support for his war drive.

The interaction between the governed and the government is primarily determined by the ways in which people organize themselves into collectivities. Their decisions to mobilize around their economic, ethnic, regional, religious, or racial affiliations largely determines the national political dynamic. These forms of mobilization may gain organizational sophistication as groups form parties and coalitions in pursuit of their interests. Political interests may be advanced through the formation of associations, unions, media outlets, armed bands, economic networks, international relations, and so on. Ultimately, however, the articulation of groups' interests and their interactions with government and other pressure groups remains the most fundamental aspect of politics (Figure 7.2).

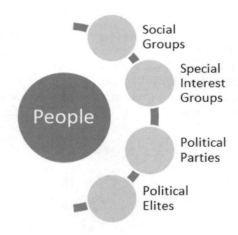

Figure 7.2 The structure of political mobilization

To correspond to the interests of diverse groups and transform popular will into laws and policies, governments have been established with a **trifecta** consisting of legislative, executive, and judicial branches (Figure 7.3). The elected legislative branch makes the law, the executive branch enforces the law, and a judiciary arbitrates fairness and constitutionality of the law and its enforcement. Yet, as discussed in Chapter 1, the orientation of each branch and its interaction with

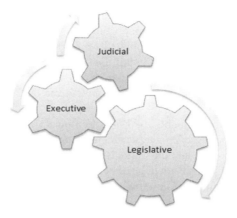

Figure 7.3 Branches of government

other branches of government are often determined based on the distinctive social attributes of the concerned society. In some countries, the branches are established with intentions of upholding the principle of separation and balance of powers. However, it is often the case in presidential systems that the executive branch appears more central to politics than other branches. According to the same rationale, many parliamentary governments have a legislative branch that takes on a heavily significant role in determining the shape and life terms of other branches.

The Lebanese constitution declares that Lebanon is a parliamentary democracy. The country's National Pact frames the practice of democracy within the context of sectarian consociationalism, in which the highest offices are proportionately reserved for sectarian representations. The constitution provides for the separation and balance of power, limited presidential terms, free and fair elections, and respect for human rights. According to the constitution, political parties can be formed within the jurisdiction of Lebanese law. Parliamentary seats are allocated along sectarian lines, so most parties are formed around sectarian affiliations and political interests. Direct parliamentary elections are held every four years. The constitution stipulates that the Parliament elects a Speaker for its duration. In addition, the Parliament is designated with the task of electing a President for a single non-renewable six-year term. The Taef Constitution delegated to the President the power to name the Prime Minister only after mandatory parliamentary consultation and approval. The assigned Prime Minister takes on the role of forming the government. Parliament must approve the inauguration of the new government through a majority vote.

Thus, the dominant mode of political mobilization has taken the sect as a prime agency in the pursuit of group's interests. As a consequence, the Lebanese popular will has been deeply fragmented along with, often at times, a non-accommodating orientation. This fragmentation has denied majoritarian politics through which a popular will is manifested in government. The result is a divided government, hardly subject to public oversight, with political elites determining its destiny. These conditions entail the manipulation of public outlooks and attitudes towards the government. Sectarian consociationalism has imprinted political wheeling and dealing among elites and formalized its dynamic in all aspects of power sharing.

During the first sectarian republic of 1943, the powers vested in the Maronite President undermined both the legislative and judiciary branches. The presidency was the most powerful office and the Sunni Prime Minister and the Shi'a Speaker played secondary roles. The President hand picked not only the ministers, but also the members of the judiciary. The struggle against political Maronism by the Muslims, confronted by the Christian campaign for its preservation, was among the key issues that colored politics during the first pact republic, leading in part to the civil war.[1]

The Taef accord aimed to balance the various branches and bring to an end the civil war, while redistributing powers evenly between Muslims and Christians. Significant power shifts occurred during this era; from the Maronite President in favor of the Sunni Prime Minister and indirectly to the Shi'a Speaker. A new dilemma soon emerged, represented by a Sunni–Shi'a struggle this time, over the power vested in the hands of the Sunni Prime Minister and the significant distribution of power within the Council of Ministers. Efforts to end this struggle culminated in the Doha Agreement, aimed at a new redistribution of power between the three major sectarian groups through electoral redistricting and redistribution of ministerial portfolios. The agreement meant a tradeoff between the right of the Shi'a to maintain their weapons and pursue special relations with Iran, while the Sunni preserved the power of the Prime Minister in running economic and domestic affairs. The Doha-stipulated electoral law brought greater representation to the Christians and the ministerial distribution provided the Maronite President with a partial share. Once again, however, this agreement proved to be short lived, and the struggle over the power vested in premiership raged on. The Lebanese populace would continue to be fragmented, manipulated, and sectarian-charged.

Politics since 1943

Hardly anyone in Lebanon doubts that political sectarianism is the primary reason behind Lebanese continuous disagreements and political struggle. Efforts to alter or abolish the confessional system of allocating power along sectarian lines have been at the center of Lebanese politics for decades. However, no one has been able to achieve any serious reformulation in the direction of non-sectarian politics. Despite a 15-year civil war and the proclamation of the Taef Accord under Article 95 to move the country toward a non-sectarian national state, sectarianism has only grown in strength. Sectarian fears, particularly those of "minorities" from an emerging tyrant majority, are to blame. Sectarian parties and elite have used this fear to consolidate their grip over all aspects of their respective shares of power and to bluff out a collective popular will.

If anything, post-Taef politics have been fixated on the struggle for the formulation of a **"troika"** between the Sunni, the Shi'a, and the Maronites. Of course, during the "era of Syrian tutelage", this distribution was determined based on a competition to gain the support of Damascus. After the withdrawal of Syrian troops from Lebanon, sectarian struggle for determination of the power share only intensified. Immediately after the 2005 electoral victory of the March 14 coalition and the appointment of anti-Syrian Prime Minister Saniora, a staunch struggle began against Syria's loyalist President Emile Lahoud. Interpretations of presidential powers in relation to those of the prime minister became a primary source of political contentions. Ambiguity made it very difficult for the ruling March 14 coalition to govern the country alongside Lahoud. In turn, the President was able to undermine the March 14 rule and to impose three ministers within the cabinet formation. While in office, Lahoud was able to prevent the majority coalition from unilaterally purging the judiciary and military officer corps, both of which were heavily vetted by the Syrians.

Interestingly, while most traditional Maronite political and religious leaders were generally supportive of the March 14 coalition in 2005, they have staunchly opposed its attempts to circumvent Lahoud's authority, fearing that the political precedent and loss of institutional prestige in favor of the prime minister would permanently weaken the last vestiges of Christian executive privilege. In their view, no short-term political gain was worth taking this long-term existential risk.

The ongoing sectarian polarizations generally resulted in greater segregation across the social spectrum. Within political parties, places of residence, schools, media outlets, and even workplaces, there is a lack of regular interaction across sectarian lines to facilitate the exchange of views and promote understanding. Increasingly, calls for political and administrative decentralization of the government have been gaining ground, to provide for greater sectarian autonomy. Most Sunnis, however, have not shown much enthusiasm, while being geographically dispersed. The Shi'a, on the other hand, have established a political duality where they have come to practice significant political autonomy in their areas of demographic concentration in the South, Bekaa, and Southern District of Beirut while, at the same time, extending their influence over national state and government.

Palestinians have also played a significant role in shaping Lebanese government and politics. Since their deportation to Lebanon, their struggle for the liberation of Palestine has influenced many Lebanese, both sympathizers and opponents. They have played a central role during major historic junctures, and particularly in the establishment of their power base in Lebanon since the late 1960s. Most Christians, and lately the Shi'a, have feared the growth of Palestinian influence and their potential nationalization. This factor was a primary cause for the denying of Palestinian many human and civil rights in Lebanon. Threat of mostly Sunni Palestinians attaining Lebanese national citizenship and consequently upsetting the sensitive sectarian balance is often cited.[2] The struggle of Lebanese women to win the right of providing citizenship to their offspring is also denied on the grounds that this may lead to massive naturalization of Palestinians.

Post-Syriana politics: A tale of two Lebanons

Since the momentous events of 2005, particularly the assassination of Prime Minister Rafik Hariri and the withdrawal of Syrian troops after a near 30-year presence, Lebanon has been caught in a power struggle between the March 14 Alliance led by the Future Movement and the March 8 coalition led by Hezbollah (Figure 7.4). This is reflective of the sharp divisions along increasingly sectarian lines and incompatible visions of Lebanon's past, present, and future. Tensions between these two alliances escalated steadily after Hariri's murder, culminating in the armed clashes of May 2008, during which Hezbollah and its allies captured West Beirut and laid siege to Future offices and institutions. The crisis was defused by the Qatar-brokered Doha Accord, which paved the way for the election of President Michel Suleiman and the formation of a national unity government. Large-scale civil conflict was averted and a period of relative calm prevailed from May 2008 until the fall of 2010.

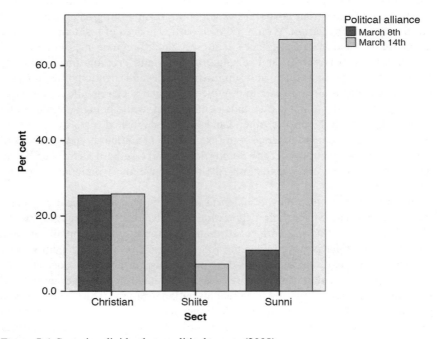

Figure 7.4 Sectarian divide along political camps (2008)

Lebanon experienced largely peaceful legislative elections in 2009, in which March 14 reemerged as a majority and Saad Hariri, son of the slain leader, was named Prime Minister. With the wounds of the May clashes still fresh, the Sunni community rallied solidly behind the Future Movement, which became the largest bloc in parliament, followed by Michel Aoun's Free Patriotic Movement (FPM), a close Hezbollah ally. Negotiations over cabinet formation dragged on for five months, until a formula brokered by Syria and Saudi Arabia was accepted by the two sides. Just one month after the polls, Walid Jumblatt of the Progressive Socialist Party (PSP) withdrew from the March 14 coalition, diluting the significance of Hariri's electoral victory. The Druze leader expressed regret for past remarks against Syria in an about-face that reflected larger regional and international realignments. After Doha, Syria was credited with facilitating the election of a new president and gradually emerged from world isolation. Saudi–Syrian rapprochement led Hariri himself to make overtures to Syria and to declare that blaming Damascus for his father's murder had been "a political accusation."[3]

After the relative calm that reigned post-Doha, tensions once again came to a head in early 2011, amid reports that the Special Tribunal for Lebanon (STL), established by the United Nations to investigate Rafik Hariri's assassination, was preparing to issue its first indictment, widely believed to implicate Hezbollah members. As the identity of the presumed culprit shifted from Syria to Hezbollah, the latter's initial skepticism towards the STL turned into virulent opposition. The possibility that some of its members might be indicted presented Hezbollah with a set of critical challenges. Domestically, those in Lebanon who until then had tolerated the organization's "state-within-a-state" status might be provided with an incentive to rally behind March 14's insistence that Hezbollah be disarmed and its broader influence curbed. Regionally, credible evidence that Hezbollah was implicated in the assassination of the most prominent Sunni figure in the Levant would damage its standing in Arab public opinion, leaving it more isolated than ever.

Faced with what it viewed as an existential threat, Hezbollah stepped up its efforts to discredit the STL, denouncing the tribunal as an instrument of US–Israeli interests and insisting that the evidence the STL had gathered was fabricated or tainted, including telecommunications data (a reference to the uncovering in 2010 of an Israeli spy ring that had infiltrated Lebanon's telecoms sector, which provided Hezbollah with new evidence to support that claim). Hezbollah also reminded its audience that in its early stages, the United Nations probe had relied heavily on "false witnesses" that were later discredited. Concluding that the STL's true purpose was not (or no longer) to reveal the truth about Hariri's assassination, the opposition demanded that the Government of Lebanon suspend cooperation with the tribunal.[4] As March 8 and March 14 adopted increasingly irreconcilable positions vis-à-vis the tribunal, Syria and Saudi Arabia attempted to defuse tensions and find an acceptable compromise. The US Obama administration, however, made explicit its opposition to any initiative that might be viewed as seeking to protect Lebanese stability at the cost of maintaining the integrity of the STL process.

Harriri was, thus, confronted by hard decisions to make. Refusal to comply with Hezbollah's demand that he disavow the tribunal might prompt the March 8 bloc to withdraw support from his government, bringing about its downfall. On the other hand, suspending Lebanon's cooperation with a tribunal investigating the assassination of his father would be described as a personal and political humiliation. It would threaten his position as the clear leader of the Sunni community, antagonize the Obama administration, and deprive the March 14 bloc of a key source of external support. Moreover, a Government of Lebanon decision to stop cooperation with the STL would mean that Lebanon would find itself in breach of its cooperation protocol with the United Nations, which could result in economic sanctions (at a time when the country is already burdened by a US$50 billion public debt).[5]

When Hariri rejected Hezbollah's demands, the March 8 bloc pulled its ten ministers from his cabinet, followed by one of the four ministers appointed by President Suleiman, bringing about the latter's collapse on January 13, 2011. At that point, the cabinet lost its constitutional legitimacy, since less than two-thirds of the 30-member cabinet seats were filled. Under the Lebanese Constitution, if and when that happens, the cabinet no longer has a mandate to govern the country. March 14 denounced the move as a Hezbollah-orchestrated "coup" and Hariri supporters poured into the streets in a "day of rage" against the ousting of their leader. Aided by their newfound parliamentary majority since Jumblatt's defection from March 14, the March 8 coalition nominated Tripoli tycoon Najib Mikati as Prime Minister designate. March 14 announced that it would boycott Mikati's government after the latter refused to make a formal, public commitment not to end Lebanon's cooperation with the STL. Mikati's intent regarding the STL remained vague despite public proclamations of support.

Following his government's collapse, Hariri upped the rhetoric against Hezbollah and declared himself the leader of the "new oppositio". At a March 13, 2011, mass rally marking the six-year anniversary of the Cedar Revolution, Hariri reiterated his bloc's commitment to the STL and refusal to capitulate to Hezbollah's "blackmail." Borrowing from the popular slogan chanted by the Tunisian and Egyptian protesters who brought down **Zine El Abidine Ben Ali** and **Hosni Mubarak** ("the people want to topple the regime"), Hariri's supporters chanted that "the people want to topple the supremacy of the arms," a reference to Hezbollah's weapons. Meanwhile, the Arab revolutions were in full swing and the two Lebanons would find themselves caught in the middle of the storm.

Fearing for his life, and after news of a series of financial collapses of his companies abroad, Hariri decided to leave Lebanon and lead his campaign from his residences in France and Saudi Arabia. In the meantime, Mikati was able to form a government that divided power between March 8 coalition and that of his centrist-claimed alliance made up of the PSP, the President, and his close Tripoli members of parliament. The new government was largely identified by the opposition as the by-product of a coup d'état that overthrew the Doha stipulations and brought to the ministership a Sunni Prime Minister backed by the Shi'a members of parliament rather than the Sunnis. The Mikati government has, thus, been accused of being formulated in Syria and Iran and sponsored in Lebanon by Hezbollah. Yet, Mikati's government was able to rule out criticism and sustain itself by claiming to provide salvation and security for Lebanon. This claim would be undermined by the 2011–13 revolution in Syria and its implications on Lebanon, which are discussed further in Chapter 13. In the following chapters, a detailed examination of contemporary institutions shaped by sectarian politics of modern Lebanon will be given.

Summary

Democratic government is founded on the ideal of public will. However, this ideal has been contested by the fact that differential powers may influence government and, ultimately, shape the forms and manifestation of public will. In a plural and divided society, group competitions can fragment and manipulate the public will. Lebanese politics encompasses this dilemma, which has been clearly reflected in the country's sectarian-driven competition for power. Early periods witnessed a strong presidency that concentrated power in the hands of the Maronites. Muslim resentment was responsible for periods of deep polarization and civil violence, which ended only after a serious government reconstruction that shifted power in favor of the Sunni-held seat of Prime Minister and his Council of Ministers. The change also implicated greater parliamentary power to the advantage of the Shi'a-held seat of the Speaker. After the Taef, however, the office of the Prime Minister and Council of Ministers were subject to emerging contentions, this time with both Shi'a and Christians demanding greater share. Once again, periodical confrontations imprinted the Taef period and reached an alarming degree after the pullout of Syrian troops from the country. Another rearrangement of political power was sought in the Qatari-brokered agreement known as the Doha Accord. This time, both Shi'a and Christians were able to secure a greater share of the executive power by redistributing ministerial portfolios to the disadvantage of the Sunnis. Yet, the Doha's stipulation of power sharing was soon proven unsustainable. A new sectarian struggle was looming, causing the collapse of the national unity government in favor of a Shi'a-led March 8-dominated government. This time, Sunni grievances had grown and the Syrian revolution of 2011 only exacerbated sectarian tension in the country. The concentration of power in the hands of one sect or another in government has resulted in a chronic situation of instability and a weak state. Striking a balance of power among the different sects has been perceived as the ultimate aim of consociationalism. The attainment of this objective has yet to be achieved.

References

1   El-Khazen, F. (2000) *The Breakdown of the State in Lebanon, 1967–1976*. London: I. B. Tauris in association with Centre for Lebanese Studies.
2   Haddad, S. (2003) *The Palestinian Impasse in Lebanon: the Politics of Refugee Integration*. Sussex Academic Press: Brighton and Portland.

3   Los Angeles Times. (2010) 'Lebanon: Supporters Stunned as Hariri says Syria Didn't Kill his Dad', *Los Angeles Times*, September 7, http://latimesblogs.latimes.com/babylonbeyond/2010/09/lebanon-hariri-assassination-hezbollah-syria-iran-tribunal-bomb.html (accessed March 28, 2013).

4   Berti, B. (2011) *Hezbollah on Trial: Lebanese Reactions to the UN Special Tribunal's Indictments*. Philadelphia: Foreign Policy Research Institute. August, 2011 E-Notes issue. http://www.fpri.org/docs/alt/201108.berti_.hezbollah.pdf (Accessed: February 22, 2013). See also report by Chatham House, December 2010. The Special Tribunal for Lebanon and the Quest for Truth, Justice and Stability. London: Chatham House.

5   Associate French Press (2011) 'Lebanon Crisis Over Funding of the Special Court', *allvoices*, October 27. Available online at www.allvoices.com/contributed-news/10720740-lebanon-crisis-over-funding-of-the-special-court (accessed March 28, 2013). See also Daily Star (2011) 'Lebanon Public Debt Reaches $53.4 Billion up to October', *Daily Star*, November 12, 2011. Available online at www.dailystar.com.lb/Business/Lebanon/ 2011/Nov-12/153821-public-debt-reaches-$534-billion-up-to-october.ashx# ixzz2M67eaYsr

8 The international affairs of Lebanon

The chapter addresses the issue of domestic realignments in light of shifting foreign allegiances. National identity has undergone major transformations as the public repositions its alliances. This came amid dramatic global and regional power shifts, which had a significant and resounding impact on the formation of Lebanese nationalism. After all, the country needed to cope with different regional and international struggles for influence. Syria, directly and indirectly, has played the most determinant role in shaping Lebanese politics and institutions. Its hegemony has been backed and supported by other regional and international powers such as Iran and Russia (and previously the USSR). Israel, France, the United States, and Saudi Arabia, among others, have been confronting Syrian influence in Lebanon. The international struggle over Lebanon has been manifested in a variety of ways, ranging from economic, cultural, and political influence to direct military intervention. This chapter examines Lebanon's relations vis-à-vis key player countries.

The geopolitics of Lebanon

Due to its geopolitical position, Lebanon draws the interest of regional and international powers. It has historically stood in the midst of various struggling civilizations that have torn its domestic landscape between different loyalties. As far back as the Phoenician civilization (1550–300BC), which thrived on commerce throughout the eastern coast of the Mediterranean, cities and regions were subjugated to different regional political and religious influences (Persian, Egyptian, Greek, Roman, Byzantine, Arab, Ottoman, European). Its geographic location represented an important commercial route linking Europe, North Africa, Arabia, and Persia. Its mountainous and agricultural environment made it of military strategic significance for regional control and the protection of commerce. Thus, its territory drew major battlegrounds among rival civilizations. Religious convictions, conversions, and affiliations represented a major aspect of societal political mobilizations and struggles for economic influence. Of course, the emerging centrality of Jerusalem among the three monolithic religions (Islam, Christianity, and Judaism) and their grand struggle to claim the region has only added to the contemporary and permanent contentions in the global power struggle for political, economic, and religious influence and control.

Lebanese geography has also contributed to the country's political diversity, which has proven conducive to foreign meddling. Lebanon's mountainous and forested environment has provided historic shelter and safe refuge for many persecuted religious groups and communities. Christian monasteries took refuge in the northern mountains and steep valleys of Annoubin against the various Muslim invasions and rules. The Druze community has also resorted to the Chouf Mountains to escape prosecutions from the various coastal Sunni rules. The most contemporary groups who have sought refuge in Lebanon include Armenians, Iraqi Chaldeans, Palestinians, Kurds, Alawis, and various Orthodox communities. As a consequence, the country has come to shelter diverse groups from different religious and cultural backgrounds, who have soon discovered that their domestic survival is subject to a complex and competitive communal environment. Taking advantage of Lebanon's strategic location, most have come to present themselves as allies to one regional power or another. This has served two purposes. First, on the domestic level, groups have come to gain protection from foreign sponsors and shield themselves from internal prosecutions by rival groups. Second, they have come to exchange economic and strategic benefits with their foreign sponsors. The religious affiliation of these groups has served as a central aspect in this **patrimonial relationship** (also referred to as compradorialism).

Global and regional polarities

International struggle over the region has thus taken many shapes and forms: civilizational, colonial, imperialist, and post-colonial. Modern political expressions have referred to contemporary international political power struggle within the context of a global polarity, as well as regional and sub-regional influence. The post-World War II international system, during which most modern nation states have emerged, has been referred to as a **bipolar world system**, where countries divided along the USSR or United States' spheres of influence. Following the disintegration and collapse of the USSR and the emergence of the United States as an indisputable hegemonic global power, the international system has been often referred to as a **unipolar international system**. The description of early twenty-first century international system as a **multi-polar system** has gained prominence with the rising power of Russia and China. World politics has also been divided along various regional areas, such as Latin America, South East Asia, Europe, Eastern Europe, Africa, and the Middle East and North Africa (MENA) among others. In turn, each has been divided into sub-regions such as Levant, the Gulf, and North Africa in the MENA region. Polarity, whether global, regional, or sub-regional, has been described according to the number of dominant or hegemonic powers. Accordingly, cross regional and sub-regional and even cross-global international politics have emerged to shape the national political dynamic.

Relevant to this discussion is the comprehensive nature of Lebanon's position within the context of these various global power formations and their intersections. Previous chapters have briefly examined the historic role of international regional powers in the determination of Lebanese politics. Lebanon's geopolitical significance and its social diversity have, evidently, played a major role in the attraction and the intertwining of global, regional, and sub-regional interests. The post-World War II bipolar system was a driving cause behind the US and Soviet interventions in Lebanon, starting with the era of Chamounism, where a direct US military intervention occurred in the 1950s, and again in the 1980s to curb the Palestinian power base and consolidate pro-Western President Amin Jemayel's administration. The USSR, on the other hand, extended significant military and financial support to its left-wing Lebanese and Palestinian allies in Lebanon confronting US influence throughout the same periods. Other global powers, such as France, also played important roles within the context of bipolarism and post-colonial influence. Regional and sub-regional MENA powers, such as Iraq, Syria, Saudi Arabia, Libya, Israel, and lately Iran and Turkey, have also provided support to different proxy groups and figures to pursue regional power advantage versus rival countries. Thus, Lebanese political parties and groups have come to strategize themselves within the context of international, regional, and sub-regional polarity. Their political outlooks, mobilizations, activities, and sustainability have been genuinely linked and determined by the different levels of polarities.

Shifting national allegiances directly linked to foreign affiliations

It is within this realm of the rise, fall, and struggle of hegemonic powers and polarities that Lebanese intra-sectarian relationships and views toward the state have been nurtured. The development and transformations of Lebanese national identity has been directly associated with varying foreign allegiances.

Annual public opinion surveys at the Lebanese American University (2007–2012) show a significant shift in perceptions and allegiance to the nation and the state. In the 2007 survey, for example, respondents expressed strong national patriotism, expressing attachment to Lebanon (76 per cent) over their Arabism, religion, social class, locality, or clan. Despite this overwhelming patriotism, however, deviation emerged in their religious and political proximity toward foreign countries. Traditional Muslim affiliation with "pan-Arabism" was now divided by an Iranian–Shi'a versus Saudi–Sunni religious and political closeness. Christians, on the other hand, emerged to have maintained their traditional foreign affiliation with Western countries and religious centers (Figure 8.1).

The Lebanese American University survey reveals the dynamic of an ever-evolving Lebanese national identity constantly reformulated by the balance of the regional power struggle. The latest reformulation is a shift away from pan-Arab and secular nationalist affiliation (Nasserism, Ba'athism, "Palestinianism", communism) in favor of a deepening and fragmented regional sectarian-driven nationalism influenced by the public's closeness to Saudi Arabia (Sunni), Iran

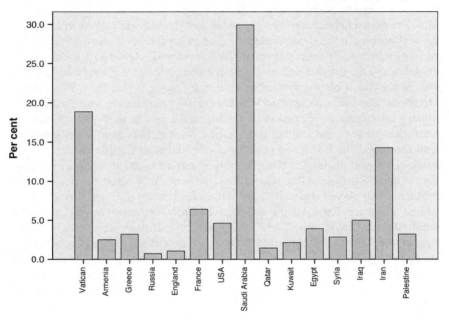

Figure 8.1 Survey of Lebanese public opinion examining the impact of foreign affiliations on the contemporary formation of the Lebanese national identity (2008)

(Shi'a), and the Vatican and the West (Christians). The **Arab Spring** revolutions have further unleashed region-wide, sectarian-based, polarity.

Lebanese public opinion emphasizes the fact that its confessional system is strongly receptive to foreign influence, yielding a permanent state of political and national identity flux. Consequently, the manifestation of a unifying Lebanese national identity and loyalty to the state has not been achieved within the context of a plural, yet divisive, confessional political system. Examining the different roles played out by foreign countries in Lebanon will shed further light on this national dilemma.

Syria

Both states, Lebanon and Syria, were geopolitically established by French colonialism from land gained from the Ottoman Empire after World War I. Significant pan-Arab and pan-Syrian opposition to this post-colonial national formation emerged throughout the post-state periods (post-World War II). This opposition reached its climax when the pan-Arab Nasserite movement in Egypt (1950s) and

Ba'ath Party in Syria (1960s) claimed power. Both Syria and Egypt attempted to defy colonial geopolitical establishment and, together, formulated a United Arab Republic. Syria, under the Ba'ath reign, rejected colonial Arab state divisions and only recognized Lebanese sovereignty in 2008, followed by the exchange of embassies. Syria's role in shaping Lebanese politics, however, was overwhelming, particularly after its direct military intervention in the country that lasted from 1976 until 2005.

In 1976, an invitational intervention of Syria into Lebanon was requested by the former Maronite president Suleiman Frangieh, to prevent the total defeat of Christian forces battling domestic left-wing, Muslim, and Palestinian groups. The request was soon answered by a massive military intervention under the auspices of the Arab League. Syrian intervention represented the beginning of 30 years of Syrian hegemony over all aspects of Lebanese state and society. Syrian rule ended only after public and international pressure converged in February 2005, following the largely suspected Syrian-sponsored assassination of Lebanese Sunni leader and former Prime Minister Rafik Hariri, to demand the end of Syria's military presence in the country. Anti-Syrian public protests on March 14, 2005, known also as the Cedar Revolution, reflected a wide public discontent and disapproval of continuous Syrian presence in the country and exerted an additional pressure against Syria's role in Lebanon.

Syria's forced military pullout in April 2005, however, did not end its political and even military influence in shaping domestic Lebanese politics. This role was attained through its allies and loyalist proxy groups led by Hezbollah, who played a vicious opposition role against the newly formed and the largely perceived anti-Syrian Saniora government. The Sunni–Shi'a struggle in Lebanon emphasized the growing regional struggle through sectarian means. The ruling and predominantly Alawi regime in Syria, and in coordination with the Shi'a regime in Iran, sought closer alliance with Shi'a groups in Lebanon, such as Hezbollah and Amal. A series of political maneuvers played out by Syria's allies prevented its foes from monopolizing political power. These maneuvers resulted in the election of a "consociationa" Lebanese president, Michel Suleiman, in 2008, the reelection of Syrian loyalist Nabih Berry to the Speaker's post in 2009, the formation of a government where Syrian supporters held a veto power over its fate and decisions in 2009, and eventually the overthrow of the pro-Western Hariri government in favor of a pro-Syrian Mikati government in 2011. This is despite the fact that pro-Syrian Shia and Christian alliance was defeated in both the 2005 and 2009 Parliamentary elections in favor of the anti-Syrian Sunni-Druze-Christian coalition.

Formal diplomatic relations between both countries were established in 2008 as part of a political deal achieved in Doha during the same year. The Doha Agreement preserved a significant power share of Syria's allies in a national unity government. Diplomatic relations were formalized and embassies and ambassadors were exchanged. Afterwards, political relations between the countries improved, the newly elected anti-Syrian Prime Minister and Sunni leader Saad Hariri visited Syria and met with President Bashar Assad in 2009 in a bid to restart stalled relations between both countries. In 2011, however, the Hariri government collapsed in favor of a pro-Syrian government under the new Prime Minister Najib Mikati, which also promised the restoration of strong ties between both countries. Prior to the Syrian turmoil that began in 2011, Syria represented the primary economic partner to Lebanon with bilateral agreements fostering the free transfer of products, goods, capital, and labor across the borders.

Israel

Ever since the initial flight of Palestinian refugees into Lebanon and the formation of the state of Israel in 1948, both countries have been in a state of war. This situation has come to cost both sides devastating economic, human, and political losses. Lebanon has come to view the state of Israel as an expansionist and illegally formed entity, with the aim of controlling Lebanon's water and land. It has demanded the right of all Palestinian refugees to return to their homeland in compliance with United Nations Security Council (UNSC) Resolution 171. Israel, on the other hand, has accused Lebanon of harboring hostile Palestinian terrorist groups aimed at the destruction of the state of Israel.

Military confrontations and their intensities between both countries have varied throughout their long struggle. Despite the fact that Lebanon did not participate in the 1967 Six-Day War with Israel, a war of attrition between both countries followed, with Palestinian guerrillas crossing borders and attacking Israeli posts and settlements. Israel carried out military operations against Palestinians and their Lebanese supporters deep inside Lebanon. Israel, soon after, became further engaged in Lebanese domestic politics. In 1975, it began to support a largely Christian Lebanese Army contingency in South Lebanon opposed to a Palestinian armed presence in the country. South Lebanon became a major theater of military skirmishes between Lebanese and Palestinian armed groups. In 1979, Israel waged a major military operation against Palestinians and left-wing allies in Southern Lebanon and established a security zone controlled, in part, by the South Lebanon Army. Israel became increasingly entrenched in Lebanese domestic politics in supporting anti-Syrian and anti-Palestinian Christian groups fighting other Lebanese. In 1982, Israel waged a massive invasion into Lebanon aimed at ousting the Palestinian military presence in the country. It succeeded in dismantling most Palestinian bases in the country and forcing the evacuation of the Palestinian Liberation Organization fighters from Beirut. Lebanese national resistance to the Israeli occupation began to assemble and deliver serious blows to the occupation. Syrian and Iranian support to Shi'a Hezbollah led to the formation of the Islamic Resistance Movement and the eventual defeat of Israel in Southern Lebanon. In 2000, Israel completed its full withdrawal in compliance with UNSC Resolution 425 and its loyalist South Lebanon Army was totally dismantled. Disputes over the total Israeli pullout from Lebanon, however, remained a source of contention, providing pretexts for Hezbollah's continued armed presence. Limited military engagements continued after the 2000 pullout. In 2006, and in retaliation of Hezbollah's abduction of three Israeli soldiers, Israel launched a major military offensive against the party in South Lebanon and Southern District of Beirut. A devastating 33-day war led to the displacement of over one million people and the serious destruction of Lebanon civilian infrastructure.[1] An end to hostilities was finally called for in UNSC Resolution 1701 and an agreement to swap three Lebanese prisoners in Israeli jails with the bodies of three Israeli soldiers killed by Hezbollah was finally reached. Israel continues to consider Hezbollah's armed presence in Lebanon, while being supported by Iran, as one of most significant threats against its security.[2]

Saudi Arabia

Lebanon shares important historic, cultural, linguistic and geographic links with the Arab world. The Arab Gulf States are among the most important economic partners of Lebanon, providing the most important market for Lebanese goods and services, with Saudi Arabia taking the lead. Saudi–Lebanese relationships were strengthened after the Kingdom turned into a major exporter of oil. Lebanon was initially considered as a site for the export of crude oil to Europe and North America through its Mediterranean ports. Major oil pipelines, known as tapelines, transported oil from Saudi Arabia through Syria and Lebanon from 1950 until the mid-1970s. Lebanon also attracted Saudi investors and tourists, owing to its open economy, strong banking sector, and moderate weather. Saudis purchased summer houses and apartments and many families traveled to Lebanon for vacation or their children's education. The presence of a large Sunni sect in Lebanon became an important medium for strengthening economic and cultural ties between both countries. Lebanon exported both skilled and unskilled labor and professionals to Saudi Arabia, together with its various local agricultural and commercial products.[3] Saudi Arabia received tens of thousands of Lebanese Muslim pilgrimages every year to visit its holy sites and perform one of the most sacred pillars of Islam, *Al Hajj*. Saudi–Lebanese intermarriage became common as both countries shared significant cultural and religious ties. Saudi Prince Talal bin Abdul Azziz Saud married the sister of Lebanon's former Prime Minister Rashid Al Solh. Their son, Talal, became one of the major successful global entrepreneurs and billionaires. He played a critical political, economic, and social role in Lebanon through his various foundations, media companies, hotels, and other business ventures. Others, such as former Minister Rafik Hariri, established big construction companies in Saudi Arabia that worked in close association with the ruling Saudi family. His huge fortune and close ties to Saudi Arabia turned him into a major Sunni leader and one of the most important political players in Lebanese political history.

Saudi Arabia's close political alliance with the United States and Europe and opposition to Nasserism, Ba'athism, and Communism turned its support to Lebanese Christians and particularly Chamounists during the 1950s and even in the 1970s. However, Saudi's major role in Lebanese politics developed in the late 1980s in a bid to help end the civil war in Lebanon. Saudi efforts bore fruit after it succeeded in assembling the main Lebanese warring factions in its city of Taef to formulate a new constitutional agreement and to rearrange political power in the country and, consequently, put an end to the war. Since then, Saudi involvement in the country's domestic affairs has only accelerated. First, Saudi Arabia helped its close ally and Sunni billionaire Rafik Hariri became the country's prime minister in 1992. Second, it provided significant financial support and investments in order to rebuild the country after its devastating civil war of 1975–1989 and the later Israeli war of 2006. Third, Saudi Arabia became even more entrenched in Lebanese domestic affairs in its drive to curb Iranian and Shia influence in Lebanon, Iraq, Syria, and Palestine.

Iran

It is believed that Iranian–Lebanese relations can be traced back to the sixteenth century when the Safafid dynasty in Persia sought to adopt Twelvers Shiism as a state religion. Then, Safafid Shahs imported scholars from Lebanon and the Gulf state to help in the spread of Shiism and its theological principles throughout Persia.[4] The presence of Shi'a holy sites in various Iranian cities attracted Lebanese pilgrimages and theological learning through the twentieth century. The rise of Lebanese–Iranian relationship reached its peak after the victory of the Iranian Islamic Revolution of 1979. Iranian Shi'a **Ayatollah Khomeini** claimed *Wilayat-al-Faqih* (Supreme Jurist) and established it as the duty of every Muslim to fight Israel and liberate Palestine.[5] Many Lebanese Shi'a were inspired by the Iranian revolutionary model, and thus adopted Khomeini's new theological interpretations and became subject to his emulations.[6] Iranian efforts to export the revolution to surrounding countries reached Lebanon in the early 1980s with young Shi'a Lebanese joining training camps set up in the Bekaa Valley by Iranian Revolutionary Guards. The aim was to turn these newly radicalized youths into a fighting force in the holy war (*Jihad*) against the Israeli occupation of Lebanon and Palestine and to establish an Islamic State in Lebanon. In 1985, several radicalized factions grouped together and declared the formation of Hezbollah.[7] The new party became the subject of extensive Iranian military and financial support. After its various successful military operations against Israeli occupation forces, the party gathered significant popularity and support among the Shi'a community. In 2000, the party claimed to have been responsible for the defeat and forced withdrawal of the Israeli forces from Lebanon, thanks to Iranian and partly Syrian support.

Hezbollah continued to gain strength and momentum, with Iranian interests well served in undermining Israeli influence in the region. Hezbollah's operation soon extended to reach out to other areas, further advancing Iranian hegemony. The most significant role the party came to play is in assisting Palestinian Hamas fighters in Gaza and helping to strengthen ties between Syria, Iran, and the Palestinians. In 2010, the Egyptian regime of Hosni Mubarak succeeded in capturing and dismantling a major Hezbollah-led weapons smuggling operation in favor of Hamas across the Egypt–Gaza border and arrested one of its main operatives. The slain Hezbollah leader in Syria, Imad Moughneyah, was known to be one of the main architects behind military coordination between Iran, Syria, Hamas, and Hezbollah.[8] Other activities of the parties, serving Iranian interest in the region further expanded to various Arab Gulf states including Iraq, Kuwait, and Bahrain.

The Iranian–Lebanese relationship was strengthened as major Iranian support came to finance the various Hezbollah social networks and activities among the Shi'a community. These include the financing of schools, hospitals, real-estate ventures, as well as several economic activities between both countries. Following the 2006 war in Lebanon, Iran financed many of the reconstruction projects in southern Lebanon that included the rebuilding of destroyed buildings, bridges, roads, rehabilitation centers, and mosques.[9]

Iran and Lebanon have taken steps to enhance economic cooperation in certain sectors. For instance, representatives from both countries signed a memorandum of understanding in June 2010, agreeing to continue to hold committee meetings to examine economic ties every four months. The agreement was completed after a follow-up meeting of the sixth joint economic commission between the two countries.

The Iranian–Lebanese relationship reached its high peak following the repeated Israeli threats to attack Iran's nuclear facilities. Iran found a strategic deterrence role to play in the position of Hezbollah and the Shi'a community along the Lebanese–Israeli borders. Iranian missiles placed in Hezbollah processions stood ready to be launched against Israel in retaliation against any Israeli attack targeting Iran. The 2006 war provided a vivid reminder for Israel regarding the ability of Hezbollah to attack vital and major sites deep inside Israel. This has strongly discouraged any Israeli military ventures in Iran.

Of course, the support of Iran to Hezbollah and the Lebanese Shi'a community has alarmed other sectarian groups who fear a sectarian imbalance in favor of the Shi'a. This is particularly the case because such a support involved significant armament of the Shi'a community without the control of the state or its elected institutions.

France

Europe represents the home of traditional colonial powers. For Lebanon, it has contributed to a significant cultural and political influence over all aspects of its life. Being the home of the Vatican, it provided continuous religious aspirations to the large Lebanese Catholic community with its various dominations. France, however, can be singled out as the major European power playing the most significant role in shaping Lebanese politics and society throughout the twentieth century. After all, modern Lebanese geopolitical foundation owes its origin to French colonialism. It was under the French Mandate that both Lebanon and Syria were declared as two political administrative entities under colonial rules, and later became independent countries recognized by the United Nations. Despite its relatively short colonial reign over Lebanon, France left major marks in the foundation of the state and society. Almost every aspect of modern

Lebanese government was set up by the French including its constitution, Parliament, and administrative districts.

Like Iran and Saudi Arabia, France's imprints stems from the presence of a substantial Catholic, mostly Maronite, community linked to the Vatican and Europe. French protectionism role of the Maronite in Lebanon began during the Ottoman period and was advanced after the country fell under the French Mandate following World War I. The French–Lebanese ties rapidly strengthened, with the French language being adopted as the second language of the country. A **Francophone** Lebanon, under a dominant Maronite political establishment, boosted its cultural, political, and economic cooperation with France. France intervened militarily and politically several times either in support of the Maronites during the civil war in Lebanon or to provide peace-keeping forces as part of the multinational forces that attempted to help the evacuation of Palestinians from Lebanon in 1982, or as part of the United Nations Interim Forces in Lebanon (UNIFIL) during various periods of the Israeli–Lebanese fights.

The climax of the Lebanese–French relations was only reached after the election of French President Jacques Chirac, a close friend of the Lebanese Sunni Prime Minister Rafik Hariri. French support to Lebanon became extensive as expressed in three major economic summits aimed to provide international support for the rebuilding and economic reforms of Lebanon. They provided the country with over ten billion dollars in financial incentives and aid, of which 7.5 billion was pledge in the 2007 Paris III Summit alone.[10] France also intervened to pressure Israeli military restraints against Southern Lebanon and forged the famously known April 1996 Rules of Engagement, which prohibited attacks on civilian populations on both sides of the border. In January 23, 2010, French and Lebanese officials approved the framework of a security agreement that, besides improving bilateral relations, included cooperation for the prevention of drugs and arms trafficking, illegal immigration and cybercrimes.[11]

The Chirac–Hariri relations represented a major shift in the traditionally established French–Lebanese rapprochement, which has historically relied on Lebanese Christian leadership. Before this shift, Sunni and Shi'a sects viewed French policies with suspicions, believing that France sought to reestablish its colonial influence through the Maronites in Lebanon. These suspicions were emphasized as the Maronites refused to identify with Arabism and insisted on their close cultural association with the Christian West, and particularly France. The Hariri era in Lebanon, however, reconstructed this alignment, particularly after France began to develop a critical view against Iran and its extended hegemony over traditionally French post-colonial spheres of influence (Lebanon and Syria). France began to see in the Sunnis, who were threatened by growing Iranian and Shi'a influence, a crucial ally. The result of this rapprochement is that Lebanese sectarian landscape became differently divided with regard to French role, having most Sunni and Druze and half of the Christian community standing in favor while opposed by mostly Shia and the other half of the Christians.

United States of America

The United States' interaction with Lebanon goes back to events of the 1958 Lebanese crisis, when US Marines landed on its shores to support the pro-Western government's position of Camille Chamoun against his pan-Arab opponents. US President Eisenhower authorized Operation Blue Bat on July 15, 1958, to aid the government of Lebanon. This was the first application of the Eisenhower Doctrine under which the United States announced that it would intervene to protect countries "threatened by international Communism".[12]

In the early 1980s, following the start of the 1975 Civil War and the Israeli invasion of 1982, the United States, once again, intervened in Lebanon to aid the newly **inaugurated** pro-Western president Amin Jemayel and to undermine his domestic opponents. Suicide attacks on US Marine barracks claimed the lives of close to 240 US soldiers and, consequently, forced US withdrawal from the country.

Anti-US sentiments grew, leading to various incidents including the hijacking of a TWA airplane, as well as various abductions and killing of US professors teaching in Lebanese universities. The United States withdrew most of its diplomats from the country and issued various travel bans.

The Cedar Revolution of 2005 and the forced withdrawal of Syrian troops from Lebanon opened up the opportunity for the United States to renew its role in the country and to provide support for the newly established pro-Western government of Fuad Saniora. Despite the 2006 war between Israel and Hezbollah, the United States continued to provide Lebanon with significant financial and economic assistance. US President Bush's Administration requested and Congress appropriated a significant increase in US assistance to Lebanon. the United States pledged 890 million dollars in military and economic support for Lebanon during Paris III summit.[13] US–Lebanese relations continued to improve following the beginning Premiership of Saad Hariri in 2009 with increasing financial support provided.[14]

Despite the fact that the population in Lebanon is less than four million, it has been ranked as the 64th largest market for US exports and tenth largest receiver of foreign aid. In early 2009, the United States exported close to one billion dollars-worth of goods to Lebanon. These included vehicles, mineral fuel and oil, machinery, electrical appliances, and cereals. Lebanon has a free-market economy and a strong laissez-faire commercial tradition.[15]

The US policy towards Lebanon has centered on containing Iran's and Syria's influence. The United States has placed Hezbollah on its terrorist list, banning the party from any American financial or political support. Various anti-American Lebanese figures are also included on the US "black list", denying them visa entry into the United States and placing their financial accounts under scrutiny. Lebanese financial and banking institutions have also been placed under the close watch of the United States, fearing money laundering and transactions that finance anti-American or "terrorist" activities.

In terms of sectarian relations, and throughout the Cold War era, the United States has stood in support of Christian Maronites, who have opposed Arab nationalism and Soviet influence in the region. During the same period, most left-wing nationalist and Muslim contingencies have attributed to the United States an imperialist character, most clearly revealed in its support and assistance to Israel against the aspirations of the larger Arab and Palestinian populations. Imperialist intentions were also indicated in US strategic interest in controlling the sources, flow, and prices of Middle Eastern oil. US support to monarchies and oppressive Middle Eastern regimes such as the Iranian rules under the Shah increased the popular conviction of a US double standards in the promotion of democracy around the region. Following the victory of the Iranian Islamic Revolution, the Shi'a community in Lebanon became increasingly hostile to the United States. Not only because the Shi'a Iranian leader Ayatollah Khomeini proclaimed the United States as the great Satan, but also because the United States continued to shield Israel from international condemnation for its occupation of the largely Shi'a area of Southern Lebanon throughout the 1980s and 1990s. Shi'a hostility toward the United States was further exacerbated following the rise of the pro-Western Sunni leader Rafik Hariri into premiership. Hariri led a major realignment of his Sunni sect in favor of a rapprochement toward Western countries. A modernist entrepreneur, Hariri sought economic liberalism, openness, and western investment in the rebuilding of Lebanon. Hariri's position alarmed the Shi'a as well as some of the Christians, who have seen in Sunni–Western alliance a decline of their strategic role vis-à-vis western interest in the region. In retaliation, Christian leader Michael Aoun sought a closer alliance with Hezbollah, Iran, and Syria, following his 2005 return from exile in France. Lebanese Christian relations with the United States severely declined amid deep Christian division over Aoun's strategy.

Russia

Russia draws from its previous empire, the USSR, most of its contemporary foreign policy clues. Throughout the Cold War era, the USSR sought to gain influence in the region. A strong anti-colonial tradition along with the spread out of liberation ideologies among economically and politically deprived youth population represented a strong incentive for the spread out of communism in the region. Large Communist, as well as anti-imperialist, social nationalist parties were formed in most Arab countries. The Lebanese Communist Party, with a strong link to the Soviet Union, was established in October 24, 1924.[16] The Soviet Union extended its influence throughout the Arab countries, challenging US and European spheres of post-colonial influence. A bipolar world strongly shaped Middle Eastern politics during the Cold War era. Revolutions and coups against pro-Western regimes were backed by the Soviets. Following Nasser's takeover in 1952, the Soviet Union established a strong bilateral military and economic agreement with Egypt replacing the British-backed monarchy of King Farouk. Soviet support was translated in military and diplomatic support for Egypt in its confrontation with Israel and the West over Sinai and the Suez Canal. Similarly, the Soviets extended their supports toward other newly formed Arab nationalist governments in Iraq, Syria, Libya, Algeria, and Southern Yemen. Most Arab countries appeared as satellite states orbiting the two world superpowers. As a consequence, Lebanon appeared evenly divided between a left–pan-Arabism, mostly Muslim, coalition backed by the Soviet Union and its various regional allies confronting a Western-supported right–nationalist alliance made out of primarily Christian groups.

Most important to Soviet foreign policy development in the region is its backing of the Palestinian struggle for an independent state; this is despite the fact that the Soviet Union was among the first countries to recognize the state of Israel and to have helped in the migration of hundreds of thousands of Russian Jews into it. At the same time, significant support for the Palestinians and the Palestine Liberation Organization (PLO) was provided. In Lebanon, and since the 1960s and throughout the Lebanese Civil War, the USSR provided critical support to the PLO–left-pan-Arabism alliance on all military, financial, and political fronts.

Russia's foreign policy diverged from the previous position of the USSR, yet it continued to pursue alliances that served its interests in the Middle East North Africa region. Despite the loss of traditional USSR allies, such as that of South Yemen and Iraq, Russia maintained strong linkages with Libya and Algeria. The losses were subsidized by increasing support to Syria and Iran, through whom it reestablished important role in the region, especially in Yemen, Sudan, Iraq, Lebanon, and Palestine.

In Lebanon, Russia continued to support Syrian tutelage over the country and to criticize Israeli policies. After the 2005 Syrian pullout, Russia's role declined in the country, yet appeared to implicitly support March 8 coalition and oppose the anti-Syrian alliance.

Both countries have signed several agreements such as an agreement on trade and payment, agreement on air traffic, cooperation in the tourism industry, non-double taxation treaty, and procedures for forwarding of diplomatic mail without the escort of diplomatic couriers.[17]

In light of deepening sectarian awakening and rifts in the region, the sizable Christian Orthodox community in Lebanon and Syria, along with that of the Armenian Orthodox communities, has increasingly entertained the prospect of greater Russian Orthodox's sponsorship in the region. Establishing stronger relations with Russia as a co-sectarian patron similar to other sects has increasingly emerged as an attractive option amid regional sectarian polarizations. This is particularly the case as Russia's support to both Iran and Armenia converges with that of its support to Alawi, Shi'a, and Orthodox alliance in both Lebanon and Syria.

Turkey

Turkey is the modern inheritor of the Ottoman Empire, which ruled most of the world during its peak periods. For over five decades, the Ottomans ruled the entire Middle East North Africa region, including all areas of modern Lebanon, exerting extensive influence over all aspects of political and cultural life. The challenging presence of diverse sectarian and religious communities in Lebanon was approached by the Sunni Ottoman rule via the establishment of the Millet system. It provided non-Muslim minorities (*duhimi*) with limited autonomy and exclusion from military services in exchange of higher taxes. Most Christians and Jews, including those of Lebanon, were able to save their presence and practices from forced conversions. This occurred despite widespread discriminatory Sharia laws and recurring periods of prosecutions. The influence of this system on Lebanese history and contemporary political practices was significant. Most importantly, it provided the different groups with the abilities to perform their own religious and cultural practices within the feudal political context. Secondly, it engaged the different groups in a competitive episode in order to win the support of the central Ottoman authority. Thirdly, and during the downfall of the Empire, these Millets were turned into unitary political entities establishing external economic, cultural, and political ties with other empires.

The period that followed the defeat of the Ottomans and the establishment of modern Turkey witnessed a gradual withdrawal of its foreign interests from the MENA region. Turkey's later affiliation with NATO against the Soviet Camp brought it closer to Israel and to Western alliance, and thus undermined its role in most MENA regions, including Lebanon. Following the disintegration of the Soviet Union, Turkey made a strong bid to join the European Union (EU). EU's rejection, however, and the growing Iranian regional influence with the emerging power of the Kurds in Northern Iraq, which followed the downfall of the strong centralized rule of Saddam Hussein, seriously alarmed Turkey. By the twenty-first century, Turkey began to turn its attention again to the region, playing a major role in MENA affairs. The Arab Spring provided Turkey a new opportunity to display its Islamic Sunni solidarity with most revolting populations. In Palestine, Lebanon, and Syria Turkey began to emerge as a major power directly intervening in most of their affairs. Lebanese–Turkish relations have witnessed important economic and political cooperation, particularly after the rise of Rafik Hariri into the Premiership in Lebanon. Hariri's family itself established sizable investments in Turkish telecommunication networks.[18]

In 2010, Turkey's President Recep Tayyip Erdogan visited Lebanon and was received by a massive popular reception that displayed Turkish flags throughout the country. Of course, the sizable Armenian community, which is largely made up of decedents of those who had fled Turkey after the Ottomans waged a genocide campaign aimed at their extermination in early twentieth century, demonstrated against the visit. Turkey has continued to deny the occurrence of Armenian massacres and refused to provide retribution or apology. In addition to the Armenians, the Shi'a expressed serious suspicion from the visit, fearing Turkey's new role would strengthen Lebanese Sunni position and undermine Iranian influence in the country.

The United Nations

Lebanon is a founding member of the United Nations, established in 1945. The Lebanese-UN relations are rooted in the continuous assistance provided by 40 UN agencies, funds, programs and offices in various domains. Many UN entities have established offices and regional headquarters in Beirut, such as the Economic and Social Commission for Western Asia and the Education, Scientific, and Cultural Organization. Other UN agencies have been active in assisting Palestinian refugees for decades, most significantly the Relief and Works Agency that serves 455,000 registered Palestinians in 12 camps throughout different regions in Lebanon. Many others have provided extensive assistance and support to the Lebanese government and population such as the Development Program, the Office of the High Commissioner for Human Rights, the High Commissioner for Refugees Agency, Human Settlements Programme Agency, World Health Organization, International Labor Organization, and UNIFIL, among others. All UN agencies in Lebanon are members of the country team that coordinates efforts among the different teams.

Lebanon has been prominent in the region in its ratification of UN conventions such as the Convention Against Torture, the Convention on the Rights of Child, and Convention on the Elimination of All Forms of Discrimination against Women (CEDAW) among many others. Conversely, these conventions have often come to challenge sectarian norms and practices, and even laws. Religious laws, for instance, have rejected various stipulations of the CEDAW, including sometimes domestic violence and rape. Thus, confessional laws that govern civil status have prevented the government from either signing or applying international conventions.

Over the years, Lebanon's internal domestic strife and conflicts with Israel have also resulted in various UN interventions including the passages of UNSC Resolutions, some of which were adopted under Chapter 7 of the UN Charter. It is not an exaggeration to claim that relative to its small size and population, Lebanon has taken a central stage in UN work and attention. Between 2004 and 2012 the UNSC has passed 20 Resolutions pertaining to Lebanon.[19]

Landmarks among these Resolutions are:

- 1559 (2004): Calls for Syrian withdrawal from Lebanon, disarmament of non-state entities in the country, and transparent elections.
- 1595 (2005): Establishes a special international independent investigation commission to assist the Lebanese authorities in the investigation of Rafik Hariri's assassination.
- 1757 (2007): Affirms under chapter 7 the establishment and work of the Special Tribunal for Lebanon to prosecute those responsible for the assassination of Rafik Hariri and other anti-Syrian figures (See Appendix D).
- 1701 (2006): Establishment of the 15,000-member UNIFIL to monitor and enforce the end of hostilities between Lebanon and Israel.

Implementation of these Resolutions is far from satisfactory. The Lebanese public has been divided on the issue of the Resolutions. Shi'a in particular, under Hezbollah, have expressed much opposition against almost every resolution, in whole or in part. The Resolutions have implied the disarmament of Hezbollah (1559), its withdrawal from areas in the South (1701), and have implicated the party in the assassination campaign carried out against Hariri and March 14 political figures (1595 and 1757). Other sects have, on the other hand, supported the Resolutions. Yet, deterioration in public support began to increase following Michael Aoun's defection from March 14 in favor of the 8. Fearing a clash with the Shi'a, the small Druze community under Jumblatt also began to pull its support from the Special Tribunal as the latter passed its indictment against Hezbollah members, holding them responsible for most assassinations. Lebanon–UN relations continue to experience turbulence as the work of the Special Tribunal has come to deepen the division between Lebanese sectarian groups.

Summary

Lebanese domestic politics captures the dynamic and antagonism of global, regional, and sub-regional struggles. The fact that Lebanon has been strategically positioned between world civilizations and nations, while at the same time hosting diverse and competing sectarian communities, turned its political environment into a conductive medium for international power rivalry. As a consequence, Lebanon has attracted world attention like no other country, compared with its small size and population. Sensing the country's geopolitical significance, communal groups often manipulated international antagonism to advance respective domestic interests. Most sectarian political groups have acted as states within the state, building their own international relations and extending sectarian economic, cultural, educational, and even military collaborations with foreign powers. Thus, and since its independence, international and regional actors have intervened in Lebanon. International involvements have included direct military interventions to protect ally political groups, such as that of US intervention to support the Chamoun administration in the 1950s, or in the forms of peace keeping missions, such as that of UNIFIL in Southern Lebanon. Economic aid and loans to Lebanon have been massive with various regional actors supporting proxy political and sectarian groups or the government itself. Iran and Saudi Arabia, among others, have provided significant financial backing to the government and allied political parties. Education and cultural influences have been immense, with the country's large and widespread diaspora playing a significant role in Lebanese modernization. Both the West and the ex-Soviet bloc countries have hosted thousands of Lebanese students and have influenced the education and cultural system(s) in the country. UNSC Resolutions pertaining to Lebanese sovereign and stability are many; some have been passed under chapter 7 of the UN Charter. In turn, the country's communal plurality, amid deeply rooted power competition, has helped the least in achieving a consensual and inclusive vision over the meaning of Lebanese nationalism. The country's efforts to attain a coherent Lebanese national identity under a unified state and society has been repeatedly stalled.

References

1   Hutson, R., Kolbe, A., Haines, T., Stringer, B., Shannon, H., and Salamey, I. (2009) 'Testing Received Wisdom: Perceptions of Security in Southern Lebanon' in Small Arms Survey (eds) *Small Arms Survey 2009: Shadows of War*, Cambridge: Cambridge University Press, pp. 317–35.
2   Salamey, I. (2009) 'Middle Eastern Exceptionalism: Globalization and the Balance of Power', *Journal of Democracy and Security*, 5 (3): 249–60.
3   Baroudi, S. (2005) 'Lebanon's Foreign Trade Relations in the Postwar Era: Scenarios for Integration (1990–Present)', *Middle Eastern Studies*, 41 (2): 201–25.
4   Salamey, I., and Othman, Z. (2011) 'Shi'a Revival and Welayat El-Faqih in the Making of Iranian Foreign Policy', *Politics, Religion and Ideology*, 12 (2): 197–212.
5   Salamey, I., and Othman, Z. (2011) 'Shi'a Revival and Welayat El-Faqih in the Making of Iranian Foreign Policy', *Politics, Religion and Ideology*, 12 (2): 197–212.
6   Salamey, I., and Othman, Z. (2011) 'Shi'a Revival and Welayat El-Faqih in the Making of Iranian Foreign Policy', *Politics, Religion and Ideology*, 12 (2): 197–212.
7   Salamey, I. and Pearson, F. (2007) 'Hezbollah: A Proletarian Party with an Islamic Manifesto – A Sociopolitical Analysis of Islamist Populism in Lebanon and the Middle East', *Journal of Small Wars and Insurgencies*, 18 (3): 416–38.
8   Levitt, M. and Schenker, D. (2008) *Who Was Imad Mughniyeh?* Policywatch 1340. Washington, DC: Washington Institute. Available online at www.washingtoninstitute.org/policy-analysis/view/who-was-imad-mughniyeh (accessed March 28, 2013).
9   Fulton, W., Farrar-Wellman, A., and Frasco, R., August 5, 2011. *Lebanon–Iran Foreign Relations*. Washington, DC: American Enterprise Institute. Available online at www.irantracker.org/foreign-relations/lebanon-iran-foreign-relations (accessed March 28, 2013).
10 Republic of Lebanon, Ministry of Finance (2009) *International Conference for Support Lebanon – Paris III: Eleventh Progress Report*. Beirut: Ministry of Finance, p. 24.
11 France, Ministry of Foreign Affairs (2013) Lebanon: Cultural, Scientific and Technical Cooperation. Available online at www.diplomatie.gouv.fr/en/country-files/lebanon-294/france-and-lebanon/cultural-scientific-and-technical-6063/ (accessed April 28, 2013).
12 Douglas L. (1996) 'His Finest Hour? Eisenhower, Lebanon, and the 1958 Middle East Crisis', *Diplomatic History*, 20 (1); 27–54; Yaqub, S. (2003) *Containing Arab Nationalism, the Eisenhower Doctrine and the Middle East*. Chapel Hill: The University of North Carolina Press.
13 Republic of Lebanon, Ministry of Finance (2009) *International Conference for Support Lebanon – Paris III: Eleventh Progress Report*. Beirut: Ministry of Finance, p. 25.
14 Addis, C. (2011) *Lebanon: Background and US Relations*. Washington, DC: Congressional Research Services, p. 4.
15 Addis, C. (2011) *Lebanon: Background and US Relations*. Washington, DC: Congressional Research Services, pp. 12–15.

16   Suleiman, M. (1967) 'The Lebanese Communist Party', *Middle Eastern Studies*, 13 (2): 134–57.
17   Oron, Y., ed. (1961) *Middle East Record*. Jerusalem: Reuven Shiloah Research Center, p. 410; see also Mattar Law Firm (2000) Russia Non Double Taxation Treaty With Lebanon. Available online at www.mattarlaw.com/lebanon-non-double-taxation-treaties/create-a-company-in-lebanon-non-double-taxation-treaty-russia.htm (accessed April 28, 2013).
18   Levine, G. (2005) 'Billionaire-Owned Telecom Wins Turk Telecom', *Forbes*, January 7. Available online at www.forbes.com/2005/07/01/0701autofacescan09.html (accessed April 28, 2013).
19   See United Nations Special Coordinator for Lebanon. Security Council Resolutions on Lebanon. Available online at http://unscol.unmissions.org/Default.aspx?tabid=9481&language=en-US (accessed April 28, 2013).

9 Elections and parties

This chapter introduces the Lebanese electoral system. Elections are discussed in terms of the electoral system, including electoral districts, distribution of seats, and major challenges confronting political reform in the country. An explanation is also provided for the Lebanese party system, with reference to the sectarian cleavages and competition that are conducive to sectarian populism. The chapter includes an account of Lebanon's various political parties, explaining their natures and functions as well as their alliances.

Electoral system

Most electoral systems in the world are distinguished by being either majoritarian or proportional. The Lebanese electoral system is a majoritarian bloc-vote, first-past-the-post system, in which voters choose as many candidates as there are allocated sectarian seats to their district. In principle, the system has been designed to minimize inter-sectarian competition and to maximize cross-confessional cooperation; candidates are opposed only by co-religionists, but must seek support from outside of their own faith in order to be elected.

The electoral system embodies the compromise between confessional elites that dates back to the National Covenant of 1943, which was updated in the Taef Accords of 1989. The fundamental purpose of these agreements was to mitigate latent conflict between militant sectarian groups. The Taef Accords stipulated a one-to-one ratio between Muslims and Christians within the unicameral 128-seat National Assembly (Chamber of Deputies). The seats allocated to these broad religious communities are further subdivided amongst the various sects within them (Table 9.1).

The parties' typical campaign practices include the distribution of respective affiliated candidates list within a specific district. The voters are then left with the options to vote for the entire list "as is" (straight **bloc vote**), to cross out certain candidates (partial bloc vote), or to cross-list candidates from competing lists (mixed bloc vote). Polling booths or *al-aklam* are typically separated in polling stations by voters' registration numbers and sectarian affiliations, a system that allows political parties to indirectly monitor and track voters' voting records. The

Table 9.1 Pre- and post-Taef allocation of sectarian seats in parliament

Confession	Before Taef		After Taef	
	(n)	*(%)*	*(n)*	*(%)*
Maronite	30	30.30	34	26.56
Greek Orthodox	11	11.11	14	10.94
Greek Catholic	6	6.06	8	6.25
Armenian Orthodox	4	4.04	5	3.91
Armenian Catholic	1	1.01	1	0.78
Protestant	1	1.01	1	0.78
Other Christians	1	1.01	1	0.78
Total Christians	54	54.55	64	50.00
Sunni	20	20.20	27	21.09
Shi'a	19	19.19	27	21.09
Druze	6	6.06	8	6.25
Alawite	0	0.00	2	1.56
Total Muslims	45	45.45	64	50.00
Total	99		128	

Source: Krayem, H. The Lebanese Civil War and the Taef Agreement, Digital Documentation
   Center at AUB in collaboration with Al Mashriq of Høgskolen i Østfold, Norway:
   http://ddc.aub.edu.lb/projects/pspa/conflict-resolution.html

absence of official, preprinted ballots constrains voters to the structured choices presented to them by sectarian parties.

Through this means, a multi-member district system is formed to allocate a specific number of seats to each major sect. District drawing practices have been characterized by sectarian and political gerrymandering that has guaranteed sectarian elites' and parties' grip on power.

Since the 1992 election, parliamentary seats have been divided among six mid-sized administrative districts and subdivided into smaller electoral districts. In the 2000 and 2005 elections, the number of electoral districts expanded to 14. In the June 2009 elections, the number of districts expanded to 26 in the application of 1960 election "*Qada*" law (small district) and in stipulation of the Doha Accord, which redistricted Lebanon to guarantee closer sectarian representation and to undermine the Sunni influence in Beirut. The districts differed in size and by number of seats; varying between two seats in small districts, such as Saida, and ten seats in large districts, such Baalbeck-Hermel. This distribution was the outcome of various political and sectarian considerations and negotiations between the different groups.

The Baabda-Aley constituency district, established for the 2000 election, is an example of electoral gerrymandering. The predominantly Druze district of Aley was combined, in a single constituency, with the predominantly Christian area of Baabda. This merging of the two districts secured a slight majority advantage for the Druze community. Majority Druze voters were able to determine the fate of all district seats, including those dedicated to Christians. The same process in the South provided the predominantly Shi'a community with electoral command in determining Christian-allocated seats. All electoral seats in Beirut were determined by majority Sunni voters, including those dedicated to other sectarian groups.

This political establishment has strongly opposed major electoral reforms, such as proportional representation (PR), that threaten its electoral manipulation by providing smaller parties with greater chances to compete. Thus, and despite their flirtations with the discourse of electoral reforms, the sectarian elites have resisted the kinds of changes that could empower non-dominant sectarian parties.

The Lebanese political system has thus been resting on electoral engineering designed to perpetuate the confessional elites' control over state's representative institutions. Elections and electoral laws are among the institutional mechanisms deployed by these elites to preserve the confessional system's **clientelistic** nature and to neutralize attempts to move away from sect-based politics. It is little wonder that the formula for converting votes into parliamentary seats – the bloc vote – has been preserved since the birth of the republic, and that PR has emerged as an unattainable primary reformist demand.

By contrast, PR would allow for more inclusive representation of political forces, including those independent of the confessional elites, and for the possible emergence of inclusive national political parties that appeal to a broader base of constituents.[1] The changes stipulated by the Taef Agreement are set out in Table 9.1.

Parliamentary elections

Lebanon is administratively divided into six governorates (*Muhafazat*). Each governorate has been administered by a Governor (*Muhafiz*) appointed by the Council of Ministers upon a proposal from the Ministry of the Interior. The governorates are further subdivided into 25 districts (*Qada*), each of which is presided over by a District Chief (*Qa'em Maqam*). In the 1992 and 1996 elections, parliamentary seats were divided among six mid-sized administrative districts and subdivided into smaller electoral districts. In the 2000 and 2005 elections, the number of electoral districts expanded to 14. They differed in size and number of seats; varying between six seats in small districts, such as Beirut District 2, and 17 seats in large districts, such as that of North Lebanon District. This distribution emerged as an outcome of various political and sectarian considerations and negotiations between the different groups. Elections are conducted according to a single list (bloc vote) system with the voter having the choice to cross-list candidates from competing lists within the districts. During the Syrian era, the districts were redrawn prior to each election to secure a majority of pro-Syrian candidates. Since the Syrian withdrawal, the confessional elites have focused on how changes in the form and size of the districts affect the standing of each political grouping, gerrymandering districts accordingly, much like the Syrians and their cronies had done.

In 2009 election, and per the stipulation of the Doha Agreement, districts were changed to 26 smaller *Qada*-based districts. The number of seats in each has varied between two in small districts, such as Batroun, and ten in larger ones, such as in the joined *Qadas* of Baalbeck-Hermel. Parliamentary elections are held every four years. Debate over appropriate districting and electoral law has continued to divide the political landscape of the country.

The *Qada*-based districts vary widely in the size of their electorates: the largest one, Baalbeck-Hermel, has over 250,000 voters while the smallest, Bsharri, has just under 45,000 voters.[2] The drawing of district lines has thus led to large discrepancies in the number of voters per district, giving unequal weight to each vote. The districting, the bloc vote, and the closed-list features of existing electoral laws have favored the hegemony of the main political parties. Independent candidates face extremely high barriers of entry and have slim chances of winning unless they join one of the electoral lists concocted by the political parties, often at a price (monetary, political, or both).

Despite the move toward small *Qada*-based elections, most districts' constituents and allocated seats remained sectarian heterogeneous (Table 9.2). Yet, the presence or absence of a sectarian majority in a district has determined, to a large degree, contested elections. In the mixed sectarian district of Zahle, where no group held a numeric edge, for example, the 2009 electoral battle over the seven parliamentary seats was among the fiercest. Five percent of votes represented the winning margin difference. This stands in sharp contrast to election held for the predominantly Shi'a (88 per cent) three-seated district of Bint Jbeil where 49,000 votes (93 per cent of votes) were cast to the third winner, compared with 600 (1 per cent) to the first losing candidate, resulting in a winning margin difference of 92 per cent.[3]

Given the country's geographic and demographic realities, with the majority of Muslims spread over a larger territory, Muslim sects prefer large electoral districts, while Christian sects prefer smaller *Qada* ones. This has tended to restrict political representation among the Muslim sects, while creating more intra-religious and intra-sectarian competition among Christian sects. The issue of representation is all the more contentious in multi-confessional districts, leading confessional minorities to complain that their representatives often capture seats based on votes from confessions other than their own. For example, in a district with a Sunni majority and a Maronite minority, it is the Sunni votes that ultimately determine which of the Maronite candidates win.

While it was meant to foster cross-sectarian cooperation in principle, the bloc-vote system has in effect encouraged the formation of short-lived electoral alliances that are based on maximizing the candidates' collective chances of winning seats rather than on shared political ideology or policy platforms. It is not uncommon for political parties to form an electoral alliance in one district and to run as opponents in another.

Still, the major deficiency has remained that of the detachment of a significant portion of the electorates from their place of residence. For instance, the system assigns voters to electoral districts of origin not to residence, namely to their villages and remote areas under sectarian control. Most voters who reside in mixed religious neighborhoods in Beirut or its suburbs have been driven to vote

Table 9.2 Allocation of seats in the 2009 election for the Parliament of Lebanon (*Majlis an-Nuwwab*)

		Total	Maronites	Shia	Sunni	Greek Orthodox	Druze	Armenian	Greek Catholic	Alawite	Protestant	Other Christians
Beirut 19	Beirut 1	5	1	—	—	1	—	2	1	—	—	—
	Beirut 2	4	—	1	1	—	—	2	—	—	—	—
	Beirut 3	10	—	1	5	1	1	—	—	—	1	1
Bekaa 23	Baalbeck–Hermel	10	1	6	2	—	—	—	1	—	—	—
	Zahle	7	1	1	1	1	—	1	2	—	—	—
	Rashaya + West Bekaa	6	1	1	2	1	1	—	—	—	—	—
Mount Lebanon 35	Jbeil	3	2	1	—	—	—	—	—	—	—	—
	Kisrawan	5	5	—	—	—	—	—	—	—	—	—
	North Metn	8	4	—	—	2	—	1	1	—	—	—
	Baabda	6	3	2	—	—	1	—	—	—	—	—
	Aley	5	2	—	—	1	2	—	—	—	—	—
	Chouf	8	3	—	2	—	2	—	1	—	—	—
North Lebanon 28	Akkar	7	1	—	3	2	—	—	—	1	—	—
	Dimiyeh and Minieh	3	—	—	3	—	—	—	—	—	—	—
	Bsharreh	2	2	—	—	—	—	—	—	—	—	—
	Tripoli	8	1	—	5	1	—	—	—	1	—	—
	Zgharta	3	3	—	—	—	—	—	—	—	—	—
	Kurah	3	—	—	—	3	—	—	—	—	—	—
	Batroun	2	2	—	—	—	—	—	—	—	—	—
South Lebanon 23	Saida	2	—	—	2	—	—	—	—	—	—	—
	Tyre	4	—	4	—	—	—	—	—	—	—	—
	Zahrani	3	—	2	—	—	—	—	1	—	—	—
	Hasbaya and Marjeyoun	5	—	2	1	1	1	—	—	—	—	—
	Nabatiyeh	3	—	3	—	—	—	—	—	—	—	—
	Bint Jbeil	3	—	3	—	—	—	—	—	—	—	—
	Jezzine	3	2	—	—	—	—	—	1	—	—	—
Total 128		128	34	27	27	14	8	6	8	2	1	1

Source: Republic of Lebanon, Ministry of Interior and Municipalities. 2009 Election Results: www.elections.gov.lb/Parliamentary/Elections–Results/2009–Real–time–Results/-الانتخابات-النيابية-الإنتخابات.aspx

Map 9.1 Lebanon's 2009 electoral districts

Source: International Foundation for Electoral System (2011)

for sectarian candidates running in their respective villages and hometowns of origin. This process has not only undermined geographic linkages between the candidates and their constituents; it has also tied voters to sectarian politics and has further perpetuated traditional sectarian leadership. Emerging urban secular and cross-confessional communities have thus been denied political representation. Worse, this electoral mechanism has weakened residential ties to the living space, establishing exclusionary sectarianism and a fragmented sense of national identity.

Municipal elections

Municipal elections are held for members of the Municipal Council and *Mukhtars* concurrently for six-year terms. The bloc-vote system is implemented in local elections in the same manner as that of Parliament. However, seats are not allocated along sectarian lines. After being elected, the Municipal Council elects its president (mayor) and officers. Most municipalities have more than one *Mukhtar*.

The number of the Municipal Council members and *Mukhtars* is determined by the size of the municipal population. *Mukhtars* do not play much of a governance role and work individually to process applications, mostly notarization services for residents related to issues of personal status. Municipalities are administratively grouped within the 25 *Qadas*.

Municipalities constitute, typically, communities of at least 500 inhabitants. In 2009, there were 945 municipalities managed by approximately 11,000 council members with limited autonomy.[4] Municipal governments are charged with the tasks of managing and advocating local concerns. However, their jurisdictions have been curtailed by a strong centralized system that concentrates power within the hands of few sectarian chiefs. Sectarian leaders along with their elected members of parliament have overshadowed local governments' roles. Calls for local empowerment and decentralization have largely been aborted by the sectarian and political leadership. This is despite the fact that the Taef Agreement stipulated decentralization among governance reform strategies.

Electoral challenges and reform efforts

A weak legal framework has left ample room for corrupt practices such as vote-buying, which is reportedly rampant, as well as pressures on voters to cast their ballots in favor of certain electoral lists. Vote-buying can take various forms, from cash payments to voters, to flying in diaspora Lebanese with all expenses paid by political parties, a practice that is believed to have contributed to the large influx of expatriates in the last parliamentary polls. In the current electoral system, paying for the loyalty of a few thousand voters can be enough to win slim majorities in some districts, affecting the balance of power in parliament. PR would make this a lot more difficult as it would create a situation in which parties would have to buy tens of thousands of votes to actually affect election results.

In addition, the absence of an official, preprinted ballot has had major consequences on electoral behavior. Ballots are prepared by political parties running on the same electoral list and are usually distributed by party agents outside polling stations, or through families and community leaders ahead of an election. The use of prepared ballots undermines the secrecy of the vote as the ballots can be traced back to the voter (e.g., based on paper color or the order in which candidates are listed). It also allows party agents to exert undue influence on voters and opens the door to selective protests since many of the ballots are technically objectionable under the law (for example, the law stipulates that only white-colored paper should be used, but this is disregarded).

In 2006, the government-appointed Boutros Commission brought together some of the country's preeminent electoral experts to draft a comprehensive law that, if adopted, would have signaled wholesale reform of the electoral system. It included such measures as partial PR, preprinted ballots, single-day voting, campaign spending limits, media regulations, establishment of an independent electoral commission, lowering of the voting age from 21 to 18, out-of-country voting, a women's quota, and polling station access for persons with disabilities.[5]

Civil society organizations mobilized as soon as the Boutros Commission unveiled its ambitious proposal in 2006, forming a wide-ranging coalition under the banner of the **Civil Campaign for Electoral Reform** to push for adoption of the recommendations. Recurrent political crises and violent conflict derailed these efforts, however, including the 2006 war with Israel, a prolonged political stalemate that shut down parliament, and the May 2008 clashes.

The Doha Agreement aborted the Boutros Commission's electoral reform recommendation in favor of the *Qada*-based bloc vote system. However, the new system introduced various technical reforms, including the adoption of single-day voting; better voting procedures (such as the use of transparent ballot boxes and indelible ink); as well as campaign finance and media regulations, which were monitored by a newly formed Supervisory Commission on Electoral Campaigns. In addition, the 2009 elections marked the first time that international and domestic election observers were formally accredited, effectively institutionalizing non-partisan election observation.

Parliament did vote in favor of lowering the voting age to 18, but the constitutional amendment required to put this into effect was not promulgated. The 2008 law also required access for the disabled, but this was not effectively implemented due to logistical constraints. Out-of-country voting was deferred to the 2013 parliamentary election, but remains unlikely for political reasons.

Though electoral reform is an uphill battle with no guaranteed outcomes, the prospect of additional reform, possibly including some form of PR, is not far-fetched. Reform efforts by various stakeholders, such as civil society groups, have gained ground in demanding the establishment of an independent electoral commission to oversee the electoral process free from sectarian political influence. Another electoral reform that has been advocated is the introduction of PR. Activists and political groups demanding PR have differed on whether this should be introduced within the country as one electoral district (typically called for by secularists and Muslim groups) or as many. Also, differences exist regarding whether PR should be implemented according to sectarian allocation of seats or should be implemented based on non-sectarian electoral law. The latter has been stipulated by Article 95 of the Taef Constitution, but its implementation is yet to be realized. The use of preprinted ballots is another typical reform demand that has been advocated for in order to ensure a secret ballot and protect the voter from intimidations. Stronger campaign finance and media regulations are also on the reform agenda. The adoption of a women's quota on candidate lists or allocated parliamentary seats has been advocated, as female members of parliament have never exceeded 2 per cent of the total. The inclusion of diaspora in the electoral process as well as lowering the voting age to 18 and providing access to voters with disabilities has also been included among reformists' demands. Yet, the establishment of residence as the base for voting districts remains one of the radical measures that have hardly attracted any of the reform demands.

Ahead of the 2013 scheduled election, proposed reforms have focused on the establishment of an electoral law that provides for accurate sectarian representation. The draft "Orthodox Law" was introduced to parliamentary committees

---

Local election reforms proposed by former minister Ziad Baroud

Reform advocate and former Minister of Interior and Municipalities Mr Ziad Baroud (2009–2011) considered it necessary to introduce some amendments to the local electoral process that include:

- the election of the president and vice-president of the municipalities by direct vote;
- the adoption of the proportional representation in larger municipalities to ensure proper representation;
- the introduction of the quota of 30 per cent (seats) for women as specified in the Beijing Declaration of 1995, also specified in Article 4 of the Convention on the Elimination of All Forms of Discrimination against Women, ratified by Lebanon in 1996;
- the adoption of preprinted ballots;
- reduction of the mandate of municipal councils and *Mukhtars* to five years.

Source: Now News: https://now.mmedia.me/lb/en/nownews/an-nahar_publishes_draft_of_new_municipal_electoral_law1 (accessed April 28, 2013).

---

which called for the implementation of sectarian proportional representation, whereby each sect would vote exclusively for its own candidates. The proposal, sponsored by all Christian political parties and backed by the Shi'a parties, was opposed by both Sunnis and Druze. The latters feared potential electoral loss and internal divisions.

Types of political parties

Parties are of different types and can be distinguished by being either cadre or mass-based parties. The two types have coexisted in many countries, particularly in Europe and the United States, where cadre-based Communist, socialist, religious and various ideological parties have emerged alongside modern mass-based conservative and liberal parties. Most parties do not fall exactly into either category but combine some characteristics of many, such as the Social-Democratic and Christian-Democratic parties. Parties can also be distinguished as either system or anti-system parties. While the formers seek to win elections and introduce reforms, the latter aim to topple the entire political regime through revolutionary means. Still, the general distinction remains between cadre and mass parties.

Cadre-based parties were most common prior to the nineteenth century's Western introduction of universal suffrage. Economic, gender, regional, age, and racial affiliations' voting requirements produced various types of aristocratic, racial, and revolutionary (anti-system) cadre-based parties. Parties' membership was confined to particular social groups who adhered to ideological views regarding the preservation or overthrow of social order and the state. Mass-based parties, on the other hand, emerged following the eradication of voting restrictions to unite hundreds of thousands of followers, sometimes millions. Thus, it became increasingly difficult for cadre-parties to win in open elections against the more moderate and wide reaching political mass-parties. The United States party system provides the clearest demonstration of mass party (Democratic and Republican parties) advantages in capturing mass votes and winning elections throughout the twentieth century compared with other cadre-based parties who have been electorally marginalized (Communist, religious, and white-supremacist parties). The introduction of party primary elections in the United States, where nominating party candidates to national election is opened to public voters, has served the purpose of establishing mass parties very well.

Number of political parties

Party systems are distinguished according to the number of existing political parties in a country. System classifications can vary as one-party (China), two-party (United States), two-and-half (Canada), and multi-party (Belgium). In most democratic countries, the electoral system may encourage or discourage the formation of parties. As a general rule, the existence of a majoritarian electoral system with large electoral districts undermines the ability of smaller parties to compete and win election. Thus, a limited number of mass parties are typically established, such as the case in the United States, where a majoritarian electoral system in relatively large electoral districts with limited number of seats consolidated its two-party system. In contrast, a proportional electoral system, with a small electoral threshold requirement, insinuates the formation of many parties and the establishment of a multi-party system. The historic/cultural/ethnic/religious/economic diversity and political cleavages of the constituents add to the plurality of the party system. The latter factor also provides for the successful formation of either mass or cadre parties. Political polarization boosts the chances of cadre parties to win constituents and undermine moderate mass parties' ability to accommodate diverse groups. Thus, in such situations many parties are formed. In summary, two factors determine the number and type of parties in a particular country: political polarity and the electoral system.

The Lebanese party system

The Lebanese bloc vote, with its first-past-the-post electoral system, has provided a moderate form of majoritarianism. Its multi-member, small-district structure has further contributed to its inclusionary and consociational nature. At the same time, strong sectarian political polarity has fragmented the country's party system. An electoral law that allocates seats to sects has further consolidated sectarian-based divisions. The combined impact of sectarian polarity and the moderate majoritarian electoral system has resulted in a multi-party system which includes aspects of sectarian-based cadre and mass party politics. Nineteen political parties won seats in the 2009 parliamentary election. Six major sectarian political parties captured most votes and the 128 parliamentary seats were divided among the following parties: the predominantly Sunni Future Movement (26), the Shi'a parties of Hezbollah (12) and Amal (13), the predominantly Maronite Free Patriotic Movement (19), together with the Lebanese Forces (8), and Phalange Party (5), and the Druze's Progressive Socialist Party (7). Although these parties have aggressively competed to win mass votes and used all possible incentives to attract voters, their membership, as well as their appeal, has been largely confined to closed sectarian constituencies. Strict cadre-based parties have remained small in size, particularly those who advocate cross-sectarian ideologies, such as the secular groups of the Lebanese Communist Party, the Left Democratic Movement, the Syrian Social Nationalist Party, and the Ba'ath Party, among others.

Most of the sectarian parties are personality-based, comprising followers of a present or past charismatic political leader or warlord. The personalization of political leadership has often led to family-run parties and the spread of kinship succession in leadership. The Hariri family, for instance, has come to control most political leadership roles among the Future Movement. Former Prime Minister Saad Al-Hariri inherited his post in government and the leadership of the Future Movement after his father Rafik Hariri. Walid Jumblatt succeeded his father Kamal Jumblatt in the leadership of the Progressive Socialist Party. Amin Jemayel succeeded his brother Bashir Jemayel as President of Lebanon, and as the head of the Kataab party after his father. Family members of former interim-President Michael Aoun are placed in key leadership positions within the Free Patriotic Movement. General Secretary of Hezbollah, Sayyed Hassan Nassrallah combines both religious and political authority among his Shi'a followers. He represents the ultimate religious scholarship for emulation for Shi'a who submits to the Iranian brand of Twelvers and, at the same time, assumes the role of party leader.

Although partisan politics in Lebanon has been a long-practiced tradition that stretches back to pre-independence, contemporary sectarian populist politics emerged in the 1950s and was represented by Chamounism, in reference to popular Christian Maronite President Camille Chamoun (1900–1987). Chamounism was mainly opposed by Kamal Jumblatt, another leader who headed the mainly Druze "Socialist Progressive Party." They were followed in the late 1960s by the emergence of a Shiite movement, called the Movement of the Disposed (Harakat al-Mahroumeen), founded by the charismatic religious leader Imam Moussa Sadr. Chamounism developed in the context of defending the Christians' (mainly Maronite) upper hand in the running of the state and economy in the face of a growing challenge by local and regional Nasserite forces. Both the Phalange Party (Al-Kataab) and the Party of Liberal Nationalists (Al-Ahrar) won Christian followings. The Movement of the Disposed (Amal), on the other hand, represented an attempt by the Shiite community to increase its share of the state resources. Subsequently, in the seventies, particularly after the outbreak of the civil war in April of 1975, the Christian populist movement regrouped itself and resurfaced, initially as the Phalange Party, then, towards the end of the 1970s, as the Lebanese Forces, led by the populist and short-lived President Bashir Jemayel. After the signing of the Taef Accord and the end of the civil war in 1989, new developments spurred the burgeoning of a new Shi'a populist movement led by Hezbollah. In 2005, after the assassination of Prime Minister Rafik Hariri and the withdrawal of Syrian troops from Lebanon, two other populist movements emerged, the Christian-based "Free Patriotic Movement" led by Michel Aoun and the Sunni-based "Future Movement" led by Saad Al-Din Al-Hariri.

Lebanese sectarian populism has served as a vehicle that transcends group grievances. It has strengthened individual communities in the sectarian power struggle, and has established a strong communal check and balance against the emergence of an overwhelmingly dominant state authority. Hence, sectarian politics within this matrix of Lebanese electoral and party systems, as well as the presence of strong personalized political leadership, have served to entrench sectarian populism as the dominant mode of political behaviors.

Lebanese parties

Given this context of Lebanese politics, sectarian populist parties in Lebanon have come to acquire a unique character; they could never be elevated to become inclusive nationalist political groups because the nationalism of each one has typically been subsumed under an overriding sectarian identity, be it Christian Maronite, Sunni Muslim or Shiite Muslim. More importantly, they have always emerged around communal claims condensing a plurality of demands raised by the party itself and constituting the ultimate goal for "hegemonic" politics.

Hence, despite the parties' general aims of winning elections and advancing communal interests, the Lebanese communal/sectarian character of populism produced a peculiar relationship between the parties and the state. The parties' attitudes towards the state have typically been contradictory, depending on their capacity to control its resources. Hence, when they secured the capacity to position state resources under their control, they stood positively toward the state, which contrasts with populist classical anti-statist views. Yet, if they lacked such control or satisfactory benefit, they would undermine state legitimacy to the extent of engaging it and oftentimes bringing about its total demise. In both cases, however, the state has been perceived and dealt with ultimately as an institution subordinate to the overriding legitimacy of the populist leaders and their sectarian parties.

Thus, political parties have used various tactics to strengthen their power positions and maximize their share of state resources. This, however, has required that populist parties present themselves as the sole and ultimate representative of respective sectarian communities. Intra-sectarian rivalry has been perceived as undermining the party's leverage and jeopardizing sectarian advantage. Thus, extensive efforts toward securing the parties' grip over their own respective sectarian communities have been made throughout Lebanese political history. They have come to consume all possible strategies to undermine and suppress rising or existing rivals. Intra-sectarian competition in the 1980s led to devastating consequences and violence which claimed thousands of casualties during the Hezbollah–Amal fight over the leadership and influence in the Shi'a community. Intra-sectarian fighting produced similar consequences in the power struggle between the Lebanese Forces, the Marada, Al-Ahrar, the Kataab, and the Aoun-led Army to establish hegemonic leadership over the Christian community.

The parties' communal mobilization has relied on various incentives including ideological indoctrination, fighters' recruitment, public jobs and services, social support and welfare, economic incentives, vote buying, and so on. The outcome is the establishment of relatively autonomous sectarian communal infrastructure networks whose maintenance and sustainability have been closely associated by the prevalence of a nepotistic relationship of patronage existing between members of the sectarian community and the populist leader.

Contributing to political party jockeying and scheming based on narrow sectarian self-interests is the absence of a political party law. As a result, political parties have not been regulated. They have only been legally required to register under the 1909 Law of Associations (the same law applied to non-governmental organizations), but the latter has no bearing on their political functions. The open framework for the operation of political parties permits them to receive unlimited funds from domestic and foreign patrons, and allows for the unusual situation in which a group like Hezbollah can be both a legal political party and an armed entity.

The parties' organization structures have varied between one group and another. Most, however, share the leadership structure of having a general secretary or a president who heads a party's political bureau and/or a central committee. They are typically elected during an annual party convention or conference. Most are also organized on a regional level, starting with the lowest party cell in a neighborhood or a village, then regionally grouped according to a *Qada* or *Muhafaza*. Depending on the party, some may even have a military security organizational structure, such as Hezbollah. Most large parties develop a division of labor among their leadership to carry out the various functions of the party, such as fundraising, media campaigns, public relations, recruitments, and so on. Lebanese parties have advanced to the level in which they come to own and operate large business enterprises to support their activities financially and to provide salaries to thousands of members. Gas stations, mini-markets, import-export companies, cement companies, security companies, real-estate operations, schools, media outlets, as well as illegal activities such as money laundering, drug and cross-border smuggling are common. Most parties publish newspapers, magazines, and have online sites. At least five major satellite television networks and more than five radio stations have been privately owned and operated by large parties employing hundreds of followers, such as Future TV, NBN, Al-Manar, and OTV.[6]

Political alliances

In order for parties to achieve their goals, they resort to various alliance formation strategies which can add to their relative strength and advance their position vis-à-vis their inter- and intra-sectarian rivals. Of course, approaches vary between formal and informal means. The latter includes forging common goals in neighborhoods and sectarian turfs with local business interests in return for financial backing and support or with influential individuals, religious figures, families, and clans who may require political protection and influence. The former, on the other hand, includes more politically and institutionally recognized processes. Among the formal alliances are those that formed with allies, and sometimes foes, in order to win university or other national syndicate association elections, such as that of the lawyers, the teachers, the engineers, the dentists, the doctors, and the pharmacists. These engagements provide the parties with a pre-election barometer as well as an assessment of public moods and required alliance strategies on the ground in order to develop effective campaigns and coalitions in crucial election battles.

Parties develop "electoral machines" whose aim is to solicit and monitor the votes. These machines become active on various fronts, such as voter mobilization, buying votes, campaigning, and election monitoring. Most importantly, they observe the compliance of allies in voting for the common list during local and national elections.

Electoral lists provide the first immediate alliance that parties formulate to win election. This has become most urgently needed in contested and political mixed electoral districts, whether for local or national elections. In safe districts, parties may establish a list with minor allies as a tradeoff for the latter's support in electorally undetermined districts. This same strategy has been often used with foes to best serve parties' national electoral calculations. Electoral lists have also taken various compositions to insure the winning chances of the alliance. Sometimes, locally oriented lists have served the purpose such as "Zahle in the Heart," which won the closely contested Zahle district election in 2009. This list was made out of local influential individuals and March 14 political parties who competed for the votes under local development slogans.

Following parliamentary national elections most electoral lists are transformed into parliamentary blocs, often with few modifications. They are typically headed by a dominant political sectarian party and overshadowed by the party chief. An example of a parliamentary bloc is "Change and Reform", which is led by its dominant party the Free Patriotic Movement under the Maronite leader Michael Aoun. The bloc includes various minor groups such as the Armenians' Tashnaq Party and the Druzes' Lebanese Democratic Party. Both legislative and government's affairs became the subject of the Bloc's activism.

Parliament blocs are reconfigured around larger parliamentary groupings that establish majority and minority alliances. This division in the Lebanese Parliament has been essential in the making of crucial political decisions amid deep political divisions. They include the nomination and election of President, Prime Minister, and Speaker. Other crucial decisions are those of approving government's lineup, policy statement, public appointments, budget, international agreement, and crucial expenditures and policy decisions. Critical legislation and confidence in government also hinges on the coherence of the majoritarian coalition.

These formal electoral and parliamentary alliances have been generally culminated in the national division of society behind two political camps. Past national coalitions were divided on the question of the country's identity and association with Arab nationalism versus Western modernism (1950s–1980s); at other times their polarization was centered on the role of Syrian "protectionism" in Lebanon (1980s–2000s), and most recently on the legitimacy of non-state armed groups (Hezbollah, March 8 groups, Sunni Jihadists) and Lebanon's regional and international relations (Syria, Iran, Saudi Arabia, United States, among others).

Summary

The formation of parties represents one of the most sophisticated aspects of the political process. Parties channel group interests within the political process, with aims of translating popular will into policies. Thus, winning elections and formulating the government's agenda and deciding policies constitute the fundamental purposes of any system party. However, a party's road to power is often shaped by the existing electoral system. The system may encourage the formation of many or few parties and shapes their ideological or mass orientations. The Lebanese bloc-vote electoral system, with its sectarian allocation of parliamentary seats, has encouraged the formation of many dominant sectarian political parties. In their drive to power, parties established various electoral coalitions, platforms, and lists. In parliament, they grouped themselves among regional and political blocs, as well as larger cross-regional political alliances. Lebanese parties have made use of sectarian-based mass partisanship, while, at the same time, emphasizing a strong personalized leadership structure. Undisputable populist sectarian leaders emerged, resulting in a nepotistic and a patrimonial-based politics. In order to perpetuate their grip on power, party leaders have been engaged in gerrymandering politics. They have blocked electoral reform efforts that attempted to introduce PR, which has the potential to engage additional competitors, and have prevented electoral regulations that impose restrictions on their abilities to buy the votes. Muslim and Christian parties have differed slightly on electoral reform agenda, where the former advocated laws that tap into their demographic advantages and national spreading out, the latter have sought laws that encourage the participation of their diasporic community and emphasize the localization of representation.

References

1   Salamey, I. and Tabar, P. (2008) 'Consociational Democracy and Urban Sustainability: Bridging the Confessional Divides in Beirut', *Journal of Ethnopolitics*, 7 (2): 239–63.

2   Republic of Lebanon, Ministry of Interior and Municipalities. 2009 Elections Results. Elections Official Results per District. Available online at www.elections.gov.lb/Parliamentary/Elections-Results/2009-Real-time-Results/نتايج-الانتخابات-لكافة-الاقضية.aspx (accessed April 28, 2013).
3   Republic of Lebanon, Ministry of Interior and Municipalities. 2009 Elections Results. Elections Official Results per District. Available online at www.elections.gov.lb/Parliamentary/Elections-Results/2009-Real-time-Results/نتايج-الانتخابات-لكافة-الاقضية.aspx (accessed April 28, 2013).
4   International City/County Management Association (2011) *Municipal Finance Studies Program Final Strategic Framework*. Beirut: Ministry of Interior and Municipalities, pp. 17–18.
5   Ekmekji, A.A. (2012) *Confessionalism and Electoral Reform in Lebanon Briefing Paper*. Washington, DC: Aspen Institute.
6   Salamey, I. and Pearson, F. (2007) 'Hezbollah: A Proletarian Party with an Islamic Manifesto – A Sociopolitical Analysis of Islamist Populism in Lebanon and the Middle East', *Journal of Small Wars and Insurgencies*, 18 (3): 416–38.

Part III
Political institutions

10 Lebanese legislative branch

The chapter provides an informative account on the Assembly of Representatives, the Speaker and overall legislative administration, distinguishing between the specialized committees. The Parliament's functions are discussed in the context of power division and sectarian consociational politics.

National Assembly of Representatives

Lebanon's national legislature is called the National Assembly of Representatives or Chamber of Deputies (*Majlis al-Nuwab* in Arabic) and is commonly referred to as the parliament. It was originally established as a bicameral legislative body during the French Mandate, but evolved into a unicameral assembly. It has changed its composition and structure several times. Since 1992, and following the stipulation of the Taef Agreement, its members became evenly composed of Christian and Muslim representatives. It has since maintained this distribution among its 128 members. It convenes twice a year in ordinary sessions in March and in October. Extra parliamentary sessions are called for by the Speaker. During the Assembly, members discuss vital national legislations and vote on proposed laws, commonly introduced by the Council of Ministers. Among its most important functions is to vote for a new president, nominate a new prime minister, approve a new government's lineup and **policy guidelines**, discuss and vote on the government's annual budget, vote on key governmental appointments, and approve and amend critical legislations such as electoral laws.

The parliament has remained a unicameral, confessionally elected assembly throughout its history. The Taef Accord stipulated that a higher chamber or a senate (*Majlis al Sheyoukh*) should be established alongside a lower chamber. The senate was supposed to represent the various sectarian interests, while the Chamber of Deputies would be elected on a non-sectarian basis. This stipulation was incorporated into the constitution in the 1990 amendments (Article 22), but these stipulations were never implemented.

Owing to the fact that the Council of Ministers is typically formed and approved by the majority of parliamentary political groupings, it emerges as a major legislative player. In fact, it has come to draft and introduce most bills. Although members of parliament can sponsor, support, and introduce proposed laws to the

Chamber, this function has been largely dominated by the Council of Ministers. Even after approval of legislation by the required majority of members of parliament, the Prime Minister and concerned ministers must sign the legislation before it can be referred to the President for final approval. Once signed by the president, the new law can be promulgated and published in the **Official Gazette**. The President may express reservations against certain legislation and may refer it back to parliament for reconsideration. However, if parliament passes it again by two-thirds majority, it can overcome presidential veto and become a law.

Seats in the parliament are confessionally distributed but elected by **universal suffrage**. Each sectarian group has a quota of parliamentary seats. Yet, parliamentary candidates are voted for by confessionally mixed constituents. The system was designed to minimize inter-sectarian competition and maximize cross-confessional cooperation. In highly mixed districts, candidates seek the support of various sectarian groups who can sway the election result in their favor against the competing groups. Owing to the likelihood of election advantages in districts being highly predetermined, based on sectarian composition, the practice of gerrymandering has been highly implemented in the sectarian elite's power bargains. Since the Chamoun era, district drawing has been manipulated to serve the power advantage of a political or sectarian group. This became most evident during the Syrian tutelage over Lebanon, where districts were drawn to boost the electoral advantages of their proponents against its Christian critics. Some electoral laws have been publicly referred to by the names of Syrian officers who intervened in all political and economic aspects of the country, such as the **Ghazi Kanaan** Law.

The Lebanese Parliament

Parliament:

- is elected by popular vote for four-year terms on the basis of proportional representation for the various confessional groups;
- proposes legislation;
- levies taxes and approves the budget;
- can impeach the prime minister and ministers for high treason, or for serious neglect of their duties (the decision to impeach can only be taken by a two-thirds majority of the total membership);
- can question ministers on policy issues;
- can withdraw confidence from certain ministers;
- can be dissolved by a joint decision of the president and the council of ministers if it fails to meet during one of its regular periods and fails to meet throughout two successive extraordinary periods, each longer than one month, or if it rejects an annual budget plan with the aim of paralyzing the government; new elections must be held within three months of dissolution.

The practice of gerrymandering was an additional effort by the ruling Syrian security apparatus to marginalize their Christian opponents. The Taef Accord has reconfigured the political power-sharing formula in the country, which empowered the Shi'a speaker and the Sunni prime minister at the expense of the Maronite president. For example, the president used to nominate every member in the cabinet, but since the Taef Accord, the cabinet formation requires the Speaker to call for parliament's approval.

The Speaker

The Speaker of the Parliament, who by custom must be a Shi'a Muslim, is now elected to a four-year term. Prior to the Taef Agreement, the Speaker was elected to a two-year term. The consociational system provides the Speaker, being the head of the Shi'a sect and often referred to as President of Parliament, extraordinary powers that include the ability to veto the political process. Speaker Nabih Berri (1992–present), one of the longest lasting Speakers in his post, is the head of Amal's political and armed wings. The Speaker's powers include that of legislative referral of draft laws to parliamentary committees, in a very similar way to that of the US House Speaker. The Speaker's power is drawn from the ability to delay or influence the tabulation of referred legislation. This provides the Speaker with a bargaining power in negotiating and determining the prospect of legislation with the various political groups opposed or favoring draft legislation. This legislative power of the speaker is further consolidated by administrative jurisdictions that provide the office with the supervision of every aspect of parliament's work. The Speaker's office is in charge of the General Secretariat, whose role includes setting legislative agenda, convening of the chamber, supervising internal finances, determining personnel recruitment and appointments of staff, interpreting the rules when needed, and maintaining records of undisclosed parliamentary committee meeting records.

Thirteen consecutive Speakers have presided over Parliament since independence (Box 10.1). All with the exception of Habib Abou Chahla were Shi'a. All have played a prominent role in the politics of Lebanon. However, the power given to the Parliament, the limits imposed on presidential powers, and the extended and unlimited term given to the Speaker by the Taef Constitution have freed the former from the influence of the President. Internal rules have also given the Speaker an inordinate amount of power over the legislative process. These circumstances have, unprecedentedly, made the Post-Taef Speaker, Nabih Berri, the most powerful political figure in the country.

Parliamentary committees

In the Parliament, there are 16 specialized Standing Committees, with sessions closed to the public and meeting records kept undisclosed (Box 10.2). Most Committees have been formed to coincide with existing ministries in the Council of Ministers. Others have been established for particular purposes, such as that of

Box 10.1 Speakers after independence

Sabri Hmede: September 21, 1943 to October 22, 1946
Habib Abou Chahla: October 22, 1946 to April 7, 1947
Sabri Hmede: June 9, 1947 to March 20, 1951
Ahmed Alassad: June 5, 1951 to May 30, 1953
Adel Osseiran: August 13, 1953 to October 15, 1959
Sabri Hmede: October 20, 1959 to May 8, 1964
Kamel Alassad: May 8, 1964 to October 20, 1964
Sabri Hmede: October 20, 1964 to May 9, 1968
Kamel Alassad: May 9, 1968 to October 22, 1968
Sabri Hmede: October 22, 1968 to October 20, 1970
Kamel Alassad: October 20, 1970 to October 16, 1984
Hussein eltoHusseini: October 16, 1984 to October 20, 1992
Nabih Berri: October 20, 1992 to present

Source: Lebanese Parliament: www.lp.gov.lb [Arabic]

Box 10.2 Parliamentary Standing Committees

*   Environment
*   Information Technology
*   Women and Children
*   Human Rights
*   Youth and Sports
*   Media and Communications
*   Economy, Trade, Industry, and Planning
*   Displaced Persons
*   Defense, Internal Affairs, and Municipalities
*   Public Health, Labor, and Social Affairs
*   Education and Culture
*   Public Works, Transport, Energy, and Water
*   Foreign Affairs and Emigrants
*   Administration and Justice
*   Budget and Finance
*   Agriculture and Tourism

Source: Lebanese Parliament: www.lp.gov.lb [Arabic]

Information Technology and Displaced Persons. There are also 13 Committees formed to strengthen Lebanese relations with a particular foreign country and these are called Friendship Committees.

Every Committee is headed by a chairperson. All chairpersons are typically appointed through a political negotiation linked to the formation of a new government. Trades-off are made between the various political groups in their shares of ministerial portfolios, as well as committee memberships and chairmanships. According to the legislative by-laws, a member of parliament cannot be a member in more than two permanent committees, unless the third is the Human Rights Committee. Committee votes are taken by majority; in the event of a tie, the chairperson casts the decisive vote, although customary practice has made decisions by consensus. The meeting quorum requires a majority attendance. The committee meetings, agenda, and minutes are all kept secret and are not publicly publishable, although outside experts or civil society groups may be invited to attend meetings. Committees' reports are submitted to the General Secretariat. Secret records have invited the criticism of many civil society groups and international oversight agencies. Many arguments have been advanced in favor of publishing records, a practice traditionally followed in most democracies, in order to strengthen parliamentary accountability and public transparency. Arguments against this have centered on the need to shield the committees' legislative performance from over-politicization, which would undermine their technocratic performance. Regardless, the current practice has empowered the Speaker with the ability to keep or publicly expose the records at will.

All draft laws pass through the most powerful committee: the Administration and Justice Committee, which reviews their compliance with the Constitution and with existing legislation. The same Committee handles any major political reform legislation, including electoral reform. In this sense, the committee acts as a legislative gatekeeper and is sometimes referred to as the "kitchen committee" because of its ability to "cook" most of the legislation. The Finance and Budget Committee, second in importance, leads approval, oversight, and review of the national budget and expenditures. It may call on any minister, including the very powerful Finance Minister, for cross-examination and questioning. From 2005 until 2013, however, the Finance and Budget Committee has failed to approve the government budget. Deep political division has prevented the different groups from agreeing on a new distribution of public funds. Government operations, therefore, have been sustained by what is called "the twelfth rule", which allows the government to maintain the same distribution of funds as that of the last approved budget. Extra public expenditures called for by the Council of Ministers would require a special parliamentary session for approval. Other more recent committees (for example, Environment, Human Rights, Information Technology) are active and have shaped a number of draft laws.

Legislating: A bill becomes a law

Almost all draft bills are prepared by the Council of Ministers, and then submitted to parliament for consideration, although technically at least one, or at most ten members of parliament, can sponsor, support and advance a proposal for a law to the Chamber. Because of Lebanon's plural confessional politics, the executive engages in informal consultations and consensus-building with parliamentary blocs ahead of introducing draft laws. As a result of the dominance of sectarian considerations, most policy issues are settled outside parliament. Major legislative decisions, such as electoral law and budget, are decided on by sectarian patrons outside of parliament. Parliament often acts as a rubber stamp for decision taken by the country's political elites.

Following the introduction of proposed legislation, the bill flows as in most parliaments, where the Speaker of the Chamber and his Secretarial Committee decide on its merit and importance. Accordingly, it is referred to special parliamentary committees to have it further reviewed and appropriately edited according to internal rules. Subcommittees and joint committees might be formed in this process for that purpose. A large amount of draft legislations that referred to committees is "buried" there, as legislations require consensus before being presented to the entire chamber for discussion and vote. Proposed legislations that pass both committees and Chamber are presented to the Prime Minister and relevant minister in the Council of Ministers for approval before being submitted for the President's signature. In each step of this process, legislation may be negotiated back and forth for further reconsiderations. Finally, the President's signature, along with the Prime Minister and the concerned Minister, turn a bill into a law published in the Official Gazette. Presidential veto may kill a bill unless overruled by absolute parliamentary majority.

Oversight

Lebanon's parliament is held in low esteem, and public perceptions of members of parliament also suffer, as they are increasingly perceived as appointees of the sectarian patrons. They are seen as establishing clientelist functions to serve supporters rather than establishing the essential functions of legislation and oversight. This perception has been emphasized by the special allowances and life-long salaries for members of parliament who serve more than one term. The legal immunity for members of parliament has only increased public suspicion of corrupt practices. Years of wars and foreign intervention have reduced public interest in the function of the state and have left the state subject to the manipulation of militia and elite cartels.

Despite the end of the war and the pullout of foreign troops from Lebanon in 2005, Lebanese division continued to attract foreign meddling and, consequently, maintain fragmented and weak government institutions. Impasse over the election of a new President in 2007, for example, divided parliament and undermined its ability to convene and elect a new head of state. The presence of organized armed groups – linked, financed, and armed by foreign sponsors – further undermined the emergence of a strong representative and transparent institution capable of performing an oversight function. Efforts to reform parliament's internal rules have been blocked by a strong suspicion regarding the possible undermining of the Shiites' power in the state in favor of other sects. Thus, the parliament's functions have continued to be jeopardized by deeply polarized sectarian politics.

Parliament's performance of executive oversight, for example, has been minimal, and checks and balances in the political system have been inadequately institutionalized through the National Assembly. Part of the problem is that the confessional preserves of influence mitigate against effective oversight, since the heads of the legislative and executive branches have been designated to belong to particular sectarian groups. However, while the president is himself somewhat shielded in this regard, other members of the Council of Ministers have been subject to more intense scrutiny. The Cabinet undergoes repeated oversight sessions, where attacks and criticism against its performance are televised by the opposition to undermine the ruling executive. Sometimes this has actually forced resignations, as when Omar Karami's Cabinet collapsed after parliamentarians took to the Chamber's stands to criticize the handling of Hariri's assassination in 2005.

The lack of effective oversight is particularly acute with regard to the review of the national budget and other financial matters. There is a notable absence of a fiscal review office or facilities in the parliament. Members of parliament themselves are not capable of systematically reviewing the budget or expenditures, and they lack the means to engage specialists on an ongoing basis. International development agencies, such as the United Nations Development Programme, the European Union, and United States Agency for International Development have established programs to strengthen and build the capacities of both parliamentarians and parliament itself to perform stronger oversight functions. Yet internal rules and political manipulations have continued to challenge sustainable development in this area.[1]

The election of politicians rather than technocrats and their appointments to committees is an additional hurdle standing against their role to play in their overnight functions, which require specialization for review and detailed examination of the budget. In addition to the internal lack of specialized expertise in budgetary analysis, the executive is not forthcoming with the necessary information in a timely fashion.

Representation

In order to understand the dynamics of the parliament and the nature of confessional representation within the legislature, it is essential to have a grasp of the key relevant features of the current electoral system.

The main purpose of the various electoral systems introduced throughout the various periods in contemporary Lebanon was to provide a balance between the confessional elites and avoid conflict. But by structuring electoral representation on a "quota-ed" confessional basis, the composition of the parliament, in effect, further reinforced sectarianism. Political elites were able to draw upon the fears of domination by other confessional groups to protect their own status as defenders of their groups versus leaders from other religious factions.

While this "quota-ed" system helped to dampen the potential for conflict in the short and medium terms, it institutionalized incentives and structures that were detrimental to political development. For one thing, sectarian politics has continued to undermine the possibilities of developing broader consensus over policy issues between the various groups. Indeed, even within confessional groups, policy platforms are rarely clearly articulated, since voters simply tend to cast their ballots for the leaders of their own sect.

Criticisms are often voiced against the current electoral "confessionally quota-ed" system. The three most obvious ones are:

- the subordination of the list to dominant sectarian leaders (a situation sometimes described as an enforcement of **political feudalism** – *Ekta'a Al-Seyasee*);
- the subordination of sectarian minority candidates within mixed districts to those of the majority through "packaged lists" (often referred to as *Al-Mahdalah* or "steamroller" lists);
- unequal representation of candidates emerging out of different sized districts (fueling the debate for small-*Qada* vs. large-*Muhafaza* voting districts and various electoral system options).[2]

Many Christians view this law as unfair to them, since the seats allotted to the Christians are mostly voted on by Shi'a and Sunni electorates. The Christians chafe against their quotas being filled by candidates selected on Muslim lists, and in addition, the Muslims tend to complain about the voting age being set at 21 years rather than 18 years. The numerical advantage that Muslims have would be increased if the voting age was reduced, since demographically their numbers are increasing among young people. In contrast, Christians have demanded the right for Lebanese expatriates worldwide to be able to vote, since the expatriates are mostly Christian and this would therefore help reverse domestic demographic trends.

The representation of women in parliament has hardly exceeded a 3 per cent margin. A male-dominated politics, in addition to the absence of an electoral quota for women, has prevented female candidates from having a fair chance. Only women connected to powerful traditional political families have been able to make their way into parliament through parliament. These include Bahia, the sister of Rafik Hariri, Streda Geagea, the wife of Lebanese Forces leader Samir Geagea, Nayla Moawad, the widow of Lebanese President Rene Moawad, Solange Jemayel, the widow of Lebanese President Bashir Jemayel and Nayla Tueini, the daughter of assassinated member of parliament Gebran Tueni.[3]

Composition of the 2005 and 2009 parliaments

The parliamentary elections of May–June 2005 were the first since 1992 that were not manipulated by Damascus. The new elections introduced changes in the political makeup of the parliament in favor of an anti-Syrian majority. The broad coalition known as the March 14 Alliance that originally won 72 of the 128 seats was led by Saad Hariri, the son and political heir to Rafik Hariri, and included the Druze faction led by Walid Jumblatt and several Christian groups (Table 10.1). The Shi'a split their votes evenly between the Amal Party and Hezbollah, gaining about 35 seats (in favor of their March 8 Alliance) between the two parties. The other large group in the new parliament was led by Michel Aoun, who was vehemently anti-Syrian, but has since moderated his position following his break with the March 14 coalition and his attempts to establish closer ties with Hezbollah to gain an edge over his intra-sectarian Christian rivals (Table 10.1).

Table 10.1 2005 and 2009 parliamentary political distributions of seats

Bloc	Leading party/ affiliation	Predominant confession in the bloc	Seats			
			2005		2009	
			(n)	*(%)*	*(n)*	*(%)*
March 14			72	56	71	55
	Future Movement and allied independents	Sunni	38	30	39	31
	Progressive Socialist Party[1]	Druze	15	12	11	9
	Lebanese Forces	Maronite	5	4	8	6
	Phalange Party and Quornat Shehwan	Maronite	8	6	6	5
	Ramgavar and Hunchack	Armenian	4	3	3	2
	The Democratic Left	None/secular	1	1	1	1
	Renewal Democratic Movement	Sunni	1	1	0	0
	Islamic Group	Sunni	0	0	1	1
	Michael Murr[2] and Independent	Orthodox	0	0	2	2
March 8			56	44	57	45
	Amal Movement	Shi'a	15	12	13	10
	Hezbollah	Shi'a	14	11	13	10
	Marada Movement	Maronite	0	0	3	2
	Lebanese Democratic Party	Druze	0	0	3	2
	Arab Socialist Baath Party	None/secular	1	1	2	2
	Syrian Social Nationalist Party	None/secular	2	2	2	2
	Kataab (pro-Syrian)/ Solidarity Party	Maronite	1	1	1	1
	Nasserites	Sunni	1	1	0	0

Table 10.1 continued

Bloc	Leading party/ affiliation	Predominant confession in the bloc	Seats 2005 (n)	2005 (%)	2009 (n)	2009 (%)
Reform and Change (Aoun)[3]						
	Free Patriotic Movement	Maronite	15	12	18	14
	Ilyas Skaff	Maronite	4	3	0	0
	Tashnaks	Armenian	2	2	2	2
	Michael Murr[1]	Orthodox	1	1	0	0
Total			128	100	128	100

Sources: European Union Election Observation Mission, *Parliamentary Elections Lebanon 2005: Final Report*. International Foundation for Electoral Systems Lebanon (June 2008) *Briefing Materials for Assessment Missions*. Lebanese Ministry of Interior and Municipalities (June 2009).
Notes:
1 Claimed independent political position after election of 2009.
2 Switched alliance in 2009 election.
3 Switched alliance and joined March 8 or the "Opposition" in 2006.

In the subsequent June 2009 elections, the parliamentary polls resulted in a majority of 71 deputies aligned with March 14 and an opposition of 57 deputies aligned with March 8. However, the balance of power began to shift when Jumblatt, who had been a March 14 stalwart since 2005, announced the adoption of a "centrist" position while expressing continued support for Hariri as prime minister. In 2011, however, he broke his stance and voted in favor of nominating Mikati against Hariri, following the latter's government collapse. With the defection of the Progressive Socialist Party and the Tripoli Gathering, which includes Mikati himself, March 8 was able to command a newfound parliamentary majority.

Summary

The constitution proclaims Lebanon as a parliamentary democracy. Indeed, legislative assemblies where established in the early twentieth century under the French Mandate and were governed by the 1926 Constitution. The establishment of a confessional politics institutionalized after independence divided all first grade public posts between Muslims and Christians on a five to six ratio in favor of the latter. This also applied to parliamentary seats. This was later adjusted into an even distribution following the Taef Agreement, which entrusted to Parliament a greater role. The post-Taef Parliament was empowered by the ability to elect not only the President, but also the Prime Minister, and to approve both his ministerial lineup and government's policy statement. Parliament was further relieved from the ability of the President to dissolve it without a constitutional reason and the approval of the Council of Ministers.

Headed by the Shi'a Speaker, Parliament was to convene twice annually in regular sessions or as needed irregularly. The mission is to legislate, perform an oversight role over the conduct of the cabinet, and represent the nation. Organized along 16 specialized Standing Committees, each headed by a chairman and divided into sub-committees. The Speaker plays a vital role in the life of Parliament, particularly after having the Taef extending his stay in office to a renewable four-year instead of a two-year term. The current Speaker, member of parliament Nabih Berri is one of the longest serving Speakers in the world, first elected in 1992. Representing the Shi'a, he holds vital powers such as tabulating and referring legislations as well as convening Parliament into sessions. The latter power has granted the speaker indirect veto power over vital parliamentary work, which has been used in 2007 to prevent Parliament from convening to elect a President by the March 14 parliamentary majority, deemed hostile to the Shi'a. In terms of its functions, Parliament has been slow to approve laws and has been constrained from performing oversight roles. The fact that legislations are mostly introduced by the Council of Ministers, which represents the parliamentary majority, Parliament has served a rubber-stamping role for legislations engineered outside of its Chamber. Instead of conducting legislation and oversight functions, parliamentarians have focused on social activities and services where they pursue constituents' interests and provide favors, such as attending funerals and pressuring ministries to perform services to respective districts. The 2009 Parliament has produced two governments: a national unity headed by Saad Hariri (2009–2011) and a majority by Najib Mikati (2011–2012).

References

1   Salamey, I. and Payne, R. (2008) 'Parliamentary Consociationalism in Lebanon: Equal Citizenry vs. Quotated Confessionalism', *Journal of Legislative Studies*, 14 (4): 451–73.

2   Salamey, I. and Payne, R. (2008) 'Parliamentary Consociationalism in Lebanon: Equal Citizenry vs. Quotated Confessionalism', *Journal of Legislative Studies*, 14 (4): 451–73.

3   Joseph, S., (2011) Political Familism in Lebanon. *Annals of the American Academy of Political and Social Science*, 636 (1): 150–63.

11 Lebanese executive branch

The chapter provides a detailed account of the functions and roles of the president and prime minister. The Council of Ministers is also examined in terms of its power, process of formation, portfolios, general organization, constitutional terms, contemporary role, political makeup, and types of policy issues under its jurisdictions, required quorums, relations to legislative and judicial branches, and the current political and sectarian make-up of the Council. Local government is also discussed – particularly its local municipal roles, powers, and its various administrative formations.

Presidential versus parliamentary systems

Democracies are distinguished by being presidential or parliamentary. In a presidential system, the head of state is the president, who is directly elected by the entire population of the country. Typically, significant power is vested in the office of the president, who can claim direct and sole national allegiance as reflected in the ballot box. Members of parliament, on the other hand, are elected by geographically limited constituencies. In Egypt, for example, the president is the only public servant elected by the entire population. As a representative of the whole national will, he summons in his office very significant powers that often overwhelm other branches of government. In the United States, the president heads the cabinet and appoints all its members. Because of his very powerful role and powers, the US President becomes the head of the party and leads a very active role in directing the Congressional legislative agenda, as well as making a significant number of public appointments, while also representing the country internationally.

In a parliamentary system, however, the population does not directly elect the president. Parliament is the only governmental entity elected directly by the population, and thus, it claims significant power relative to other branches of government. In fact, it is the parliament who elects the president and the prime minister. In most parliamentary systems, the executive branch is divided between both the president and prime minister, though the president is entitled with a symbolic national role while the prime minister oversees the entire process of the executive branch. Both the president and prime minister report back to the parliament and seek its approval in most critical issues, such as the formation of government, its guidelines, and its budget. Still, the prime minister plays the most significant national leadership role. In most parliamentary states, such as Israel, the president hardly plays any significant role, while the office of the prime minister and his cabinet overwhelmingly dominate the executive branch.

It is sometimes the case in countries with presidential systems, yet with strong parliamentarianism, such as France, that a power struggle emerges between the president and the prime minister. This is particularly the case when elections yield a president and a parliamentary majority of opposite political parties. The **Fifth Republic of France** attempted to establish a clear division in the jurisdictions of each office in a bid to undermine potential power struggles.

The Lebanese constitution declares Lebanon to be a parliamentary republic. Parliament elects the president and nominates the prime minister. However, the pre-Taef Constitution entrusted the president with significant powers, including that of appointing the prime minister and other ministers, and dictating most executive and legislative agendas, including the ability to dissolve the parliament altogether. Having the post reserved for a Maronite, the system emerged closer to a presidential system throughout the period prior to the Taef Agreement. After the Taef, however, the powers of the executive branch were divided between the Maronite president and the Sunni prime minister, with the latter gaining significant grounds on the account of the former. An impasse between the president and prime minister emerged following the withdrawal of the Syrian troops in 2005, with the prime minister and president representing opposite political camps. The election of the consociational President Michel Suleiman, as part of a political deal reached between the Marches in the Doha, was the only way out that facilitated the marriage of convenience between both poles of the executive.

The President of Lebanon

Lebanon's political system is based on the separation of power into executive, legislative, and judicial branches. Executive power is divided between the president of the Republic and the Council of Ministers. The president is the head of state, and a symbol of the nation's unity; s/he is in charge of safeguarding the Constitution. The Taef stipulated that the president shall designate the prime minister, but only after binding consultations with parliament whose approval is required for the formation of a new cabinet. The premier, who is the head of the government, forms a Council of Ministers after consulting the main parliamentary political blocs. The Council of Ministers has the authority to ensure the execution of laws, propose bills, dismiss parliament, deploy the army, and ratify international treaties (all of which were prerogatives of the president before the 1989 Taef Agreement). Since the Council of Ministers is composed of sectarian leaders, or their representatives, inter-sectarian disputes can paralyze the cabinet and parliament for months whenever they occur.

The president is elected by the National Assembly for a six-year, non-renewable term. Lebanon's presidential term limit has been an exceptional practice among Arab heads of state. Only three presidents in Lebanon have been able to extend their stay by extra-constitutional amendments for an additional three years; they were Presidents Bechara El Khoury (1943–1952), Elias El Hrawi (1989–1998), and Emile Lahoud (1998–2007). Yet, political culture has strongly opposed an extended stay, because the sects feared the emergence of a strong autocratic president. Presidential attempts to extend their stay in office have been often confronted by strong political and sectarian opposition. A two-thirds majority approval is required for such an extra-constitutional amendment.

The presidential election is a two-round process. A candidate must win two-thirds of parliament's vote in the first round, otherwise a second round with a simple majority vote suffices (see list of Presidents in Table 11.1). Among presidential powers is the delegation to parliament's nominated prime minister of the task of forming a Council of Ministers. Another power of the president is the ability to promulgate or veto laws passed by the parliament, as well as issuing decrees with the approval of the prime minister or the relevant minister. The president may also negotiate and ratify treaties in coordination with the prime minister. S/he may convene, in consultation with the prime minister and the Council of Ministers in extraordinary sessions. The president also has the ability to request from the Council of Ministers to revise decisions or to dissolve parliament if it fails to perform critical functions such as passing the annual government budget. Yet, none of these requests are binding, and in fact, parliament has failed to approve government's annual budget from 2005 until 2013. At the same time, the president has not requested its dissolution, knowing that the Council of Ministers would not approve its own demise. Other powers include issuing **pardon** by decree and acting as a commander in chief of the armed forces.

On November 23, 2007, the term of Emile Lahoud, the tenth President of Lebanon, came to an end. At the time, the Lebanese political spectrum was deeply polarized, with virtually all parties being divided either as the government loyalists (March 14), or the opposition (March 8). The two camps could not come to an agreement as to who should become the country's eleventh president. As a result of a provision in the country's constitution, the powers of the presidency transferred to the government in the expectation that an agreement would be reached shortly.

Several names were advanced as potential candidates for the presidency, including Michel Aoun, Nassib Lahoud, Boutros Harb, among others, each of whom was affiliated either to the March 14, 8 camps. It soon became apparent, however, that only a consociational candidate would be acceptable to both sides. Michel Suleiman was generally viewed as the only consensual candidate. Most Lebanese commentators and policy makers agreed that Suleiman had successfully won the trust of both camps and the support of most countries in the Arab region, as well as most Western countries. However, his election was achieved only after a number of concessions made by both Marches and concluded in the Doha Agreement. These include the agreement to establish a national unity government after presidential inauguration that would prepare for a parliamentary election under a new electoral law (known as the 1960 electoral law). On May 25,

Table 11.1 Presidents of the Republic of Lebanon (1943–2013)

#	Name	Year of birth–year of death	Date inaugurated	Date left office	Political affiliation
1	Bechara Khoury	1890–1964	22 November 1943	18 September 1952	Constitutional Bloc
	Fuad Chehab (acting)	1902–1973	18 September 1952	22 September 1952	Military
2	Camille Chamoun	1900–1987	23 September 1952	22 September 1958	National Liberal Party
3	Fuad Chehab	1902–1973	23 September 1958	22 September 1964	Military
4	Charles Helou	1913–2001	23 September 1964	22 September 1970	Chehabist
5	Suleiman Frangieh	1910–1992	23 September 1970	22 September 1976	Marada Movement
6	Elias Sarkis	1924–1985	23 September 1976	22 September 1982	Chehabist
	Bachir Jemayel[1]	1947–1982	–	–	Kataab Party
7	Amine Jemayel	1942–	23 September 1982	22 September 1988	Kataab Party
	Selim Hoss (acting)	1929–	22 September 1988	5 November 1989	Independent
8	René Moawad	1925–1989	5 November 1989	22 November 1989	Independence Movement
	Selim Hoss (acting)	1929–	22 November 1989	24 November 1989	Independent
–	Michel Aoun (acting)	1935–	23 September 1988	13 October 1990	Military
9	Elias Hrawi	1925–2006	24 November 1989	24 November 1998	Independent
10	Émile Lahoud	1936–	24 November 1998	23 November 2007	Independent
	Fuad Saniora (acting)	1943–	23 November 2007	25 May 2008	Future Movement
11	Michel Suleiman	1948–	25 May 2008	Present	Independent

Source: Presidency of the Republic of Lebanon: www.presidency.gov.lb

Note:
1 Elected but was not inaugurated.

2008 Suleiman was elected and inaugurated as the 11th President of Lebanon. He was voted by an absolute majority of 118 members of parliament.

The Prime Minister of Lebanon

The prime minister is appointed to form a government by the president after binding consultations with parliamentary blocs, with parliamentary majority nominating successful candidate. The president plays a ceremonial role in this appointment, simply declaring the prime minister as the winner of majority's nomination. The prime minister spends extensive time in forming the government. Ministerial composition must be satisfactory in order for government to win the support of a parliamentary majority. Some formation processes have taken months, others have led to the acquittal of the nominated prime minister after failing to form the government. Saad Hariri, for example, failed his first effort to form a government after the 2009 election, but he was renamed by parliament to renew his efforts and finally succeeded months later. No time limit is imposed by the constitution to complete this process. After the approval of parliament and the president, the prime minister diverts efforts to formulate policy guidelines, according to which his government must present to and gets approved by parliament.

The prime minister is the second head of government, and has vested power as part of the sectarian power sharing formula. As a Sunni, the prime minister has come to acquire a significant role after the Taef Agreement. He resides over the Council of Ministers and sets its agenda, although this role is shared with the president. The prime minister must countersign all decrees and laws along with the president of the Republic, including international treaties. The prime minister nominates individuals to ministerial portfolios before the approval of parliament. The office of the prime minister is one of the most powerful, as it maintains a significant share of governmental budget and commands various oversight and public hiring agencies. There is no term limit on the prime minister and some have spent eight terms in office, such as former Prime Minister Rashid Karami. Most of the prime minister's powers have been acquired through the Taef Agreement; where before the prime minister played mostly a subordinate role to that of the president (see list of Prime Ministers in Table 11.2).

On January 24, 2011, the March 8 alliance, together with several March 14 defected prime ministers, nominated Najib Mikati to become prime minister and to succeed Saad Hariri, whose government was brought down by the resignation of one-third of his ministers. This was the minimum number required for the dissolution of the Council of Ministers. On January 25, 2011, 68 members of parliament nominated Najib Mikati for the task of forming a new government. President Michel Suleiman then named Mikati to head a new government. On June 13, 2011, Mikati succeeded in assembling a parliamentary majority coalition to support his new government. This was his second term as a premier.

Table 11.2 Prime Ministers of Lebanon since independence (1943–2013)

#	Name	Year of birth–year of death	Date inaugurated	Date left office	Political affiliation
1	Riad Solh (1st term)	1894–1951	25 September 1943	10 January 1945	Independence Movement
2	Abdul Hamid Karami	1890–1950	10 January 1945	20 August 1945	Independent
3	Sami Solh (2nd term)	1887–1968	23 August 1945	22 May 1946	Independent
4	Saadi Munla		22 May 1946	14 December 1946	Independent
5	Riad Solh (2nd term)	1894–1951	14 December 1946	14 February 1951	Independence Movement
6	Hussein Oweini (1st term)		14 February 1951	7 April 1951	Independent
7	Abdallah Yafi (2nd term)	1901–1986	7 April 1951	11 February 1952	Independent
8	Sami Solh (3rd term)	1887–1968	11 February 1952	9 September 1952	Independent
9	Nazim Akkari		10 September 1952	14 September 1952	Independent
10	Saeb Salam (1st term)	1905–2000	14 September 1952	18 September 1952	Independent
11	Abdallah Yafi (3rd term)	1901–1986	24 September 1952	30 September 1952	Independent
12	Khaled Chehab (2nd term)	1887–1968	1 October 1952	1 May 1953	Independent
13	Saeb Salam (2nd term)	1905–2000	1 May 1953	16 August 1953	Independent
14	Abdallah Yafi (4th term)	1901–1986	16 August 1953	16 September 1954	Independent
15	Sami Solh (4th term)	1887–1968	16 September 1954	19 September 1955	Independent
16	Rachid Karami (1st term)	1921–1987	19 September 1955	20 March 1956	Independent
17	Abdallah Yafi (5th term)	1901–1986	20 March 1956	18 November 1956	Independent
18	Sami Solh (5th term)	1887–1968	18 November 1956	20 September 1958	Independent
19	Khalil Hibri (acting)	1904–1979	20 September 1958	24 September 1958	Independent
20	Rachid Karami (2nd term)	1921–1987	24 September 1958	14 May 1960	Independent
21	Ahmed Daouk (2nd term)		14 May 1960	1 August 1960	Independent
22	Saeb Salam (3rd term)	1905–2000	2 August 1960	31 October 1961	Independent
23	Rachid Karami (3rd term)	1921–1987	31 October 1961	20 February 1964	Independent
24	Hussein Oweini (2nd term)		20 February 1964	25 July 1965	Independent
25	Rachid Karami (4th term)	1921–1987	25 July 1965	9 April 1966	Independent
26	Abdallah Yafi (6th term)	1901–1986	9 April 1966	2 December 1966	Independent
27	Rachid Karami (5th term)	1921–1987	7 December 1966	8 February 1968	Independent
28	Abdallah Yafi (7th term)	1901–1986	8 February 1968	15 January 1969	Independent
29	Rachid Karami (6th term)	1921–1987	15 January 1969	13 October 1970	Independent

Table 11.2 continued

#	Name	Year of birth–year of death	Date inaugurated	Date left office	Political affiliation
30	Saeb Salam (4th term)	1905–2000	13 October 1970	25 April 1973	Independent
31	Amin Hafez	1926–2009	25 April 1973	21 June 1973	Independent
32	Takieddine Solh (1st term)	1908–1988	21 June 1973	31 October 1974	Independent
33	Rachid Solh (1st term)	1926–	31 October 1974	24 May 1975	Independent
34	Nureddine Rifai	1899–1980	24 May 1975	27 May 1975	Military
35	Rachid Karami (7th term)	1921–1987	1 July 1975	8 December 1976	National Salvation Front
36	Selim Hoss (1st term)	1929–	8 December 1976	20 July 1980	Independent
37	Takieddine Solh (2nd term)	1908–1988	20 July 1980	25 October 1980	Independent
38	Shefic Dib Wazzan	1925–1999	25 October 1980	30 April 1984	Independent
39	Rachid Karami (8th term)	1921–1987	30 April 1984	1 June 1987	National Salvation Front
40	Selim Hoss (2nd term)	1929–	2 June 1987	14 October 1990	Independent
41	Michel Aoun	1935–	22 September 1988	13 October 1990	Military
42	Selim Hoss (3rd term)	1929–	14 October 1990	24 December 1990	Independent
43	Omar Karami (1st term)	1934–	24 December 1990	13 May 1992	Independent
44	Rachid Solh (2nd term)	1926–	13 May 1992	31 October 1992	Independent
45	Rafik Hariri (1st term)	1944–2005	31 October 1992	2 December 1998	Future Movement
46	Selim Hoss (4th term)	1929–	2 December 1998	23 October 2000	Independent
47	Rafik Hariri (2nd term)	1944–2005	23 October 2000	21 October 2004	Future Movement
48	Omar Karami (2nd term)	1934–	21 October 2004	15 April 2005	Independent
49	Najib Mikati (1st term)	1955–	15 April 2005	30 June 2005	Glory Movement
50	Fuad Saniora	1943–	30 June 2005	9 November 2009	Future Movement/March 14
51	Saad Hariri	1970–	9 November 2009	25 January 2011	Future Movement/March 14
52	Najib Mikati	1955–	13 June 2011	22 March 2013	Glory Movement/March 8

Source: Presidency of the Council of Ministers, www.pcm.gov.lb

The Council of Ministers

According to Article 66 of the Constitution, only Lebanese who satisfy the conditions for deputization may assume ministerial posts. The ministers administer the Government's services and assume the responsibility for applying the laws and regulations, each one according to the affairs of his administration and what is specific to them. Ministers are collectively responsible before the Chamber for the general policy of the government and individually responsible for their personal actions.

Ministers are considered to be **grade-one public employees**, and therefore they are subject to sectarian quotas. Thus, the Cabinet is divided in the same sectarian manner as that of parliament. Though no law stipulates such distribution, it has been upheld by political norms. The formation of the Council of Ministers is considered one of the major tasks/responsibilities undertaken by the prime minister, who must forge a strong alliance with major political groups before succeeding in such a task. The satisfactory assignment and distribution of ministerial portfolios among political groups determine the success and longevity of any government lineup. This is particularly the case because ministries differ by their sizes, budget, and political importance.

The number of ministries is determined by the designated prime minister during the drive to establish a minimum winning (politically narrow government) or a maximum winning government (national unity) coalition. It is often the case that an expanded government of 30 ministers is established to satisfy the largest possible number of political groups. The latest governments have included 20 ministers with portfolios and 10 without (called ministers of state). While those with portfolios reside over sizable administrations with dedicated annual budgets, the non-portfolio ministers are included in the cabinet for voting purposes only. In theory, a Council of Ministers can last as long as the life of parliament permits, or four years. However, it requires maintaining the confidence of parliament throughout its duration, otherwise a new one may replace it.

Parties compete to win key portfolios that provide them with power and influence. Most significant among them are the so-called "sovereign ministries" that include the Interior, Defense, Finance, and Foreign Affairs. The importance of others is established based on the ability of each to contribute to parties' political influence. Ministries of secondary importance have been labeled "services ministries" and include ministries such as Roads, Transportation, and Infrastructure, where services can be traded off with political influence and favors. Others, such as the Ministry of Education and the Ministry of Energy and Water constitute job opportunity for followers. The Ministry of Telecommunications gained increasing attention among competitors after demonstrating its ability to perform significant security functions in tracing and eavesdropping on political figures and networks. Hence, the distribution of these ministerial portfolios takes an elaborate process of political negotiation toward their designation among political and sectarian parties. Of course, larger parties (such as Future Movement and Free Patriotic Movement) and those with significant power leverage to title majorities (such as Progressive Socialist Party and the President) are favored in the selection of ministries, as well as their sharing.

Sometimes, political dealings result in the offsetting of strict sectarian distribution of portfolios. A fine calculation is made by political groups to determine the number and types of ministries to be occupied. This laborious exercise has become of increased relevancy after the Taef Accord provided the Council of Ministers and ministers with greater autonomy and power. Ministers gained significant role in determining the various consultants and advisors to be hired, as well as the ability to issue decrees that have the power of law in certain occasions. Collectively, the Council of Ministers began to preside over budget spending and became the major entity in driving the legislative agenda, either through issuing decrees or presenting draft laws to parliament. The power vested in the Council of Ministers has in many ways tilted the balance of power to its advantage compared with other branches of government. Thus, the political struggle to control its composition and function has grown since the Taef Agreement.

One of the major aspects of political contentions that emerged following the 2005 Syrian pullout is the proportional distribution of the Council of Ministers between the two Marches. March 8 has been consistent in demanding a one-third portion while being in the parliamentary minority. The struggle stems from the fact that two-thirds of the Council of Ministers can determine policies considered in the constitution as being of "national significance." These policies include amending the constitution, declaring and ending a state of emergency, declaring war, signing peace agreements, signing international treaties, the annual government budget, long-term development projects, the appointment of high-level government employees, the dissolution of parliament, electoral laws, nationality laws, personal status laws, and the dismissal of ministers.

The Council of Ministers, through the Ministry of Interior and Municipalities, appoints local administrators, such as the *Muhafiz* and *Qaimmaqam* and funds most work of the municipalities.

In addition to the ministries, there are about 40 public agencies, including entities such as the Council of the South, the Higher Relief Council, and Council of Development and Reconstruction. Despite the national discourse on privatization, the main utilities are managed by public bodies, including electricity, telecommunications, Beirut's seaport and airport.

The Council of Ministers holds the power to perform oversight functions over the other branches of government. For example, it can dissolve the parliament upon request of the president if parliament, for no compelling reason, fails to meet during one of its regular periods and fails to meet throughout two successive extraordinary periods, each longer than one month, or if it rejects an annual budget plan with the aim or paralyzing the government (Article 65). It also controls the Court of Audit, which can perform various administrative and scrutinizing oversight roles over the public contracts and funds.

In June 2011, Prime Minister Najib Mikati succeeded in forming a new government (Table 11.3). The new government was supported by 68 members of parliament and opposed by 58. The new government excluded March 14 political

Table 11.3 Composition of the 2011 Mikati Government

Ministry	Minister	Political affiliation	Religious sect
Presidential Share (3/30)			
Interior and Municipalities	Marwan Charbel	Independent	Maronite
Deputy Prime Minister	Samir Mouqbel	Independent	Greek Orthodox
Environment	Nazim Khoury	Independent	Maronite
Prime Minister's share (6/30)			
Prime Minister	Najib Mikati	Glory Movement	Sunni
Finance	Mohammad Safadi	Independent	Sunni
Minister of State	Ahmad Karami	Glory Movement	Sunni
Information	Walid Daouk	Independent	Sunni
Education	Hassan Diab	Independent	Sunni
Economy and Trade	Nicholas Nahhas	Glory Movement	Greek Orthodox
Change and Reform bloc (11/30)			
Labor	Salim Jereisati	Free Patriotic Movement	Greek Catholic
Telecommunications	Nicolas Sehnawi	Free Patriotic Movement	Greek Catholic
Culture	Gaby Layyoun	Free Patriotic Movement	Greek Orthodox
Justice	Shakib Qortbawi	Free Patriotic Movement	Maronite
Energy and Water	Gebran Bassil	Free Patriotic Movement	Maronite
Tourism	Fadi Abboud	Free Patriotic Movement	Maronite
Defense	Fayez Ghosn	Marada Movement	Greek Orthodox
Minister of State	Salim Bey Karam	Marada Movement	Maronite
Industry	Vrej Sabounjian	Tashnag	Armenian Orthodox
Minister of State	Panos Manjian	Tashnag	Armenian Orthodox
Minister of State	Marwan Kheir El Din	Lebanese Democratic Party	Druze

Table 11.3 continued

Ministry	Minister	Political affiliation	Religious sect
Loyalty to the Resistance bloc (2/30)			
Agriculture	Hussein Hajj Hassan	Hezbollah	Shia
Minister of State	Mohammad Fneish	Hezbollah	Shia
Struggle Front bloc (3/30)			
The displaced	Alaaeddine Terro	Progressive Socialist Party	Sunni
Public Works and Transport	Ghazi Aridi	Progressive Socialist Party	Druze
Social Affairs	Wael Abou Faour	Progressive Socialist Party	Druze
Others (5/30)			
Health	Ali Hassan Khalil	AMAL Movement	Shia
Foreign Affairs	Adnan Mansour	AMAL Movement	Shia
Sports and Youth	Faisal Karami	Arab Liberation Party	Sunni
Minister of State	Nicolas Fattoush	Independent	Greek Catholic
Minister of State	Ali Qanso	Syrian Social Nationalist Party	Shia

Source: Lebanese Information Center, www.licus.org

forces and distributed its portfolios among the major supporters and that of the President as following: three ministers nominated by the President, six by the Prime Minister, three by the centrist Struggle Front bloc, 11 by Change and Reform bloc, and ten by remaining March 8 blocs.

Central oversight agencies

Most of the state accountability and oversight agencies were created in the 1950s and 1960s. The election of the country's third president, Fuad Chehab, in 1958 marked a turning point in the evolution of Lebanon's bureaucratic institutions. Chehab committed himself to structural changes designed to revamp the Lebanese state and instill professionalism, transparency, and accountability throughout the bureaucracy. In addition to establishing the Central Bank, he oversaw the formation of the Civil Service Board and the Central Inspection Board. Chehab quickly grew disillusioned with the confessional elites' resistance to change and submitted his resignation in 1960, which he withdrew under public pressure. Upon leaving office, he handpicked his successor, Charles Helou, to promote the functions of the institutions he had created. Helou augmented his predecessor's executive contributions by introducing the General Disciplinary Council in 1965.

Today, the control agencies of the executive branch are autonomous but under the purview of the cabinet and prime minister; they include the following institutions:

- The Court of Audit, established in 1951, performs pre- and post-audit functions and ensures the compliance of civil servants with standard procedures governing the allocation and administration of public funds. Its pre-audit checks seek to ascertain the validity and legality of transactions. Its post-audit duties mainly focus on unearthing contractual irregularities.
- The Civil Service Board is in charge of overseeing the work of civil servants and admitting new public cadres through competitive exams for third- and fourth-grade positions. The Board helps to determine personnel needs for all government departments, prepares the personnel budget, supervises and approves promotions and transfers, and designs and implements performance appraisal systems. Its prerogatives include preparing job classifications for announced vacancies and dismissing civil servants whose performance is deemed unsatisfactory.
- The Central Inspection Board is in charge of monitoring civil servants' adherence to relevant laws and regulations. The Board conducts inspections and investigations of public sector institutions and employees, prepares and monitors public tenders for works commissioned by public agencies, and advises government units on organizational structure.
- The General Disciplinary Council investigates and decides on disciplinary cases referred to it by government agencies and ministries. It the most important tool for ensuring the proper conduct of public officials through the prosecution and punishment of employees who violate the public trust.

In addition, the Ministry of Finance is the most influential instrument of financial control in the public sector through the following primary functions: a) response to requests for authorization of expenditures; b) liquidation of expenditures to verify actual occurrence of the activity; c) issuance of payment orders; and d) dispensation of payments.

Despite the relatively large number of control and disciplinary agencies within the executive branch, the state has not been able to curb corruption and mismanagement within the public administration. In fact, Lebanon ranks 127 out of 178 countries on Transparency International's Corruption Perceptions Index (2010), earning a score of 2.5, the same as Syria; the worldwide index scores countries on a scale from 10 ("very clean") to 0 ("highly corrupt").

Local government

Lebanon is administratively divided into six governorates or *Muhafazat* (North, Mount Lebanon, Beirut, Bekaa, South, and Nabatiyeh). Each governorate has been administered by a governor (*Muhafiz*) appointed by the Council of Ministers upon a proposal from the Ministry of the Interior. The governorates are further subdivided into 25 districts (*Qada*), each of which is presided over by a district chief (*Qa'em Maqam*). The 25 *Qada* are administered by 945 Municipal Councils, and managed by approximately 11,000 council members, who are elected by popular vote for a six-year term, together with Mukhtars.[1] With roots in the Ottoman Empire, *Mukhtars* are public servants in charge of personal status issues; they are roughly equivalent to justices of the peace. Each Municipal Council is headed by a president (Mayor). The Municipal Council is considered the core administrative body responsible for local governance.

In contrast to the situation at the central government level, municipal politics are more integrated and less confessional than national politics. However, a core challenge is overly centralized governance that constrains decision-making authority at the local level, making it difficult for local leaders to address the demands of their electorate. Municipalities and municipal leaders are generally eager to meet the service delivery needs of their constituents, but face a host of challenges, chief among which are a lack of funds, personnel, and capacities.

The political establishment has long recognized these constraints and calls for decentralization have been part of the parlance since the end of the civil war. Lack of significant movement in that direction is due to a combination of factors, including political instability, the primacy of other, more pressing national-level issues and disputes, the complexities and general lack of understanding of decentralization in its various forms, and, perhaps more importantly, the benefits that the confessional elites stand to derive from weak local governance, which bolsters their clientelistic powers.

Municipal councils

Municipalities vary widely in size, from a few hundred inhabitants to more than one million in the case of Beirut. The size of municipal councils, which is stipulated in the law of municipalities or municipal code (Law No. 118), likewise fluctuates between 9 and 21 members, except for Beirut and Tripoli, the country's largest cities, which have 24 council members each. Law 118 was first adopted in 1977 and has been amended on several occasions, most importantly in 1997. The 1997 amendments marginally increased the **financial autonomy** of municipalities, in principle if not in practice. Municipal Councils, with their limited resources, take on the role of providing local municipal services, including aspects of local planning, infrastructural development, and local services. Often, their functions intersect with different ministries that necessitate extensive collaboration with central government.

Local development has also been confronted with the required coordination and collective efforts with surrounding municipalities. This has led to the formation of Municipal Unions by decree from the Council of Ministers based on requests from the Ministry of Interior and Municipalities and municipalities themselves. Municipal Unions have established councils comprising the mayors of member municipalities to serve for the same term as municipalities; they elect their own union council president and vice president. All decisions taken by a union council are legally binding on member-municipalities, which contribute 10 per cent of their revenues to the union. Member municipalities benefiting from joint projects contribute an additional percentage of their revenues as set by the union council and approved by the Ministry of Interior and Municipalities. There are currently 43 municipal unions across the country.

All municipalities fall under the purview of the Ministry of Interior and Municipalities. There is no other elected body between the Ministry of Interior and Municipalities and municipalities themselves, although there is a degree of de-concentration, whereby the *Muhafiz* and *Qa'em Maqam* are both appointed by the central government to handle various administrative matters and approvals at the governorate and district levels.

In response to the Taef Accord's call for strengthening municipalities, the Government of Lebanon established the Ministry of Municipal and Rural Affairs in 1993 to support the development of local governments. It was later merged with the ministry of interior to constitute today's Ministry of Interior and Municipalities, which critics say has undermined the ministry's ability to provide an adequate level of support to municipalities. Currently, the Ministry of Interior and Municipalities is one of the most complex government ministries, handling the internal security forces, personal status issues, the civil register, refugee matters, the administration of national and local elections, and municipal affairs.

Among his prerogatives, the interior minister sets the exact dates for municipal council elections and announces the location of polling stations. According to the municipal code, the Ministry of Interior and Municipalities is also responsible for providing technical assistance and training to municipalities and municipal unions, but this has been difficult, due to lack of resources and the sheer number of municipal councils. As a result, first-time council members assume office with minimal, if any, training, and are often unfamiliar with the municipal code.

Municipalities rely on two main sources of revenue: taxes and fees directly collected by municipalities themselves, and surtaxes collected by the state on behalf of municipalities and placed in an "Independent Municipal Fund" administered by the Ministry of Finance. Legal contradictions provide central government with considerable leeway in determining the redistribution of independent municipal funds. A 1979 law specifies that 75 per cent of independent municipal funds should be allocated to municipalities and 25 per cent to municipal unions (Decree 1917 of 1979), but the practice is drastically different and municipalities typically receive a fraction of independent municipal funds to spend as they wish. Since 1995, the Council of Ministers has entrusted the Council of Development and Reconstruction and similar agencies with implementing development projects on behalf of municipalities, paid for through the Independent Municipal Fund (Decree 7425 of 1995).

Summary

The executive branch stands at the center stage of Lebanese government structure. The balance of power in government is strongly tipped in its favor, where two essential posts are held: the president and the prime minister. Although the country is founded on parliamentarian principles and implements the indirect election of the Maronite president and the Sunni prime minister by the National Assembly, its sectarian confessionalism has delegated explicit and implicitly powers to each institution. During the covenant period, strong presidentialism imprinted all aspects of Lebanese political life. This was shifted in favor of the prime minister and his Council of Ministers during the Taef era. Sectarian elites have increasingly found in the Council of Ministers a manageable platform for the deliberation of legislation and their execution. Thus, after the pullout of the Syrian troops from Lebanon, the Shi'a and some Christians became increasingly alarmed by the extended powers vested in the hand of the Sunni prime minister and his council. The Doha Accord, assured the Shi'a parties and allies in March 8 Coalition a one-third share of the Council of Ministers, which provided them with the ability to obstruct government decision on national issues, as well as the ability to dissolve government by their resignation. In addition, the Doha established presidential election by consensus, which implied, if turned into a tradition, that the 2014 presidential candidates must attain the overwhelming support of all sectarian political groups from the 2013 Parliament.

The Council of Ministers is the major active government body. Most importantly, because it commands the public budget and determines its distribution and expenditures. In addition, it can issue decrees that have the power of laws and formulate legislative agenda for parliament and approves laws. It is the Council of Ministers that determines policies of national interest, appoint public employees, collect taxes, and ratify international agreements. Its Ministry of Justice oversees and administers the entire work of the judiciary, turning the latter into a dependent branch of government. Its Ministry of Interior and Municipalities manages and supervises local governments, which undermines its much-needed decentralized functions. Because of a strong centralization, the executive branch has remained subject to elite political manipulation and competition. Despite the Taef Constitutional reforms and the Doha Agreement, the concentration of power in the executive has continued to plunge the sectarian state in turmoil. Much-needed division of power and decentralization such as empowering local governments, activating the legislative function of parliament, and establishing an independent judiciary continues to inspire the political agenda of many reformists.

Reference

1   International City/County Management Association (2011) *Municipal Finance Studies Program Final Strategic Framework.* Beirut: Ministry of Interior and Municipalities, pp. 17–18.

12 Lebanese judicial branch

The justice sector is vital for a healthy democracy. Its institutionalization in light of the Arab Spring has proven to be critical for smooth political democratic transition in countries such as Egypt and Tunisia. Its absence can lead to catastrophic consequences. The promotion of justice under various principles such as human rights, citizenship, fairness, equal application of the law, economic and political freedoms, and combating corruption, constitutes the fundamental foundation of civic culture and democratic tradition. The role of the judiciary in Lebanon is also critical because of the population's diversity and complexity. It can offer ways for arbitration and dispute mediation toward conflict resolution or transformation, hence undermining extremism and violent confrontations. Justice is the essence of political stability and coexistence in a plural society.

This chapter examines the Lebanese legal system in details, concentrating on the types of legal jurisdictions, regular courts, special courts, and councils. The separation of the judiciary and executive power is analyzed. Attention is also drawn to the Bar Association of Lebanon, legal education and training, internal security forces, and general security.

The legal system

The Lebanese legal system is a combination of Ottoman law, Canon law, the Napoleonic Code and civil law. The Constitution of Lebanon, adopted in 1926 and amended in 1990, guarantees the independence of the judiciary and the separation of powers among the three branches of government. The Taef Agreement of 1989, which is incorporated by proclamation into the Lebanese Constitution, provides that all officials and citizens are subject to the supremacy of the law. It states: "Lebanon is a republic, governed by an Executive branch consisting of the President, Prime Minister, and a cabinet, a Legislative branch consisting of the 128-member popularly elected National Assembly (*Majlis Alnuwab* or *Assemblée Nationale*), and a Judicial branch consisting of four Courts of Cassation, a Constitutional Council and the Supreme Council. The president is elected by the National Assembly".[1]

The major codes of Lebanon, specifically the Penal Code, the Code of Obligations and Contracts (which is the primary source for civil law), the Code of Commerce, the Code of Criminal Procedure, the Civil Procedure Code, the Commercial Code, the Tax Law, and the Intellectual Property Law, have all been revised or are in the process of being revised. These newly revised codes are based on democratic and market-based economic principles.

Most judges and legal professionals believe that the current Codes, as revised, are sufficiently sound and reliable, but the enforcement and application of laws is not consistent. Although there is a need to constantly upgrade the laws to meet the political and economic needs of the Lebanese society, the more pressing issue is to ensure the consistent and fair application of the existing laws.

The Constitution of Lebanon

The Constitution of Lebanon guarantees the independence of the judiciary and the separation and balance of powers among the three branches of government (Article 20). Lebanon's constitution was written before extensive provisions for judicial bodies became common. While it has been amended, there has been no attempt to detail provisions for the judiciary. As amended in 1990, Lebanon's constitution contains only three articles on the judiciary. Article 19 calls for the establishment of a Constitutional Council and Article 20 states that "judicial power is to be exercised by the tribunals of various levels and jurisdictions." Article 20 also provides for an independent judiciary, whereas Article 80 deals with trying ministers and presidents.[2] In practice, the judiciary is subject to political pressure, particularly in finance and the appointments of key prosecutors and investigating magistrates.

The justice system

The judiciary in Lebanon is divided horizontally into three main court systems and councils, each having a multilevel hierarchical structure:

- judicial court system, known as *Kadaa' Al-Adli*;
- exceptional and specialized courts;
- administrative specialized councils.

Espousing the inquisitorial scheme, Lebanese lawmakers circumscribed the role of prosecution, indictment and investigation to three legal bodies:

- public trial (or *Al-Niyaba Al-Ammah*), in which the task of commencing the community act is vested;
- preliminary inquisitorial bodies, which examine the case;
- criminal magistrates, who make a decision on the case.

In the *Al-Niyaba* system, prosecutors are considered part of the judicial corps. Public prosecution remains under the aegis of the Ministry of Justice rather than the Supreme Judicial Council. Thus, the legal process enmeshes both judicial and executive branch **jurisdictions**. The legal process under this system covers a wide range of trial cases, including civil, criminal, commercial, labor, land, military, juvenile, audit, national security, confessional, administrative, and political.

Courts of general jurisdiction

The Lebanese court system comprises both ordinary and exceptional courts (Box 12.1). The ordinary courts are arranged in a hierarchy and are subdivided into criminal (penal) and civil departments. At the base of the structure are the 56 courts of first instance (17 of which are in Beirut), each organized into a three-judge chamber, although a single judge may adjudicate civil cases of lesser value and minor criminal cases. Trials by jury are not used in Lebanon.

Judgments from the courts of first instance can be appealed to the courts of appeal, which have both appellate and original jurisdictions over felonies. The courts of appeal – one located in each governorate or *Muhafaza* (six in total) – are presided over by a chief judge and include a public prosecution department headed by an attorney general. The decisions of the courts of appeal may be appealed to the Beirut-based Court of Cassation, the country's highest appeals court. The latter also adjudicates disputes between exceptional and ordinary courts, or between two types of exceptional courts. Judgment execution courts, located in each *Muhafaza*, oversee all aspects of the implementation of court decisions and order the judicial police to take enforcement actions.

Courts with specialized jurisdiction include the confessional courts, which settle personal status affairs or "statuses of personal affairs" (e.g., marriage, divorce, child custody, inheritance, etc.) for individuals from various confessional groups. The *sharia* courts are divided into Sunni and Shi'ite sections. There are also courts for the various Christian sects, Druze, and Jews. There is no appeal mechanism for the confessional courts. The confessional courts provide the essential personal legal framework of confessionalism and many have characterized their role as robust against the establishment of a secular state and the realization of national citizenry.

Other exceptional judicial bodies include the military courts, which deal with military affairs and also have jurisdiction over civilians in espionage, treason, and other security-related cases. While international standards of criminal procedure are generally observed in the regular judiciary, the military courts largely consist of military officers with no legal training. There are also quasi-judicial or arbitration bodies for press, juvenile, labor, real estate, and customs disputes. Additionally, there are Arbitration Courts, which are mostly specialized in corporate and business disputes, whereas the Court of Audit – attached to the prime minister's office – oversees cases related to public funds.

Judicial administration is organized under the Council of State, which presides over all aspects of disciplinary proceedings that may be brought by the Disciplinary Council against judges.

Box 12.1 Judicial courts

Civil courts
- Legal Texts
- Courts of First Instance
- Courts of Appeals
- Court of Cassation
- Special Courts and Committees:
  - Arbitral Labor Council
  - Arbitral Committee examining the collective labor disputes
  - High Banking Board
  - Special Banking Court
  - Real Estate Judge/Additional Real Estate Judge
  - Arbitral Council for the private non-gratis school
  - Arbitral Insurance Council
  - Judicial Committee examining disputes
  - Disputes Settlement Committee
  - Appropriation Committees

Penal courts
Ordinary courts:
- Penal Single Judge
- Court of Appeal
- Assizes Court
- Penal Cassation Court

Special criminal courts:
- Supreme Council for prosecuting presidents and ministers
- Judicial Council
- Press Court
- The court ruling on the cases of monopoly
- The juvenile court

Military judiciary
- Military Cassation Court
- Permanent Military Court
- Unique Military Judges
- Commissioner and his Assistants
- Military Judicial Police
- Administrative Committees of the Militaries
- Exceptional, Specialized, and Administrative Courts

Source: Lebanese Ministry of Justice: www.justice.gov.lb

The Councils

Supreme Judicial Council

The Supreme Judicial Council is a ten-member body responsible for appointing, promoting and transferring judges. It is subject to the approval of the minister of justice. In addition to the role of the Ministry of Justice, the President of the Republic and the Cabinet jointly approve the appointment of eight of the ten Council members. The Supreme Judicial Council is headed by the Chief Judge of the Court of Cassation and is considered the most powerful judicial administrative establishment.

Council of State

The Council of State was formed in 1924 to try disputes between individuals and the state. In addition to serving as the highest administrative court in cases where the government or one of its agencies is party to a dispute, it also advises the government on legislation and legislative drafting.

Disciplinary Council

Under the **auspices** of the Ministry of Justice, the Judicial Inspection Unit is tasked with monitoring the performance of judges and court staff of all ordinary courts, in addition to the Council of State and Ministry of Justice departments involved in judicial functions. Cases may be brought to the attention of the Judicial Inspection Unit either by individuals or the Ministry of Justice. The Unit's mandate allows it to investigate issues of corruption, but this has rarely been the case; much of the focus has centered on reviewing the timeliness of a judge's work. All inspections are confidential, even when warnings or demotion decisions are taken, on the premise that the secrecy of the proceedings is important to preserve judicial authority and public trust. Violations are referred to the Disciplinary Council, which comprises three judges; the decisions of the Disciplinary Council may be reexamined by five Supreme Judicial Council judges without appeal. Decisions become public only when judges or court personnel are removed from office.

Constitutional Council

The Constitutional Council, created in 1990, judges the constitutionality of laws and arbitrates disputes arising from parliamentary and presidential elections. Parliament and the Cabinet select judges for this body.

Judicial Council

A tribunal of five senior judges, known as the Judicial Council, adjudicates threats to national security. The Cabinet, on the recommendation of the Minister of Justice, decides whether to bring a case before the Judicial Council, whose decisions are final and not subject to appeal.

Supreme Council

The function of the Supreme Council, a judicial body conceived after the Taef Agreement, is to try presidents and ministers. It consists of seven members of parliament elected by parliament and eight senior judges. At least two-thirds of members of parliament must vote to bring a case before the Supreme Council. Decisions of condemnation by the Council must be rendered by a majority of ten out of 15 votes.

Main interlocutors of the justice system

Ministry of Justice

The Ministry of Justice oversees the budget and administration of the courts. In addition, the Ministry plays a major role in the appointing, training, and transferring of most judges (sectarian balance into account), in addition to forming the Supreme Judicial Council and overseeing public prosecution (Box 12.2).

Judicial Training Institute

Established in the 1960s, the Judicial Training Institute administers a three-year training program for new judges. Selection of the trainees is based on written and oral exams administered by a committee comprising the president and general director of the Institute, the Supreme Judicial Council president, and two rotational Supreme Judicial Council judges. Training, which combines theory with practice, is standard, with no specialization. In-service training consists of seminars, workshops and regional and international exchange programs. Public prosecutors are considered to be judicial officers and are subject to the same training requirements at the Institute as those who become judges.

The Lebanese Bar Association

Lebanon has two **bar associations**, one located in Beirut and the other in Tripoli. The Tripoli Bar maintains jurisdiction over lawyers who practice in the North *Muhafaza*, whereas all other lawyers are registered under the jurisdiction of the Beirut Bar. All practicing lawyers, estimated at approximately 10,000, must be registered with the appropriate bar. A president, elected for a two-year term, and a 12-member council, elected for a three-year term, govern each bar. The Lebanese Bar Association is active in promoting human rights, including fair treatment of prisoners, providing legal aid for the indigent, organizing continuing education for attorneys, and handling arbitration and mediation cases.

Box 12.2 Organization of the Ministry of Justice

General Directorate of the Ministry of Justice:
- legal text
  - Director

Committee of Legislation and Consultations:
- Bodies of the Committee
- Tasks of the Committee
- Work Procedures in the Committee of Legislation

Committee of Cases:
- Tasks of the Committee
- Work Types and Actions in the committee of cases

Institute of Judicial Studies:
- The Board of Directors
- Financial and Administrative Situation of the Institute
- The Tasks of the Institute
- Competition of Admission to the Institute
- Curricula of Education and Methodology in the Institute
- Plan of the Work Process before the Institute of Judicial Studies – Judicial Judiciary
- Plan of the Work Process before the Institute of Judicial Studies – Administrative Judiciary
- Plan of the Work Process before the Institute of Judicial Studies – Financial Judiciary

Directorate of Judges and Employees Affairs

Service Job

Directorate of Prisons

Delinquent Juveniles Reform Department

Forensic Medicine and Criminal evidence Service
- Service Tasks

Source: Lebanese Ministry of Justice: www.justice.gov.lb

Prisons

Lebanese prisons, which consist of 23 penal institutions and eight detention facilities, have been recently transferred from the jurisdiction of the Ministry of

Interior to that of the Ministry of Justice, a move long advocated by human rights groups. Prison guards and administrators are members of the Internal Security Forces Operating on a regular rotational system; they are not specialized or specifically trained in prison administration. Recent estimates place the number of prisoners at approximately 7,000. Prisons are severely overcrowded and reports of human rights abuses are common. Roumieh Prison, the country's largest jail, has seen recurring riots over the past two years, leading to the deaths and injuries of several inmates. There is a vocal and active cadre of civil society groups engaged in promoting respect for human rights, including the rights of prisoners.

Legal education and training

There are five principal faculties of law in Lebanon, four of which are private, that offer a four-year law degree that is required to either practice law or assume a judicial career. Law students who want to practice law are required to engage in a three-year training program, which is conducted under the auspices of a practicing lawyer. Law students desiring to pursue a judicial career as a judge or prosecutor must partake in the three-year training program at the Judicial Training Institute.

In general, private universities are critically interested in graduating competent lawyers and judges, holding a fundamental interest in the expansion of the rule of law. Yet, the public Lebanese University Law School stipulates their curricula. Law programs are provided primarily in Arabic and French. Additionally, there is growing interest and market demand for common law practices. Thus, English programs in common law are beginning to emerge, together with English libraries and resources. Specialized journals in legal studies (e.g., *Judicial Review*) are also being published. Universities also publish occasional rulings by the high courts in Arabic.

Most universities keep close contact with civil society groups. Occasional lectures/presentations by non-governmental organizations (NGOs) and specialists are not uncommon, and students are encouraged to develop projects and engage with NGOs.

Civil society groups

Lebanon has a dynamic, active and vibrant civil society. In this country of approximately four million people, there are literally thousands of registered NGOs. Civil society groups in Lebanon have greater freedom than those of most other countries in the region and are a strong presence in sectors as varied as education, environment, economic, legal, human rights, women and youth.

Civil society groups cover the entire range of political, apolitical, secular and religious interests. Most groups are frustrated with the current state of political affairs (i.e., the ineffective institutions, unaccountable representatives, elite control of the state, and the government's lack of concern for people's social welfare, *inter alia*). The younger generations in these NGOs tend to be particularly convinced that the way forward for a democratic Lebanon lies in a secular, rather than confessional, system. In 2011, a movement to end confessionalism, in tandem with Lebanon's civil society groups, led to massive protests, mobilizing thousands of youths.

There is a clear indication of a strong political will for reform among emerging civil society groups, many of which are actively engaged in pushing for reforms and greater accountability in creative ways (with or without donor support). One of the main challenges faced by these groups is that most of them are quite small and their efforts are fragmented. Although already a force for change, civil society groups have the potential to be even stronger agents for reform – not to mention a political force in their own right – if unified.

Civil society groups are an important constituent for reform and have played an active role in rule of law programming. Civil society organizations have been engaged in watchdog roles to increase the transparency of public processes, and in promoting better public awareness of civic responsibilities and the rule of law. This is has been most salient in human rights work and in conducting various workshops and awareness campaigns around the country.

Internal Security Forces

The Internal Security Forces of Lebanon are under the control of the Ministry of Interior and Municipalities. They consist mainly of the paramilitary gendarmerie (responsible for areas outside of Beirut), the Beirut Police, and the Judicial Police (responsible for criminal investigations and executions of judicial judgments and warrants). The Internal Security Forces also include a training institute, embassy and diplomatic security.

General State Security (*Sécurité Générale*) and the Lebanese Armed Forces also handle national security matters. Prior to the 2005 Cedar Revolution and the arrest of top Syrian-loyal Lebanese security officers, the Syrian Intelligence Services exercised direct control over their Lebanese security counterparts.

The confessional system has had a pernicious effect on accountability within the security system, as well as other vectors of the government. The heads of the principal security agencies are appointed on a sectarian basis, with the head of intelligence being a Maronite and the head of General Security being a Shi'ite. This has resulted in very little coordination and communication between the different agencies. The confessional nature of the appointments meant that the lines of accountability to civilian agencies were skewed by political sectarianism.

During Lebanon's 1975–1990 civil war and the subsequent Syrian occupation, the Lebanese government's policing capacity was significantly weakened. Local communities and armed militia groups provided their own security during the civil war, while over 15,000 members of the Syrian military and paramilitary policed many parts of the country during Syria's occupation. There are still some areas of the country that are controlled and policed by Palestinian groups and local militias in place of the Internal Security Forces.

The security forces have had a historical focus on national security rather than law and order. This is evident in the training that police and gendarmerie receive. Police officers must attend three years of military academy alongside military officers. Upon graduation, they enter the police academy for a six-month course that covers police-specific issues. In an attempt to attract more people with legal knowledge into the police ranks, those with university degrees in law are now hired; they can go directly into the police academy and graduate in one year.

Under Lebanese law, police officers can remain in a position for a period not to exceed three years. Regular movement of officers occurs frequently, with changes sometimes happening on a weekly or monthly basis. Officers can thus serve as traffic police one week, prison guards the next, and criminal investigators the following week. As a result, there is virtually no specialization and many police officers do not have the skills necessary to discharge their more complex duties (e.g., cybercrime investigation). The Ministry of Interior and Municipalities, however, has been considering the development of specialized units.

Though there have been many proposed information and communications technology (ICT) initiatives, police stations and the offices of the Directorate General are not computerized on the whole. Daily, weekly, monthly and annual records are kept manually. In order to do a background check, calls are made from one area to another, something that works relatively well, given the small geography of Lebanon.

Judicial Independence

The threat to judicial independence in Lebanon emanates from two major sources. The first is the limited appointment authority of the Supreme Judicial Council, whose decisions are, under certain circumstances, subject to the approval of the Ministry of Justice. The Supreme Judicial Council and the Ministry of Justice engage in negotiations over the appointment and transfer of judges with a final decision over any conflict determined by the Council of Ministers. The second factor undermining judicial independence is the political interference in judicial decision making, particularly in the area of criminal law.

Amendments to the law governing the organization of the courts have given greater powers of appointment and transfer of judges to the Supreme Judicial Council by providing that seven-member majority votes of the Council can confer the appointment of judges. However, the Ministry of Justice continues to have some hold on the appointment process. Furthermore, the Council of Ministers continues to have the prerogative over appointing individuals to key judicial positions, such as the first president of the Court of Cassation, the president of the Council of State, and the state prosecutor. Even though the Supreme Judicial Council has greater powers over the appointment process, it still lacks institutional autonomy. More importantly, it has to adhere to sectarian equilibriums in major judicial appointments, a practice which sidelines the paragon of merit.

Furthermore, it continues to be subordinate to the Ministry of Justice over administrative and budgetary matters affecting the Lebanese judiciary.

In addition to the procedural concern over the appointment and transfer process is the substantive concern pertaining to confessional appointments. At the higher level of the courts, sectarian considerations remain prevalent in the appointment process for the sake of maintaining a confessional balance in leadership positions.

As for the second threat to judicial independence, the most common problem regarding improper influence over the judiciary remains interference by political officials in the appointments of and decision-making processes of prosecutors and investigating judges in criminal cases. However, improper influence owing to bribery is reputed to be rare. This perception is often shared not only by criminal and civil judges, but also by attorneys who stated that they generally trust judges in civil cases and in most criminal cases.

Unlike most other countries, the law in Lebanon prohibits the creation of a voluntary judges' association. The purpose of associations of judges is generally to protect and promote an independent judiciary. Indeed, the Beirut Declaration of the Recommendations of the First Arab Conference on Justice, held from June 14–16, 1999, concluded in Recommendation 10, that "Judges shall freely practice freedom of assembly in order to represent their different interests. In this regard, they shall have the right to establish an organization to protect their interests and guarantee their constant promotion".[3] The establishment of such an organization in Lebanon would be an important corollary to reform of the SJC to make it more independent.

Access to justice

Democracies with mature justice systems recognize the fundamental right of equal access to justice for all citizens and resident foreign nationals, regardless of financial status. They also recognize that without quality legal representation, the right to full and equal access to justice cannot be materialized. From these principles springs the need for legal assistance to the indigent.

Lebanon is no exception to this basic principle. The right to free legal assistance in criminal cases is guaranteed by the Lebanese Constitution and prescribed in the Criminal Procedures Code; additionally, the right to legal assistance in civil cases, based on indigent status, is prescribed in the Civil Procedures Code. Continuing legal education for practicing lawyers is presently not mandated by the Lebanese Bar Association. By law, the responsibility to provide legal aid in criminal and civil cases rests exclusively with the Lebanese Bar Association, although a handful of civil society organizations do provide *pro bono* legal assistance to their clients in cooperation with members of the bar.

Unfortunately, however, the Lebanese government provides no financial support for legal assistance to the indigent. Thus, the goal of ensuring equal access to justice has increasingly attracted the intervention of various civil society and professional groups who have been providing support to the poor and disadvantaged. The Lebanese Bar Association, for example, has set up legal aid services to help the poor in the legal process. Lawyers and judges have also been provided with ICT services to access laws and precedents so as to help them make better-informed legal decisions.

A competent, dynamic judicial corpus

In Lebanon, becoming a lawyer or judge is viewed as a prestigious career, leading many parents to encourage their children to study law at university. A growing cadre of dynamic young lawyers and judges, including women, are entering the profession, bringing a modern outlook and unprecedented ICT skills to the table.

Five faculties of law (Saint Joseph University, University of the Holy Spirit, La Sagesse, Beirut Arab University, and Lebanese University) offer a four-year law degree, which is required to either practice law or embark on a judicial career. The vast majority of students, approximately 75 percent of an estimated 12,000 law students, attend the state-owned Lebanese University, which is free of charge. The different regional campuses of the university tend to correspond to different sectarian groups, with both the southern and West Beirut campuses comprised mostly of Shi'ites, whereas the student body of the Bekaa campus is an amalgam of Lebanon's various sects). Lebanese women are increasingly joining law faculties and notably form the majority of law students at Saint Joseph University. Overall, the quality of legal education and the training requirements for joining the bar or judicial corps translates into a high level of competency in the sector.

Summary

The Lebanese legal system derives its jurisprudence from civil codes and religious laws. The sources of the civil codes are those of the Lebanese Constitution and Parliament-passed laws. The religious laws, on the other hand, are supplied by the various sectarian interpretations of Islamic Sharia. While civil codes apply to all aspects of civil conducts, the religious codes are limited to the personal status. For the Christians, informal spiritual courts by different churches have been given authorities to preside over personal status affairs as well. This plurality in the legal system has preserved the different civil and religious interpretations of the laws that respond to the various sectarian sensitivities in the country. Calls for political deconfessionalization, which was stipulated by the Taef Constitution under Article 95 did not imply the abolition of religious laws. This is one of the reasons why Muslim leaderships have supported such a drive. The call for secularization by many civil society groups, on the other hand, has implied the abolition of religious laws altogether. Because the Christian church is better positioned to maintain the same influence under secular order, it has supported secularization as opposed to the Muslim religious and political authorities.

As most judicial system in the world, the Lebanese judiciary is structured hierarchically into three tiers: lower (First Instant), appeal, and higher courts (Cassation). The courts are divided by specialty areas. Elaborate institutionalism linked to the judiciary is established that includes the powerful Bar Association, a highly developed education and training faculty of law, interactive non-governmental civil society organizations, correction facilities, in addition to a host of foreign assisted programs provided by donor countries such as European Union and the United States to assist the judiciary.

The main challenge confronting the judiciary is political and confessional. The establishment of a sectarian balanced judiciary has often been prioritized over the merit of the appointments. Yet the most serious challenge has been that of its independence. Despite constitutional stipulation of its independence, it has remained strongly dependent on the executive branch and that of the Ministry of Justice in particular. The latter has controlled all the finances and determines the appointments of various councils including the Supreme Judicial Councils that reside over the administration of the judiciary. Its members are determined by political agreements within the Council of Ministers. This political deficiency, in addition to a range of infrastructural shortages, has restricted public access to justice. The development of an independent, accessible, and transparent judiciary remains one of the key demands of judicial reform in the country.

References

1   BikeAbout (2004) 'About Lebanon'. Available online at: www.bikeabout.org/resource/lebanon.htm (accessed April 29, 2013).
2   Brown, N. J. (2001). *Arab Judicial Structures: A Study Presented to the United Nations Development Program, Programme On Governance In The Arab Region Pogar*. United Nations Development Programme. Available online at web.dubaichamber.ae/LibPublic/Arab%20judicial%20structures.pdf (accessed April 29, 2013).
3   Sherif, A. O. and Brown, N. J. (2002) *Judicial Independence in the Arab World. A Study Presented to the Program of Arab Governance of the United Nations Development Program*. Washington, DC: UNDP. Available online at www.judicial-ethics.umontreal.ca/en/textes%20int/documents/ONU_jud-independence_MONDE_ARABE.pdf (accessed April 29, 2013).

13 State consociationalism and democracy

This chapter examines contemporary challenges for the establishment of a democratic civil state in Lebanon. The characteristic of sectarian populism is highlighted as a phenomenon that has overwhelmed Lebanese communal politics and undermined Lebanon's potential to become a consensual nation state. The chapter also discusses anti-sectarian movements and provides various reform propositions to move beyond sectarianism that include electoral and administrative restructuring of government. The future of state consociationalism and sectarian power sharing arrangements is finally analyzed in light of the Arab Spring and regional transformations.

Sectarian populism in Lebanon

Since its inception in 1943, Lebanon has been torn by different and opposing sectarian interests. The "war of the sects" has taken a settled, but at other times violent, path. This struggle has resulted in a unique and complex Lebanese government and political framework. It has often called for foreign interventions to advance regional influence and other times to mediate resolution to domestic conflicts. The division of power among the various sects has required a relative balance, which prevented the hegemony of a single sect and denied **autocratic leadership**. Alternatively, and as part of its mobilization strategy, each sect developed differently styled politics determined by their intra- and inter-power struggles. Common to all are **nepotistic networks** – established around close kin, co-villagers, and fellow sectarian subjects – that have provided a suitable environment for the rise of a personalized sectarian leadership structure. It is within this context that sectarian populist political movements in Lebanon, under the patronage of charismatic leaderships, became the dominant vehicle for advancing groups' interests (Box 13.1).

Lebanese populist sectarian movements emerged in times of deep political crises that presented serious challenges to the communal power-sharing formula prevalent at the time. The populist movements that emerged were formed for the protection of the existing communal power structure or for challenging it by birthing an opposing movement. Given this context, populist movements in Lebanon acquired a unique character; they could never be elevated to become an

---

Box 13.1 Characteristics of populist movements

- Antagonism against status quo
- Anti-elitist views
- Communal orientation
- Emphasis on homogeneity of group
- Isolationist and exclusionary – clear divide between "us" and "them"
- Charismatic authoritarian leader
- Crowd action as a source of power
- Discourse ruling out compromise – no recognition or demonization of opposition
- Use of moral judgment as a source of authority
- Forced dependence on leader through lack of true empowerment of people
- Political inactivity outside election period or other transitional phase
- Lack of trust in institutionalism
- Calls for fundamental reform

---

inclusive nationalist movement because the nationalism of each one has typically been subsumed under an overriding sectarian identity, be it Christian Maronite, Sunni Muslim or Shi'a Muslim. More importantly, populist movements in Lebanon have always emerged around communal claims condensing a plurality of demands raised by the populist movement itself and constituting the ultimate goal for "hegemonic" politics. Moreover, the Lebanese communal/sectarian style of populism produced a peculiar relationship between the populist groups and the state.

The attitudes of sectarian populists towards the state have typically been contradictory, depending on their capacity to control its resources. Hence, when they secure the capacity to position state resources under their control, they stood positively toward the state, which contrasts with populist classical anti-statist views. On the other hand, if they lacked such control or satisfactory benefit, they would undermine the state legitimacy to the extent of engaging it and oftentimes bringing about its total demise. In both cases, however, the state has been perceived and dealt with ultimately as an institution subordinate to the overriding legitimacy of the populist leaders. The communal basis upon which the state in Lebanon was built impeded its development and prevented it from becoming strongly institutionalized and relatively autonomous from the fragmented social and economic fabric of the Lebanese society.[1]

The roots of sectarian populism can be traced back in Lebanese history to divisions and mobilizations under feudal chiefdoms, such as Druze historic division between "Qaysi" and "Yemeni", "Yezbaki" and "Jumblatty". The modern populist movement, however, emerged in the 1950s and was represented by Chamounism, in reference to popular Christian Maronite President Camille

Chamoun (1900–1987). It was followed in the late 1960s by the emergence of a Shi'a movement, called the Movement of the Disposed (*Harakat al-Mahroumeen*), founded by Imam Moussa Sadr. Chamounism developed in the context of defending the Christians' (mainly Maronite) upper hand in the running of the state and economy in the face of a growing challenge by local and regional Nasserite forces. The Movement of the Disposed, on the other hand, represented an attempt by the Shi'a community to increase its share of the state resources. Subsequently, in the 1970s, and particularly after the outbreak of the civil war in April of 1975, the Christian populist movement regrouped itself and resurfaced, initially as the Phalange Party, then, towards the end of the 1970s, as the Lebanese Forces, led by the populist and short-lived president Bashir Jemayel. After the signing of the Taef Accord and the end of the civil war in 1989, new developments spurred the burgeoning of a new Shi'a populist movement led by Hezbollah under its charismatic leader Sayyed Hassan Nassrallah. In 2005, after the assassination of Prime Minister, Rafik Al-Hariri and the withdrawal of Syrian troops from Lebanon, two other populist movements emerged, one Christian, led by Michel Aoun, and the other, Sunni, led by Saad Al-Din Al-Hariri.

Lebanese sectarian populism has served as a vehicle that transcends groups' grievances vis-à-vis the state. It has strengthened individual communities in the sectarian power struggle, and has established strong communal checks and balances against the emergence of an overwhelmingly dominant state authority. Yet this Middle Eastern "democratic" **exceptionalism** has prevented the foundation of an effective state capable of carrying out political reform or instituting transparent institutions. Perhaps the most evident manifestation of sectarian populism impeding state building and nationhood is a deeply fragmented society, something very apparent in the emergence of a strongly mobilized sectarian public, fiercely loyal to their own populist leaders.[2] Sectarian followers are charged with deep pessimism towards the state and its institutions, are suspicious about the intention of other sectarian groups, exhibit an exclusionist attitude in their vision of the nation and its surroundings, and display an isolationist posture in their communal orientations. A fragmented Lebanese sectarian attitude towards the state and nationhood demonstrates that sectarian populism under consociationalism has grown anti-statist with a diverged sense of belonging and nationhood, with many populist groups deeming the transition towards democracy as an impossible mission.

Sectarian populist leadership

Sectarian groups vest great trust in the person of the populist leader and his decisions. Their support for the sectarian leader stands out as one of the most evident indicators of sectarian populism.

A national opinion survey conducted in 2011 with 300 Lebanese by the Lebanese American University (LAU) revealed clear political mobilization and leadership support among the three main Lebanese sectarian groups – Maronite, Shi'a, and Sunni (Table 13.1). Respondents were clearly divided along sectarian

Table 13.1 Support of key political leaders by sect

Leader	Main sect (%)			Total
	Maronite	*Shi'a*	*Sunni*	
President Nabih Berry	1.7	29.2	3.4	12.5
Doctor Samir Geagea	23.3	–	2.7	7.5
President Najib Mikati	1.7	1.3	13.0	5.5
President Amin Jemayel	7.8	–	0.7	2.4
Mr. Mohammad Al-Safadi	0.9	–	2.7	1.2
President Michael Aoun	28.4	8.4	4.1	12.5
President Saad Al-Din Al-Hariri	4.3	2.6	52.1	20.4
Al-Sayyed Hassan Nassrallah	5.2	48.1	7.5	21.9
Al-Meer Talal Arslan	–	1.3	0.7	0.7
Mr. Suleiman Franjeyah	6.0	1.3	0.7	2.4
Mr. Houghik Mkhayteryan	1.7	–	–	0.5
President Michel Suleiman	8.6	3.9	4.8	5.5
Minister Ziad Baroud	2.6	0.6	0.7	1.2
None	4.3	2.6	4.1	3.6
Another Leader	3.4	0.6	2.7	2.2
Total	100.0	100.0	100.0	100.0

Survey question asked: Which of the following leaders most represent you?

lines in their support for sectarian populist leadership. Most Shi'as split their support between Hezbollah's General Secretary Hassan Nassrallah (48 per cent) and the President of the Amal Movement and Parliament Speaker Nabih Berry (29 per cent). The majority of Sunnis supported the Future Movement leader and former Prime Minister Saad Al-Din Al-Hariri (52 per cent), followed by Prime Minister Najib Mikati (13 per cent). A slight majority of Maronites, on the other hand, divided their support between Free Patriotic Movement leader Michael Aoun (28 per cent) and Lebanese Forces leader Samir Geagea (23 per cent). Yet, it is worth noting that Shi'as were among the most mobilized behind the sectarian leadership, casting support for two leaders (77 per cent), compared with Sunnis (65 per cent) and Maronites (51 per cent). No notable support to Druze leader Walid Jumblat was expressed by any of the respondents from the main non-Druze sectarian groups.

Most significant to this support is the degree of mobilization and following behind the person of the sectarian leader. Sectarian populism is manifested most clearly in respondents' declaration of allegiance to the person of the leader and his performance. Followers' populism is revealed by the extent to which respondents believed in their leaders' infallibility. Evidently, the LAU survey showed strong sectarian populist sentiments in this regard. Over half of the respondents considered that their respective sectarian leader had rarely or never committed a mistake over the past five years of political conduct (Table 13.2). Most Shi'as (70 per cent), compared with Sunnis (53 per cent) and Maronites (41 per cent), believed that of their leader(s). In fact, 38 per cent of Shi'a respondents considered that their leader never committed a mistake at all, compared with 19 per cent of Sunnis and 14 per cent of Maronites (Table 13.2).

Table 13.2 Sectarian loyalty to the leader

Leader	Main sect (%)			Total
	Maronite	*Shi'a*	*Sunni*	
Too many	8.7	4.0	8.2	6.8
Many	5.2	4.0	8.2	5.8
Relatively few	45.2	22.5	30.6	31.7
Very few	27.0	31.1	34.0	31.0
Never committed a mistake	13.9	38.4	19.0	24.7
Total	100.0	100.0	100.0	100.0

Survey question asked: In general, what is the proportion of mistakes committed by the leader you support over the past 5 years?

Moving beyond sectarian populism

In early 2011, thousands of young demonstrators and intellectuals took to the streets to protest against the sectarian establishment. In October 2012, another mobilization of non-aligned mostly secular activists marched under the banner "neither 14 nor 8" and demanded a civil state. These mass demonstrations, marching under the banner of "Secular Pride," can in some ways be interpreted as a rejection of an antiquated system whereby sectarian populism can dictate which football team to support, which newspapers to read, and even which cafés to attend. Unarguably, sectarian populism has accentuated the vertical segmentation of Lebanese society. On the political front, many intellectuals have come to view the confessional system as an accessory to political gridlock. Yet most sectarian communalists have argued that a confessional system is necessary to avert domestic chaos and protect numeric minorities, particularly the Christians.

The issue of political sectarianism, and the prospects of its reform, has divided Lebanese society since the country's independence. In fact, for much of the Republic's modern history, religion has been the maidservant of political expression, yielding a system wherein sectarian primacy subsumes democratic procedures.

If Lebanon's current demography is any indication, this polarization clearly reflects the deep-seated concerns of the Christian community of being relegated into a political minority, should a proportional representation electoral system emerge in place of the current one. Muslims, on the other hand, and particularly the Shi'as, are much more eager to translate their demographic advantages into political gains. Christian fears and Sunni hesitancy may have further been consolidated as a result of the contemporary rise of Shi'a populism. Whatever the specific reason may be, the common denominator underlying this apprehension seems to stem from fear of political marginalization. As a result, many sectarian partisans cannot bring themselves to deal forthrightly with a system that may potentially undermine their political power.

In the absence of a unified social contract, many Lebanese have come to view various policy initiatives through a sectarian prism. This is clearly reflected in the sectarian populist trend whereby the atmosphere of mutual distrust amongst Lebanon's sects has been nothing short of palpable, creating a stalemate ultimately defined by political paralysis and social discord. In turn, this stalemate itself has nurtured an environment of suspicion and mistrust, perpetuating the wheels of a vicious cycle and further roiling the political waters.[3]

Another consideration lies well outside of Lebanon, on the international horizon. The domestic balance of power is often tipped in favor of one sectarian group whenever the regional balance of power shifts. This has been manifested in the changes and extent of external aid in the form of financial, military, political, and diplomatic support for both the Lebanese state and its sub-state actors by different regional powers. And, of course, one cannot discuss the regional implications without accounting for major regional players (United States, France, Saudi Arabia, Syria, Iran, Turkey, etc.). For instance, since the shifting regional balance in favor of Shi'a Iran and on the account of Sunni Arab states, many Lebanese – particularly among Christians and Sunnis – fear that the political outcome will ultimately contribute to growth of Shi'a political power in the country. The Syrian revolution against President Bashar Al-Assad's rule, being primarily driven by Sunni grievances against the Alawi-controlled autocratic regime, is now providing a corresponding fear in non-Sunni sects. Thus, the question of transition toward democracy in Lebanon seems to be fundamentally linked to the wider regional development, whose latest episode is that of the Arab Spring.

Propositions for the reformation of Lebanese sectarianism

Sectarian populism has served as a major obstacle against the foundation of a cross-sectarian agenda or national vision. In fact, sectarian leaders use their populism to prevent the emergence of a cross-confessional political agenda, instigating constant fear against other sects and their potential rise to power. The politics of sectarian division is most evident in the sectarian segmentation of the population along divergent and exclusive national agendas. These differences run across every political issue from the public appointment of minor military officers or their reassignment to issues regarding the country's foreign relations and political reform agenda.

Being founded on sectarian communalism, state consociationalism privileges the representation of collective over individual rights. Political competition pits groups against one another which hinders any attempts towards a stable and peaceful political environment. More often than not, sectarian populism has been the vehicle of this political instability associated with communal violence. Often times, socioeconomic injustices provided fertile ground for the rise of populist movements. Yet their reconciliation with other groups' aspirations has demonstrated exclusionary trends conducive to recurrent violence. In other words, despite the different claims that are entertained by the populist sectarian movements in Lebanon, which are, in principle, essential to the process of building a strong and democratic state (e.g., such as equality, abolition of sectarian discrimination, the building of truly representative state institutions, sovereignty, rule of law, independence, unity of the nation), the sectarian character of these populist movements makes it inherently impossible to achieve such objectives. Populism ensures that state institutions are not only mistrusted but also replaced with a blind loyalty to individual leaders, while sectarianism divides the society along denominational lines by privileging exclusionary (sectarian) politics over inclusionary (national) politics. Through the absence of transparent politics, populist leaders have been able to establish what can be described as "authoritarian enclaves in a democratic regime". These enclaves have guaranteed that the different Lebanese sectarian communities remain isolated and suspicious of one another, while sectarian leaders emerge as indisputable saviors. There is, therefore, an inherent contradiction between consociational state building and democratization, on one hand, and sectarian populist politics, on the other.

Various scholars have pointed out important openings within the Lebanese state and society, which bear the potential to moderate the impacts of populism in favor of nation state building.[4] Political reform propositions have included strengthening the role of civil society as a path to establishing cross-sectarian movements linked to the process of democratization. Other reform initiatives have targeted institutional and legal reformulations, such as the injection of electoral and institutional reforms that may provide for integrating the voters and establishing national partisanship. Other institutional reform initiatives advocate secularizing the legal system and civilizing personal status laws, which has been viciously opposed by the religious establishment. Most secular reformists are convinced that the later reform is a prerequisite to liberate the individual from the dictation by the religious establishment over personal affairs. Other institutional reforms include that of administrative decentralization. Advocates for decentralization base their campaign on the perspective that the concentration of power in one office (the President before the Taef and the Prime Minister and his Council of Ministers after the Taef) intensifies sectarian competition over power. Thus, the distribution of power in favor of parliament and the judiciary as well as empowering municipal councils politically and economically undermines reasons for periodical struggle over government and its ministerial lineup. Localizing political competition turns the sectarian struggle inward rather than outward.

Economic reformists have also advocated privatization as a way to strengthen the emergence of a secular or cross-confessional entrepreneurship motivated by profit and economic benefits rather than sectarian political interest. These liberal reformists are convinced that the public sector is a major factor in preserving the system of sectarian patronage and corruption. International reformists have also encouraged the state to adopt international policy standards such as those of human rights and commercial practices that would strengthen citizenship and the rule of law. All these proposed reforms, if implemented properly, may favor the transition toward a democratic nation state and undermine the splintering and the authoritarian exclusionism of sectarian populism. Until then, the Lebanese will continue to quarrel about ways in which the country and the state must best be reformulated.

The Arab Spring and Lebanese sectarianism

Lebanese sectarian groups' division in supporting or opposing revolutions in the Arab region demonstrates their heightened fear or enthusiasm from potential repercussions. Part of the Lebanese Christian community, for example, has stood pessimistic over rising Sunni majoritarianism in Egypt, perceiving a consequential strict observation of Islamic Sharia laws and practices against Christian minority rights. Lebanese Shi'a, on the other hand, attribute the events leading to a "Sunni political awakening" in the region to a foreign **conspiracy** whose aim is to undermine the Iranian–Syrian "rejection front" that is confronting Western Zionism. Shi'a Hezbollah fears the loss of its Syrian Shi'a–Alawi backing and its further isolation in light of a "Sunni awakening". At the same time, Most Lebanese Shi'a have expressed strong support to the protest movement in Bahrain, where the ruling Sunni monarchy stands to lose in favor in face of a Shi'a majority. In contrast, most Lebanese Sunni attribute developments in Bahrain to an Iranian plot that aims at dividing the majority Arab Sunni world along sectarian lines. Yet, Sunni have, by large, stood optimistic about the Arab Spring in most Sunni majority countries such as Syria, Egypt, Tunisia, and Libya expecting to gain strength as a consequence.[5]

Sectarian attitudes toward the different revolutions sweeping the Arab countries were measured by a public opinion survey of 324 Lebanese, conducted in 2012 by the LAU. The survey showed that Lebanese are extremely attentive to surrounding events, spending an average of two or more hours daily following the news. Results pointed to a deep sectarian rift in the perception of the Arab Spring, most notably between Shi'a and Sunni respondents. Sunni Muslims, who share the same sect as the majority of the rebelling population in the Arab Spring, except in Bahrain, emphasized the lack of political freedom as the driving force for the protest movements. Shi'a Muslims, in contrast, cited external conspiracy behind the Arab Spring movements.

The roles played by regional and international powers (e.g., Iran, Russia, and China) in the "Arab Spring" also receive a divisive sectarian evaluation in the survey. This is particularly the case because intervening regional powers are composed of respective sectarian majorities, such as Shi'a in Iran, Sunni in Qatar and Turkey, Orthodox in Russia, Catholic and Protestants in Europe and North America. This fact has helped the least in conciliating different sectarian attitudes and, instead, heightened sectarian fears. The Shi'a–Sunni rift in this matter is quite deep and growing amid regional and international interventions.

Despite public polarization, the anti-autocratic attitude emerging out of the Arab Spring represents a major challenge to populist sectarian leadership in Lebanon. Sectarian "family rule" and the concentration of power in the hand of a single leader is expected to decline in popularity in favor of anti-elitist attitude, especially among a new generation of youth. Modern information technology has already demonstrated throughout the Arab Spring countries its effective use by young people in political mobilization and the dissemination of information independent from the control of leaders and political elites. Sectarian leaders' influence over their constituents appears to be eroding as increasing numbers of youth are being empowered by mass education, global exposures, and a mobile and hyperactive social information networking made available by the advancement and decentralization of communication infrastructure. The question remains, however, whether the Arab Spring and the modern communications infrastructure will provide an opportunity for the new generation to move beyond sectarian enclaves in favor of an alternative cross-sectarian political affiliation or simply to help reconstruct and modernize sectarianism into a more effective vehicle in transporting communal aspirations within national and regional political struggle.

Evidently, early political manifestations of the Arab Spring are adding to the complexity of Lebanese sectarian politics. While calls for freedom and the end of corruption and authoritarianism have brought the emancipatory aspirations of democratic liberalism into the forefront of the battles throughout the Arab states, the outcomes have provided an unprecedented rise and growing social influence of political Islam. The outburst of Islamist political parties in most Arab states has come to represent a major challenge confronting pluralism and secularism, as most Islamists reject civil laws in favor of Sharia. Islamists' interpretations of Sharia and Islamic rules are also contested, not only between Shi'a and Sunnis but also from within each sect and subsect. Moderates, Conservatives, Salafists, and Jihadists dispute one another. The governing implication of divergent political propositions in plural and confessionally mixed society such as Iraq has been the implementation of a mixed consociational and federal form of rule. The preservation of Syria as a nation state in light of its revolution will probably have a similar outcome as that of Iraq, where both autonomy and power sharing are ultimately institutionalized. Increasing implementation of confessionally and ethnically based power-sharing arrangements in the region emerges as an encouraging factor for a stronger confessionalism in Lebanon. Still, the Lebanese reception of regional change remains unclear. Whether Lebanese will close rank and confront increasing regional sectarian polarization and fragmentation or submerge with regional sectarian kin on the account of their nationalism is yet to be seen.

References

1   Salamey, I. and Tabar, P. (2012) 'Democratic Transition and Sectarian Populism: The Case of Lebanon', *Contemporary Arab Affairs*, 5 (4): 37–41.
2   El Khazen, F. (2003) 'Political Parties in Postwar Lebanon: Parties in Search of Partisans', *Middle East Journal*, 57 (4): 605–24.
3   Salamey, I. (2013) 'The Crisis of Consociational Democracy in Beirut: Conflict Transformation and Sustainability through Electoral Reform' in Vojnovic, I. Z. (ed.) *Urban Sustainability: Perspective*. Lansing: Michigan State University Press, pp. 177–98.

4   Salem, P. (2006) 'The Future of Lebanon', *Foreign Affairs*, 85 (6): 13–22.
5   Salamey, I. (2012) 'The Many Colors of the Arab Spring', *Columbia's Journal of International Affairs*. Available online at http://jia.sipa.columbia.edu/many-colors-%E2%80%98arab-spring%E2%80%99 (accessed on April 29, 2013).

Appendix A

Lebanon Taef Constitution

Preamble

a. Lebanon is a sovereign, free, and independent country. It is a final homeland for all its citizens. It is unified in its territory, people, and institutions within the boundaries defined in this constitution and recognized internationally.

b. Lebanon is Arab in its identity and in its association. It is a founding and active member of the League of Arab States and abides by its pacts and covenants. Lebanon is also a founding and active member of the United Nations Organization and abides by its covenants and by the Universal Declaration of Human Rights. The Government shall embody these principles in all fields and areas without exception.

c. Lebanon is a parliamentary democratic republic based on respect for public liberties, especially the freedom of opinion and belief, and respect for social justice and equality of rights and duties among all citizens without discrimination.

d. The people are the source of authority and sovereignty; they shall exercise these powers through the constitutional institutions.

e. The political system is established on the principle of separation, balance, and cooperation amongst the various branches of Government.

f. The economic system is free and ensures private initiative and the right to private property.

g. The even development among regions on the educational, social, and economic levels shall be a basic pillar of the unity of the state and the stability of the system.

h. The abolition of political confessionalism is a basic national goal and shall be achieved according to a gradual plan.

i. Lebanese territory is one for all Lebanese. Every Lebanese has the right to live in any part of it and to enjoy the sovereignty of law wherever he resides. There is no segregation of the people on the basis of any type of belonging, and no fragmentation, partition, or colonization.

j. There is no constitutional legitimacy for any authority which contradicts the "pact of communal coexistence". This Constitutional Law shall be published in the Official Gazette.

[Part] A. Fundamental Provisions

[Chapter] I. On the State and its Territories

Article 1 [Territory]
Lebanon is an independent, indivisible, and sovereign state. Its frontiers are those which now bound it:

- On the North: From the mouth of al-Kabir River, along a line following the course of this river to its point of junction with Khalid Valley opposite al-Qamar Bridge.
- On the East: The summit line separating the Khalid Valley and al-Asi River (Orontes) and passing by the villages of Mu'aysarah, Harbanah, Hayt, Ibish, Faysan to the height of the two villages of Brina and Matraba. This line follows the northern boundary of the Baalbak District at the northeastern and south eastern directions, thence the eastern boundaries of the districts of Baalbak, Biqa', Hasbayya, and Rashayya.
- On the South: The present southern boundaries of the districts of Sûr (Tyre) and Marjiyun.
- On the West: The Mediterranean.

Article 2 [Territorial Integrity]
No part of the Lebanese territory may be alienated or ceded.

Article 3 [Administrative Areas]
The boundaries of the administrative areas may not be modified except by law.

Article 4 [Republic, Capital]
Greater Lebanon is a Republic the capital of which is Beirut.

Article 5 [Flag]
The Lebanese flag is composed of three horizontal stripes, a white stripe between two red ones. The width of the white stripe is equal to that of both red stripes. In the center of and occupying one third of the white stripe is a green Cedar tree with its top touching the upper red stripe and its base touching the lower red stripe.

[Chapter] II. The Rights and Duties of the Citizen

Article 6 [Nationality]
Lebanese nationality and the manner in which it is acquired, retained, and lost is to be determined in accordance with the law.

Article 7 [Equality]
All Lebanese are equal before the law. They equally enjoy civil and political rights and equally are bound by public obligations and duties without any distinction.

Article 8 [Personal Liberty, *nulla poena sine lege*]
Individual liberty is guaranteed and protected by law. No one may be arrested, imprisoned, or kept in custody except according to the provisions of the law. No offense may be established or penalty imposed except by law.

Article 9 [Conscience, Belief]
There shall be absolute freedom of conscience. The state in rendering homage to the Most High shall respect all religions and creeds and guarantees, under its protection, the free exercise of all religious rites provided that public order is not disturbed. It also guarantees that the personal status and religious interests of the population, to whatever religious sect they belong, is respected.

Article 10 [Education, Confessional Schools]
Education is free insofar as it is not contrary to public order and morals and does not interfere with the dignity of any of the religions or creeds. There shall be no violation of the right of religious communities to have their own schools provided they follow the general rules issued by the state regulating public instruction.

Article 11 [Official National Language]
Arabic is the official national language. A law determines the cases in which the French language may be used.

Article 12 [Public Office]
Every Lebanese has the right to hold public office, no preference being made except on the basis of merit and competence, according to the conditions established by law. A special statute guarantees the rights of state officials in the departments to which they belong.

Article 13 [Expression, Press, Assembly, Association]
The freedom to express one's opinion orally or in writing, the freedom of the press, the freedom of assembly, and the freedom of association are guaranteed within the limits established by law.

Article 14 [Home]
The citizen's place of residence is inviolable. No one may enter it except in the circumstances and manners prescribed by law.

Article 15 [Property]
Rights of ownership are protected by law. No one's property may be expropriated except for reasons of public utility in cases established by law and after fair compensation has been paid beforehand.

[Part] B. Powers

[Chapter] I. General Provisions

Article 16 [Legislative Power, One Chamber]
Legislative power is vested in a single body, the Chamber of Deputies.

Article 17 [Executive Power, Council of Ministers]
Executive power is entrusted to the Council of Ministers to be exercised in accordance with the conditions laid down in this constitution.

Article 18 [Bills]
The Parliament and the Council of Ministers has the right to propose laws. No law shall be promulgated until it has been adopted by the Chamber.

Article 19 [Constitutional Council]
A Constitutional Council is established to supervise the constitutionality of laws and to arbitrate conflicts that arise from parliamentary and presidential elections. The President, the President of the Parliament, the Prime Minister, along with any ten Members of Parliament, have the right to consult this Council on matters that relate to the constitutionality of laws. The officially recognized heads of religious communities have the right to consult this Council only on laws relating to personal status, the freedom of belief and religious practice, and the freedom of religious education. The rules governing the organization, operation, composition, and modes of appeal of the Council are decided by a special law.

Article 20 [Judicial Power]
Judicial power is to be exercised by the tribunals of various levels and jurisdictions. It functions within the limits of an order established by the law and offering the necessary guarantees to judges and litigants. The limits and conditions for the protection of the judges are determined by law. The judges are independent in the exercise of their duties. The decisions and judgments of all courts are rendered and executed in the name of the Lebanese People.

Article 21 [Electoral Rights]
Every Lebanese citizen who has completed his twenty-first year is an elector provided he fulfills the conditions laid down in the electoral law.

Chapter II. The Legislative Power

Article 22 [Senate]
With the election of the first Parliament on a national, non-confessional basis, a Senate is established in which all the religious communities are represented. Its authority is limited to major national issues.

Article 23 [Eligibility to the Senate]
{Abolished 1927}

Article 24 [Electoral Laws]
(1) The Chamber of Deputies is composed of elected members; their number and the method of their election is determined by the electoral laws in effect. Until such time as the Chamber enacts new electoral laws on a non-confessional basis, the distribution of seats is according to the following principles:
   a. Equal representation between Christians and Muslims.
   b. Proportional representation among the confessional groups within each religious community.
   c. Proportional representation among geographic regions.
(2) Exceptionally, and for one time only, the seats that are currently vacant, as well as the new seats that have been established by law, are to be filled by appointment, all at once, and by a majority of two thirds of the Government of National Unity. This is to establish equality between Christians and Muslims as stipulated in the Document of National Accord [The Taef Agreement]. The electoral laws will specify the details regarding the implementation of this clause.

Article 25 [Dissolution]
Should the Chamber of Deputies be dissolved, the Decision of dissolution must provide for the holding of new elections in accordance with Article 24 and within a period not exceeding three months.

Article 26 [Location of Government and Parliament]
The Government and the Chamber of Deputies shall be located in Beirut.

Article 27 [Representation]
A member of the Chamber represents the whole nation. No restriction or stipulation may be imposed upon his mandate by his electors.

Article 28 [No Incompatibility]
A Deputy may also occupy a ministerial position. Ministers, all or in part, may be selected from among the members of the Chamber or from persons outside the Chamber.

Article 29 [Incompatibility by Law]
Cases in which persons are disqualified from becoming Deputies are determined by law.

Article 30 [Validating Elections]
The Deputies alone have competence to judge the validity of their mandate. No Deputy's mandate may be invalidated except by a majority of two thirds of the votes of the entire membership. This clause is automatically cancelled as soon as

the Constitutional Council is established and as soon as the laws relating to it are implemented.

Article 31 [Illegal Sessions]
Meetings of the Chamber outside those set for legal sessions are unlawful and *ipso facto* null and void.

Article 32 [Ordinary Sessions]
The Chamber meets each year in two ordinary sessions. The first session opens on the first Tuesday following 15 March and continues until the end of May. The second session begins on the first Tuesday following 15 October; its meetings are reserved for the discussion of and voting on the budget before any other work. This session lasts until the end of the year.

Article 33 [Extraordinary Sessions]
The ordinary sessions begin and end automatically on the dates fixed in Article 32. The President of the Republic in consultation with the Prime Minister may summon the Chamber to extraordinary sessions by a Decree specifying the dates of the opening and closing of the extraordinary sessions as well as the agenda. The President of the Republic is required to convoke the Chamber if an absolute majority of the total membership so requests.

Article 34 [Quorum]
The Chamber is not validly constituted unless the majority of the total membership is present. Decisions are to be taken by a majority vote. Should the votes be equal, the question under consideration is deemed rejected.

Article 35 [Publicity]
The meetings of the Chamber are public. However, at the request of the Government or of five Deputies, the Chamber may sit in secret sessions. It may then decide whether to resume the discussion of the same question in public.

Article 36 [Voting Process]
Votes are to be cast verbally or by the members standing, except for elections when the ballot is secret. With respect to laws in general and on questions of confidence, the vote is always taken by roll call and the responses are made in an audible voice.

Article 37 [Vote of No-Confidence]
Every Deputy has the absolute right to raise the question of no-confidence in the government during ordinary or extraordinary sessions. Discussion of and voting on such a proposal may not take place until at least five days after submission to the secretariat of the Chamber and its communication to the ministers concerned.

Article 38 [Reintroduction of Bills]
No Bill that has been rejected by the Chamber may be re-introduced during the same session.

Article 39 [Indemnity]
No member of the Chamber may be prosecuted because of ideas and opinions expressed during the period of his mandate.

Article 40 [Immunity]
No member of the Chamber may, during the sessions, be prosecuted or arrested for a criminal offense without the permission of the Chamber, except when he is caught in the act.

Article 41 [Re-election]
Should a seat in the Chamber become vacant, the election of a successor begins within two months. The mandate of the new member does not exceed that of the old member whose place he is taking; however, should the seat in the Chamber become vacant during the last six months of its mandate, no successor may be elected.

Article 42 [General Elections]
General elections for the renewal of the Chamber shall take place within a sixty day period preceding the expiration of its mandate.

Article 43 [Rules of Procedure]
The Chamber draws up its own internal rules and procedures.

Article 44 [First Session]
(1) Each time a new Chamber is elected, the Chamber meets under the presidency of the oldest member and the secretariat or the two youngest. It will then elect separately, by a secret ballot and by an absolute majority of the votes cast, the President and the Vice President of the Chamber to hold office for the length or the Chamber's term. At the third ballot, a relative majority is sufficient. Should the votes be equal, the oldest candidate is considered elected.
(2) Every time a new Chamber of Deputies is elected, as well as in the October session or each year, the Chamber elects two Secretaries by secret ballot according to the majority stipulated in the first part or this article.
(3) The Chamber may, once only, two years after the election or its President and his Deputy, and in the first session it holds, withdraw its confidence from the President of the Chamber or his Deputy by a Decision of two thirds of the Chamber, based on a petition signed by at least ten Deputies. The Chamber, at such point, must hold an immediate session to fill the vacant post.

Article 45 [Presence]
Members of the Chamber may only vote when they are present at the meeting. Voting by proxy shall not be permitted.

Article 46 [Parliamentary Order]
The Chamber has the exclusive right to maintain order in its meetings through its President.

Article 47 [Petitions]
Petitions to the Chamber may not be presented except in writing. They may not be presented verbally or at the bar of the Chamber.

Article 48 [Remuneration]
The remuneration of members of the Chamber is determined by law.

[Chapter] III. The Executive Power

[Section] 1. The President of the Republic

Article 49 [Presidential Powers]
(1) The President of the Republic is the bead of the state and the symbol of the nation's unity. He shall safeguard the constitution and Lebanon's independence, unity, and territorial integrity. The President shall preside over the Supreme Defense Council and be the Commander-in-Chief of the Armed Forces which fall under the authority of the Council of Ministers.
(2) The President of the Republic shall be elected by secret ballot and by a two thirds majority of the Chamber of Deputies. After a first ballot, an absolute majority shall be sufficient. The President's term is for six years. He may not be re-elected until six years after the expiration of his last mandate. No one may be elected to the Presidency of the Republic unless he fulfills the conditions of eligibility for the Chamber of Deputies.
(3) It is also not possible to elect judges, Grade One civil servants, or their equivalents in all public institutions to the Presidency during their term or office or within two years following the date of their resignation or their leaving office for whatever reason.

Article 50 [Oath]
Upon assuming office, the President of the Republic shall take an oath of fidelity before the Parliament to the Lebanese Nation and the constitution in the following terms:

> "*I swear by Almighty God to observe the Constitution and the laws of the Lebanese Nation and to maintain the independence of Lebanon and its territorial integrity*".

Article 51 [Promulgation of Laws]

The President of the Republic promulgates the laws after they have been approved by the Chamber in accordance with the time limits specified by the constitution. He asks for the publication or these laws, and he may not modify these laws or exempt anyone from complying with their provisions.

Article 52 [Negotiation of International Treaties]

The President of the Republic negotiates international treaties in coordination with the Prime Minister. These treaties are not considered ratified except after agreement of the Council of Ministers. They are to be made known to the Chamber whenever the national interest and security of the state permit. However, treaties involving the finances of the state, commercial treaties, and in general treaties that cannot be renounced every year are not considered ratified until they have been approved by the Chamber.

Article 53 [List of Additional Presidential Powers]

(1) The President presides over the Council of Ministers when he wishes without participating in voting.
(2) The President designates the Prime Minister in consultation with the President of the Chamber of Deputies based on parliamentary consultations which are binding and the content of which the President formally discloses to the Prime Minister.
(3) The President alone issues the Decree which designates the Prime Minister.
(4) He issues, in agreement with the Prime Minister, the decree appointing the Cabinet and the decrees accepting the resignation of Ministers.
(5) He issues, on his own authority, the decrees accepting the resignation of the Cabinet or considering it resigned.
(6) He forwards to the Chamber of Deputies Bills that are delivered to him by the Council of Ministers.
(7) He accredits ambassadors and accepts the credentials of ambassadors.
(8) He presides over official functions and grants official decorations by Decree.
(9) He grants particular pardons by Decree, but a general amnesty cannot be granted except by a law.
(10) He addresses, when necessary, letters to the Chamber of Deputies.
(11) He may introduce, from outside the agenda, any urgent matter to the council of Ministers.
(12) He may, in agreement with the Prime Minister, call the Council of Ministers to an extraordinary session, whenever he deems this necessary.

Article 54 [Countersignature]

The decisions of the President must be countersigned by the Prime Minister and the Minister or Ministers concerned except the Decree designating a new Prime Minister and the Decree accepting the resignation of the Cabinet or considering it resigned. Decrees issuing laws must be countersigned by the Prime Minister.

Article 55 [Dissolution of Parliament by Decree]

(1) The President of the Republic may, in accordance with the conditions stipulated in Articles 65 and 77 of this constitution, ask the Council of Ministers to dissolve the Chamber of Deputies before the expiration of its mandate. If the Council, based on this request, decides to dissolve the Chamber of Deputies, the President issues the Decree dissolving it, and in this case, the electoral bodies meets as provided for in Article 25, and the new Chamber is to be called to convene within fifteen days after the proclamation of the election.

(2) The administrative staff of the Chamber of Deputies continues to function until the election or a new Chamber.

(3) If elections are not held within the time limit specified in Article 25 of the constitution, the Decree dissolving the Chamber is considered null and void, and the Chamber of Deputies continues to exercise its powers according to the stipulations of the constitution.

Article 56 [Promulgation Time Limits]

(1) The President of the Republic promulgates the laws which have been adopted within one month of their transmission to the Government. He must promulgate laws that were declared urgent by a special Decision of the Chamber within five days.

(2) The President issues decrees and requests their promulgation; he has the right to ask the Council of Ministers to review any Decision that the Chamber has taken within fifteen days of the decision's transmission to the Presidency. If the Council of Ministers insists on the Decision or if the time limit passes without the Decree being issued or returned, the Decision or Decree is considered legally operative and must be promulgated.

Article 57 [Presidential Veto]

The President of the Republic, after consultation with the Council of Ministers, has the right to request the reconsideration of a law once during the period prescribed for its promulgation. This request may not be refused. When the President exercises this right, he is not required to promulgate this law until it has been reconsidered and approved by an absolute majority of all the members legally composing the Chamber. If the time limits pass without the law being issued or returned, the law is considered legally operative and must be promulgated.

Article 58 [Urgent Bills]

Every Bill the Council of Ministers deems urgent and in which this urgency is indicated in the decree of transmission to the Chamber of Deputies may be issued by the President within forty days following its communication to the Chamber, after including it on the agenda of a general meeting, reading it aloud before the Chamber, and after the expiration of the time limit without the Chamber acting on it.

Article 59 [Adjourning the Chamber]
The President of the Republic may adjourn the Chamber for a period not exceeding one month, but he may not do so twice during the same session.

Article 60 [Responsibility]
(1) While performing his functions, the President of the Republic may not be held responsible except when he violates the constitution or in the case of high treason.
(2) However, his responsibility in respect of ordinary crimes is subject to the ordinary laws. For such crimes, as well as for violation of the constitution and for high treason, he may not be impeached except by a majority of two thirds of the total membership of the Chamber of Deputies. He is to be tried by the Supreme Council provided for in Article 80. The functions of Public Prosecutor of the Supreme Council are performed by a judge appointed by the Supreme Council in plenary session.

Article 61 [Suspension after Impeachment]
Should the President of the Republic be impeached, he is suspended from his functions. The presidency remains vacant until the Supreme Council has settled the matter.

Article 62 [Vacancy]
Should the Presidency become vacant for any reason whatsoever, the Council of Ministers exercises the powers of the President by delegation.

Article 63 [Remuneration]
The remuneration of the President of the Republic is determined by a law. It may not be increased or reduced during his term of office.

[Section] 2. The Prime Minister

Article 64 [Responsibility and Powers]
The Prime Minister is the Head of Government and its representative. He speaks in its name and is responsible for executing the general policy that is set by the Council of Ministers. He exercises the following powers:

1. He heads the Council of Ministers and is ex officio Deputy Head of the Supreme Defense Council.
2. He conducts the parliamentary consultations involved in forming a Cabinet. He signs, with the President, the Decree forming the Cabinet. The Cabinet must present its general statement or policy to the Chamber and gain its confidence within thirty days of the date of issuance of the Decree in which the Cabinet was formed. The Cabinet does not exercise its powers before it gains the Chamber's confidence nor after it has resigned or is considered resigned, except in the narrow sense of managing affairs.

3. He presents the Government's general policy statements before the Chamber of Deputies.
4. He signs, along with the President, all decrees, except the Decree which designates him the head of the Government, and the Decree accepting the Cabinet's resignation or considering it resigned.
5. He signs the Decree calling for an extraordinary parliamentary session, decrees issuing laws, and requests for reviewing laws.
6. He calls the Council of Ministers into session and sets its agenda, and he informs the President and the Ministers beforehand of the subjects included on the agenda and of the urgent subjects that will be discussed.
7. He supervises the activities of the public administrations and institutions, coordinates among the Ministers and provides general guidance to ensure the proper progress of affairs.
8. He holds working meetings with the competent authorities in the Government in the presence of the concerned Minister.

[Section] 3. The Council of Ministers

Article 65 [Powers]

Executive authority is vested in the Council of Ministers. It is the authority to which the armed forces are subject. Among the powers that it exercises are the following:

1. It sets the general policy of the Government in all fields, prepares Bills and organizational Decrees and makes the decisions necessary for implementing them.
2. It watches over the execution of laws and regulations and supervises the activities of all the Government's branches including the civil, military, and security administrations and institutions without exception.
3. It appoints Government employees and dismisses them and accepts their resignations according to the law.
4. It dissolves the Chamber of Deputies upon the request of the President of the Republic if the Chamber of Deputies, for no compelling reasons, fails to meet during one of its regular periods and fails to meet throughout two successive extraordinary periods, each longer than one month, or if the Chamber returns an annual budget plan with the aim or paralyzing the Government. This right cannot be exercised a second time if it is for the same reasons which led to the dissolution of the Chamber the first time.
5. The Council of Ministers meets in a locale specifically set aside for it, and the President chairs its meetings when he attends. The legal quorum for a Council meeting is a majority of two thirds of its members. It makes its decisions by consensus. If that is not possible, it makes its decisions by vote of the majority of attending members. Basic national issues require the approval of two thirds of the members of the Council

named in the Decree forming the Cabinet. Basic national issues are considered the following: The amendment of the constitution, the declaration of a state of emergency and its termination, war and peace, general mobilization, international agreements and treaties, the annual government budget, comprehensive and long-term development projects, the appointment of Grade One government employees and their equivalents, the review of the administrative map, the dissolution of the Chamber of Deputies, electoral laws, nationality laws, personal status laws, and the dismissal of Ministers.

Article 66 [Ministries, Responsibility]
Only Lebanese who satisfy the conditions for deputation may assume ministerial posts. The Ministers administer the Government's services and assume the responsibility of applying the laws and regulations, each one according to the affairs of his administration and what is specific to them. Ministers are collectively responsible before the Chamber for the general policy of the Government and individually responsible for their personal actions.

Article 67 [Ministers in Parliament]
Ministers may attend the Chamber if they so desire, and they have the right to be heard whenever they request to speak. They may be assisted by whomever they select from among the officials of their Departments.

Article 68 [Vote of No-Confidence]
When the Chamber, in accordance with Article 37, passes a vote of no confidence in a Minister, that Minister is required to resign.

Article 69 [Government Resignation]
(1) The Government is considered resigned in the following circumstances:
    a. if the Prime Minister resigns;
    b. if it loses more than a third of the members specified in the Decree forming it;
    c. if the Prime Minister dies;
    d. at the beginning of the term of the President of the Republic;
    e. at the beginning of the term of the Chamber of Deputies;
    f. when it loses the confidence of the Chamber of Deputies based on the Chamber's initiative or based on the Council's initiative to gain the Chamber's confidence.
(2) Ministers are to be dismissed by a Decree signed by the President and the Prime Minister in accordance with Article 65 of the constitution.
(3) When the Council resigns or is considered resigned, the Chamber of Deputies is automatically considered in extraordinary session until a new Council has been formed and has gained the Chamber's confidence.

Article 70 [Impeachment]
(1) The Chamber of Deputies has the right to impeach the Prime Minister and Ministers for high treason or for serious neglect of their duties. The Decision to impeach may not be taken except by a majority of two thirds of the total membership of the Chamber.
(2) A special law is to be issued to determine the conditions of the civil responsibility of the Prime Minister and individual Ministers.

Article 71 [Judicial Impeachment Proceedings]
The impeached Prime Minister or Minister are tried by the Supreme Council.

Article 72 [Consequences of Impeachment]
A Prime Minister or Minister leaves office as soon as the Decision of impeachment concerning him is issued. If he resigns, his resignation does not prevent judicial proceedings from being instituted or continued against him.

[Part] C. Procedural Provisions

[Chapter] I. Election of the President of the Republic

Article 73 [Election of the President]
One month at least and two months at most before the expiration of the term of office of the President of the Republic, the Chamber is summoned by its President to elect the new President of the Republic. However, should it not be summoned for this purpose, the Chamber meets of its own accord on the tenth day preceding the expiration of the President's term of office.

Article 74 [Vacancy of Presidency]
Should the Presidency become vacant through the death or resignation of the President or for any other cause, the Chamber meets immediately and by virtue of the law to elect a successor. If the Chamber happens to be dissolved at the time the vacancy occurs, the electoral bodies are convened without delay and, as soon as the elections have taken place, the Chamber meets by virtue of the law.

Article 75
The Chamber meeting to elect the President of the Republic is considered an electoral body and not a legislative assembly. It must proceed immediately, without discussion or any other act, to elect the Head of the State.

[Chapter] II. Amending the Constitution

Article 76 [Proposal]
The constitution may be revised upon the proposal of the President of the Republic. In such a case the Government submits a draft law to the Chamber of Deputies.

Article 77 [Request]
The constitution may also be revised upon the request of the Chamber of Deputies. In this case the following procedures are to be observed:

> During an ordinary session and at the request of at least ten of its members, the Chamber of Deputies may recommend, by a majority of two thirds of the total members lawfully composing the Chamber, the revision of the constitution.
>
> However, the articles and the questions referred to in the recommendation must be clearly defined and specified. The President of the Chamber then transmits the recommendation to the Government requesting it to prepare a draft law relating thereto. If the Government approves the recommendation of the Chamber by a majority of two thirds, it must prepare the draft amendment and submit it to the Chamber within four months; it does not agree, it shall return the Decision to the Chamber for reconsideration. If the Chamber insists upon the necessity of the amendment by a majority of three fourths of the total members lawfully composing the Chamber, the President of the Republic has then either to accede to the Chamber's recommendation or to ask the Council of Ministers to dissolve the Chamber and to hold new elections within three months. If the new Chamber insists on the necessity of amending the constitution, the Government must yield and submit the draft amendment within four months.

Article 78 [Priority]
When a draft law dealing with a constitutional amendment is submitted to the Chamber, it must confine itself to its discussion before any other work until a final vote is taken. It may discuss and vote only on articles and questions clearly enumerated and defined in the draft submitted to it.

Article 79 [Majority, Promulgation]
(1) When a draft law dealing with a constitutional amendment is submitted to the Chamber, it cannot discuss it or vote upon it except when a majority of two thirds of the members lawfully composing the Chamber are present. Voting is by the same majority.
(2) The President of the Republic is required to promulgate the law of the constitutional amendment under the same conditions and in the same form as ordinary laws. He has the right, within the period established for the promulgation, to ask the Chamber to reconsider the draft, after consultation with the council of Ministers, in which case the vote is by a majority of two thirds.

[Part] D. Miscellaneous Provisions

[Chapter] I. The Supreme Council

Article 80 [Function, Composition, Organizational Law]
The Supreme Council, whose function is to try Presidents and Ministers, consists of seven deputies elected by the Chamber of Deputies and of eight of the highest Lebanese judges, according to their rank in the judicial hierarchy, or, in case of equal ranks, in the order of seniority. They meet under the presidency of the judge of the highest rank. The Decisions of condemnation by the Supreme Council is rendered by a majority of ten votes. A special law is to be issued to determine the procedure to be followed by this Council.

[Chapter] II. Finances

Article 81 [Integral Tax Law]
No public taxes may be imposed and no new taxes established or collected in the Lebanese Republic except by a comprehensive law which applies to the entire Lebanese territory without exception.

Article 82 [Rule of Law]
No tax may be modified or abolished except by virtue of law.

Article 83 [Yearly Budget]
Each year at the beginning of the October session, the Government has to submit to the Chamber of Deputies the general budget estimates of state expenditures and revenues for the following year. The budget is voted upon article by article.

Article 84 [Budget Discussion]
During the discussion of the budget and draft laws involving the opening of supplementary or extraordinary credits, the Chamber may not increase the credits proposed in the budget or in the draft laws mentioned above either by way of amendment Or by means of a proposal. The Chamber may, however, adopt, by way of proposal, laws involving further expenditures after the close of this discussion.

Article 85 [Extraordinary Credit]
No extraordinary credit may be opened except by a special law. Nevertheless, should unforeseen circumstances render urgent expenditures necessary, the President of the Republic may issue a Decree, based on a Decision of the Council or Ministers, to open extraordinary or supplementary credits or transfer appropriations in the budget as long as these credits do not exceed a maximum limit specified in the budget law. These measures are to be submitted to the Chamber for approval at the first ensuing session.

Article 86 [Provisional Budget]
If the Chamber of Deputies has not given a final decision on the budget estimates before the expiration of the session devoted to the examination of the budget, the President of the Republic, in coordination with the Prime Minister, immediately convenes the Chamber for an extraordinary session which lasts until the end of January in order to continue the discussion of the budget; if, at the end of this extraordinary session, the budget estimates have not been finally settled, the Council of Ministers may take a decision on the basis of which a decree is issued by the President giving effect to the above estimates in the form in which they were submitted to the Chamber. However, the Council of Ministers may not exercise this right unless the budget estimates were submitted to the Chamber at least fifteen days before the commencement of its session. Nevertheless, during the said extraordinary session, taxes, charges, duties, imposts, and other kinds of revenues continue to be collected as before. The budget of the previous year is adopted as a basis. To this must be added the permanent credits which have been dropped, and the Government fixes the expenditures for the month of January on the basis of the "provisional twelfth".

Article 87 [Final Financial Accounts, Auditing Bureau]
The final financial accounts of the administration for each year must be submitted to the Chamber for approval before the promulgation of the budget of the year following. A special law is to be issued for the setting up of an Auditing Bureau.

Article 88 [Public Loan]
No public loan or undertaking involving an expenditure from the treasury funds may be contracted except by virtue of a law.

Article 89 [Contracts, Concessions, Resources, Monopolies]
No contract or concession for the exploitation of the natural resources of the country, or a public utility service, or a monopoly may be granted except by virtue of a law and for a limited period.

[Part] E. Provisions Relating to the Mandatory Power and the League of Nations

Article 90 [...]
{Abolished in 1943}

Article 91 [...]
{Abolished in 1943}

Article 92 [...]
{Abolished in 1943}

Article 93 [...]
{Abolished in 1947}

Article 94 [...]
{Abolished in 1943}

[Part] F. On the Abolition of Political Confessionalism

Article 95 [National Committee]
(1) The first Chamber of Deputies which is elected on the basis of equality between Muslims and Christians takes the appropriate measures to realize the abolition of political confessionalism according to a transitional plan. A National Committee is to be formed, headed by the President of the Republic, including, in addition to the President of the Chamber of Deputies and the Prime Minister, leading political, intellectual, and social figures.
(2) The tasks of this Committee are to study and propose the means to ensure the abolition of confessionalism, propose them to the Chamber of Deputies and the Ministers, and supervise the execution of the transitional plan.
(3) During the transitional phase:
  a. The confessional groups are to be represented in a just and equitable fashion in the formation of the Cabinet.
  b. The principle of confessional representation in public service jobs, in the judiciary, in the military and security institutions, and in public and mixed agencies are to be cancelled in accordance with the requirements of national reconciliation; they shall be replaced by the principle of expertise and competence. However, Grade One posts and their equivalents are exempt from this rule, and the posts must be distributed equally between Christians and Muslims without reserving any particular job for any confessional group but rather applying the principles of expertise and competence.

[Part] G. Provisions Relating to the Election and Functions of the Senate

Article 96 [...]
{Abolished in 1947}

Article 97 [...]
{Abolished in 1947}

Article 98 [...]
{Abolished in 1947}

Article 99 [...]
{Abolished in 1947}

Article 100 [...]
{Abolished in 1947}

[Part] H. Additional Provisions

Article 101 [Greater Lebanon, The Lebanese Republic]
Beginning 1 Sep 1929, the state of "Greater Lebanon" is to be known as "The Lebanese Republic" without any other change or modification.

Article 102 [Abrogation of Old Laws]
All legislative provisions contrary to the present constitution are abrogated.

Appendix B

Security Council Resolution 1559

02/09/2004

Security Council declares support for free, fair presidential election in Lebanon; calls for withdrawal of foreign forces there

Resolution 1559 (2004) Adopted by Vote Of 9 in Favor, to None Against, with 6 Abstentions

By a vote of 9 in favor (Angola, Benin, Chile, France, Germany, Romania, Spain, United Kingdom, United States) to none against, with 6 abstentions (Algeria, Brazil, China, Pakistan, Philippines, Russian Federation), the Council adopted resolution 1559 (2004), reaffirming its call for the strict respect of Lebanon's sovereignty, territorial integrity, unity, and political independence under the sole and exclusive authority of the Government of Lebanon throughout the country.

"*The Security Council,*

"*Recalling* all its previous resolutions on Lebanon, in particular resolutions 425 (1978) and 426 (1978) of 19 March 1978, resolution 520 (1982) of 17 September 1982, and resolution 1553 (2004) of 29 July 2004 as well as the statements of its President on the situation in Lebanon, in particular the statement of 18 June 2000 (S/PRST/2000/21),

"*Reiterating* its strong support for the territorial integrity, sovereignty and political independence of Lebanon within its internationally territorially recognized borders,

"*Noting* the determination of Lebanon to ensure the withdrawal of all non-Lebanese forces from Lebanon,

"*Gravely concerned* at the continued presence of armed militias in Lebanon, which prevent the Lebanese government from exercising its full sovereignty over all Lebanese territory,

"*Reaffirming* the importance of the extension of the control of the Government of Lebanon over all Lebanese territory,

"*Mindful* of the upcoming Lebanese presidential elections and underlining the importance of free and fair elections according to Lebanese constitutional rules devised without foreign interference or influence,

"1. *Reaffirms* its call for the strict respect of the sovereignty, territorial integrity, unity, and political independence of Lebanon under the sole and exclusive authority of the Government of Lebanon throughout Lebanon;

"2. *Calls upon* all remaining foreign forces to withdraw from Lebanon;

"3. *Calls for* the disbanding and disarmament of all Lebanese and non-Lebanese militias;

"4. *Supports* the extension of the control of the Government of Lebanon over all Lebanese territory;

"5. *Declares* its support for a free and fair electoral process in Lebanon's upcoming presidential election conducted according to Lebanese constitutional rules devised without foreign interference or influence;

"6. *Calls upon* all parties concerned to cooperate fully and urgently with the Security Council for the full implementation of this and all relevant resolutions concerning the restoration of the territorial integrity, full sovereignty, and political independence of Lebanon;

"7. *Requests* that the Secretary-General report to the Security Council within thirty days on the implementation by the parties of this resolution and decides to remain actively seized of this matter."

Appendix C

Security Council Resolution 1595

07/04/2005

**SECURITY COUNCIL ESTABLISHES COMMISSION TO ASSIST
INVESTIGATION INTO BEIRUT BOMBING THAT KILLED FORMER
LEBANESE PRIME MINISTER**

Resolution 1595 (2005) Adopted Unanimously;

"*The Security Council,*

"*Reiterating* its call for the strict respect of the sovereignty, territorial integrity, unity and political independence of Lebanon under the sole and exclusive authority of the Government of Lebanon,

"*Endorsing* the Secretary-General's opinion, as expressed in his letter of 24 March 2005 to the President of the Security Council, that Lebanon is passing through a difficult and sensitive period, that all concerned should imperatively behave with the utmost restraint and that the future of Lebanon should be decided strictly through peaceful means,

"*Reaffirming* its unequivocal condemnation of the 14 February 2005 terrorist bombing in Beirut, Lebanon, that killed former Lebanese Prime Minister Rafik Hariri and others, and caused injury to dozens of people, and *condemning* the subsequent attacks in Lebanon,

"*Having examined* the report of the fact-finding mission to Lebanon inquiring into the circumstances, causes and consequences of this terrorist act (S/2005/203), transmitted to the Security Council by the Secretary-General following the declaration of the President of the Security Council of 15 February 2005 (S/PRST/2005/4),

"*Noting* with concern the fact-finding mission's conclusion that the Lebanese investigation process suffers from serious flaws and has neither the capacity nor the commitment to reach a satisfactory and credible conclusion,

"*Noting also* in this context its opinion that an international independent investigation with executive authority and self-sufficient resources in all relevant fields of expertise would be necessary to elucidate all aspects of this heinous crime,

"*Mindful* of the unanimous demand of the Lebanese people that those responsible be identified and held accountable, and *willing* to assist Lebanon in the search for the truth,

"*Welcoming* the Lebanese Government's approval of the decision to be taken by the Security Council concerning the establishment of an international independent investigation Commission, and *welcoming also* its readiness to cooperate fully with such a Commission within the framework of Lebanese sovereignty and of its legal system, as expressed in the letter of 29 March 2005 from the Chargé d'affaires a.i. of Lebanon to the United Nations to the Secretary-General (S/2005/208),

"1. *Decides*, consistent with the above-mentioned letter from the Chargé d'affaires a.i. of Lebanon, to establish an international independent investigation Commission ("the Commission") based in Lebanon to assist the Lebanese authorities in their investigation of all aspects of this terrorist act, including to help identify its perpetrators, sponsors, organizers and accomplices;

"2. *Reiterates* its call on the Lebanese Government to bring to justice the perpetrators, organizers and sponsors of the 14 February 2005 terrorist bombing, and *calls upon* the Lebanese Government to ensure that the findings and conclusions of the Commission's investigation are taken into account fully;

"3. *Decides* that, to ensure the Commission's effectiveness in the discharge of its duties, the Commission shall:

– Enjoy the full cooperation of the Lebanese authorities, including full access to all documentary, testimonial and physical information and evidence in their possession that the Commission deems relevant to the inquiry;

– Have the authority to collect any additional information and evidence, both documentary and physical, pertaining to this terrorist act, as well as to interview all officials and other persons in Lebanon, that the Commission deems relevant to the inquiry;

– Enjoy freedom of movement throughout the Lebanese territory, including access to all sites and facilities that the Commission deems relevant to the inquiry;

– Be provided with the facilities necessary to perform its functions, and be granted, as well as its premises, staff and equipment, the privileges and immunities to which they are entitled under the Convention on the Privileges and Immunities of the United Nations;

"4. *Requests* the Secretary-General to consult urgently with the Lebanese Government with a view to facilitate the establishment and operation of the Commission pursuant to its mandate and terms of reference as mentioned in paragraphs 2 and 3 above, and *requests also* that he report to the Council accordingly and notify it of the date the Commission begins its full operations;

"5. *Requests further* the Secretary-General, notwithstanding paragraph 4 above, to undertake without delay the steps, measures and arrangements necessary for the speedy establishment and full functioning of the Commission, including recruiting impartial and experienced staff with relevant skills and expertise;

"6. *Directs* the Commission to determine procedures for carrying out its investigation, taking into account the Lebanese law and judicial procedures;

"7. *Calls on* all States and all parties to cooperate fully with the Commission, and in particular to provide it with any relevant information they may possess pertaining to the above-mentioned terrorist act;

"8. *Requests* the Commission to complete its work within three months of the date on which it commenced its full operations, as notified by the Secretary-General, and authorizes the Secretary-General to extend the Commission's operation for a further period not exceeding three months, if he deems it necessary to enable the Commission to complete its investigation, and requests that he inform the Security Council accordingly;

"9. *Requests* the Commission to report to the Council on the conclusions of its investigation and *requests* the Secretary-General to update orally the Security Council on the progress of the Commission every two months during the operations of the Commission or more frequently as needed."

Appendix D

Security Council Resolution 1757

30 May 2007

Security Council authorizes establishment of special tribunal to try suspects in assassination of Rafik Hariri

Resolution 1757 (2007) Adopted by 10-0-5;
China, Indonesia, Qatar, Russian Federation, South Africa Abstain

By a vote of 10 in favor to none against, with 5 abstentions (China, Indonesia, Qatar, Russian Federation and South Africa), the Security Council, acting under Chapter VII of the Charter, adopted resolution 1757 (2007) authorizing the creation of the Special Tribunal for Lebanon. It gives the Lebanese Government until 10 June "to notify the United Nations in writing that the legal requirements for entry into force have been complied with", thus allowing Lebanese factions 10 days to reach an agreement internally before it goes into effect.

"*The Security Council,*

"*Recalling* all its previous relevant resolutions, in particular resolutions 1595 (2005) of 7 April 2005, 1636 (2005) of 31 October 2005, 1644 (2005) of 15 December 2005, 1664 (2006) of 29 March 2006 and 1748 (2007) of 27 March 2007,

"*Reaffirming* its strongest condemnation of the 14 February 2005 terrorist bombings as well as other attacks in Lebanon since October 2004,

"*Reiterating* its call for the strict respect of the sovereignty, territorial integrity, unity and political independence of Lebanon under the sole and exclusive authority of the Government of Lebanon,

"*Recalling* the letter of the Prime Minister of Lebanon to the Secretary-General of 13 December 2005 (S/2005/783) requesting inter alia the establishment of a tribunal of an international character to try all those who are found responsible for this terrorist crime, and the request by this Council for the Secretary-General to negotiate an agreement with the Government of Lebanon aimed at establishing such a Tribunal based on the highest international standards of criminal justice,

"*Recalling further* the report of the Secretary-General on the establishment of a special tribunal for Lebanon on 15 November 2006 (S/2006/893) reporting on the conclusion of negotiations and consultations that took place between January 2006 and September 2006 at United Nations Headquarters in New York, The Hague, and Beirut between the Legal Counsel of the United Nations and authorized representatives of the Government of Lebanon, and the letter of its President to the Secretary-General of 21 November 2006 (S/2006/911) reporting that the Members of the Security Council welcomed the conclusion of the negotiations and that they were satisfied with the Agreement annexed to the Report,

"*Recalling that,* as set out in its letter of 21 November 2006, should voluntary contributions be insufficient for the Tribunal to implement its mandate, the Secretary-General and the Security Council shall explore alternate means of financing the Tribunal,

"*Recalling also that* the Agreement between the United Nations and the Lebanese Republic on the establishment of a Special Tribunal for Lebanon was signed by the Government of Lebanon and the United Nations respectively on 23 January and 6 February 2007,

"*Referring* to the letter of the Prime Minister of Lebanon to the Secretary-General of the United Nations (S/2007/281), which recalled that the parliamentary majority has expressed its support for the Tribunal, and asked that his request that the Special Tribunal be put into effect be presented to the Council as a matter of urgency,

"*Mindful* of the demand of the Lebanese people that all those responsible for the terrorist bombing that killed former Lebanese Prime Minister Rafik Hariri and others be identified and brought to justice,

"*Commending* the Secretary-General for his continuing efforts to proceed, together with the Government of Lebanon, with the final steps for the conclusion of the Agreement as requested in the letter of its President dated 21 November 2006 and referring in this regard to the briefing by the Legal Counsel on 2 May 2007, in which he noted that the establishment of the Tribunal through the Constitutional process is facing serious obstacles, but noting also that all parties concerned reaffirmed their agreement in principle to the establishment of the Tribunal,

"*Commending also* the recent efforts of parties in the region to overcome these obstacles,

"*Willing* to continue to assist Lebanon in the search for the truth and in holding all those involved in the terrorist attack accountable and reaffirming its determination to support Lebanon in its efforts to bring to justice perpetrators, organizers and sponsors of this and other assassinations,

"*Reaffirming* its determination that this terrorist act and its implications constitute a threat to international peace and security,

"1. *Decides*, acting under Chapter VII of the Charter of the United Nations, that:

(a) The provisions of the annexed document, including its attachment, on the establishment of a Special Tribunal for Lebanon shall enter into force on 10 June 2007, unless the Government of Lebanon has provided notification under Article 19 (1) of the annexed document before that date;

(b) If the Secretary-General reports that the Headquarters Agreement has not been concluded as envisioned under Article 8 of the annexed document, the location of the seat of the Tribunal shall be determined in consultation with the Government of Lebanon and be subject to the conclusion of a Headquarters Agreement between the United Nations and the State that hosts the Tribunal;

(c) If the Secretary-General reports that contributions from the Government of Lebanon are not sufficient to bear the expenses described in Article 5 (b) of the annexed document, he may accept or use voluntary contributions from States to cover any shortfall;

"2. *Notes* that, pursuant to Article 19 (2) of the annexed document, the Special Tribunal shall commence functioning on a date to be determined by the Secretary-General in consultation with the Government of Lebanon, taking into account the progress of the work of the International Independent Investigation Commission;

"3. *Requests* the Secretary-General, in coordination, when appropriate, with the Government of Lebanon, to undertake the steps and measures necessary to establish the Special Tribunal in a timely manner and to report to the Council within 90 days and thereafter periodically on the implementation of this resolution;

"4. *Decides* to remain actively seized of the matter.

Appendix E

Security Council Resolution 1701

11 August 2006
SECURITY COUNCIL CALLS FOR END TO HOSTILITIES BETWEEN HEZBOLLAH, ISRAEL,
UNANIMOUSLY ADOPTING RESOLUTION 1701 (2006)
Permanent Ceasefire to Be Based on Creation
Of Buffer Zone Free of Armed Personnel Other than UN, Lebanese Forces

"*The Security Council*,

"*Recalling* all its previous resolutions on Lebanon, in particular resolutions 425 (1978), 426 (1978), 520 (1982), 1559 (2004), 1655 (2006) 1680 (2006) and 1697 (2006), as well as the statements of its President on the situation in Lebanon, in particular the statements of 18 June 2000 (S/PRST/2000/21), of 19 October 2004 (S/PRST/2004/36), of 4 May 2005 (S/PRST/2005/17), of 23 January 2006 (S/PRST/2006/3) and of 30 July 2006 (S/PRST/2006/35),

"*Expressing* its utmost concern at the continuing escalation of hostilities in Lebanon and in Israel since Hezbollah's attack on Israel on 12 July 2006, which has already caused hundreds of deaths and injuries on both sides, extensive damage to civilian infrastructure and hundreds of thousands of internally displaced persons,

"*Emphasizing* the need for an end of violence, but at the same time emphasizing the need to address urgently the causes that have given rise to the current crisis, including by the unconditional release of the abducted Israeli soldiers,

"*Mindful* of the sensitivity of the issue of prisoners and encouraging the efforts aimed at urgently settling the issue of the Lebanese prisoners detained in Israel,

"*Welcoming* the efforts of the Lebanese Prime Minister and the commitment of the Government of Lebanon, in its seven-point plan, to extend its authority over its territory, through its own legitimate armed forces, such that there will be no weapons without the consent of the Government of Lebanon and no authority other than that of the Government of Lebanon, welcoming also its commitment to a United Nations force that is supplemented and enhanced in numbers, equipment, mandate and scope of operation, and *bearing in mind* its request in this plan for an immediate withdrawal of the Israeli forces from southern Lebanon,

"*Determined* to act for this withdrawal to happen at the earliest,

"*Taking due note* of the proposals made in the seven-point plan regarding the Shebaa farms area,

"*Welcoming* the unanimous decision by the Government of Lebanon on 7 August 2006 to deploy a Lebanese armed force of 15,000 troops in South Lebanon as the Israeli army withdraws behind the Blue Line and to request the assistance of additional forces from UNIFIL as needed, to facilitate the entry of the Lebanese armed forces into the region and to restate its intention to strengthen the Lebanese armed forces with material as needed to enable it to perform its duties,

"*Aware* of its responsibilities to help secure a permanent ceasefire and a long-term solution to the conflict,

"*Determining* that the situation in Lebanon constitutes a threat to international peace and security,

"1. *Calls for* a full cessation of hostilities based upon, in particular, the immediate cessation by Hezbollah of all attacks and the immediate cessation by Israel of all offensive military operations;

"2. Upon full cessation of hostilities, *calls upon* the Government of Lebanon and UNIFIL as authorized by paragraph 11 to deploy their forces together throughout the South and calls upon the Government of Israel, as that deployment begins, to withdraw all of its forces from southern Lebanon in parallel;

"3. *Emphasizes* the importance of the extension of the control of the Government of Lebanon over all Lebanese territory in accordance with the provisions of resolution 1559 (2004) and resolution 1680 (2006), and of the relevant provisions of the Taef Accords, for it to exercise its full sovereignty, so that there will be no weapons without the consent of the Government of Lebanon and no authority other than that of the Government of Lebanon;

"4. *Reiterates* its strong support for full respect for the Blue Line;

"5. *Also reiterates* its strong support, as recalled in all its previous relevant resolutions, for the territorial integrity, sovereignty and political independence of Lebanon within its internationally recognized borders, as contemplated by the Israeli-Lebanese General Armistice Agreement of 23 March 1949;

"6. *Calls on* the international community to take immediate steps to extend its financial and humanitarian assistance to the Lebanese people, including through facilitating the safe return of displaced persons and, under the authority of the Government of Lebanon, reopening airports and harbors, consistent with paragraphs 14 and 15, and *calls on* it also to consider further assistance in the future to contribute to the reconstruction and development of Lebanon;

"7. *Affirms* that all parties are responsible for ensuring that no action is taken contrary to paragraph 1 that might adversely affect the search for a long-term solution, humanitarian access to civilian populations, including safe passage for humanitarian convoys, or the voluntary and safe return of displaced persons, and *calls on* all parties to comply with this responsibility and to cooperate with the Security Council;

"8. *Calls for* Israel and Lebanon to support a permanent ceasefire and a long-term solution based on the following principles and elements:

– full respect for the Blue Line by both parties;

– security arrangements to prevent the resumption of hostilities, including the establishment between the Blue Line and the Litany river of an area free of any armed personnel, assets and weapons other than those of the Government of Lebanon and of UNIFIL as authorized in paragraph 11, deployed in this area;

– full implementation of the relevant provisions of the Taef Accords, and of resolutions 1559 (2004) and 1680 (2006), that require the disarmament of all armed groups in Lebanon, so that, pursuant to the Lebanese cabinet decision of 27 July 2006, there will be no weapons or authority in Lebanon other than that of the Lebanese State;

– no foreign forces in Lebanon without the consent of its Government;

– no sales or supply of arms and related materiel to Lebanon except as authorized by its Government;

– provision to the United Nations of all remaining maps of land mines in Lebanon in Israel's possession;

"9. *Invites* the Secretary-General to support efforts to secure as soon as possible agreements in principle from the Government of Lebanon and the Government of Israel to the principles and elements for a long-term solution as set forth in paragraph 8, and *expresses* its intention to be actively involved;

"10. *Requests* the Secretary-General to develop, in liaison with relevant international actors and the concerned parties, proposals to implement the relevant provisions of the Taef Accords, and resolutions 1559 (2004) and 1680 (2006), including disarmament, and for delineation of the international borders of Lebanon, especially in those areas where the border is disputed or uncertain, including by dealing with the Shebaa farms area, and to present to the Security Council those proposals within thirty days;

"11. *Decides*, in order to supplement and enhance the force in numbers, equipment, mandate and scope of operations, to authorize an increase in the force strength of UNIFIL to a maximum of 15,000 troops, and that the force shall, in addition to carrying out its mandate under resolutions 425 and 426 (1978):

(a) Monitor the cessation of hostilities;

(b) Accompany and support the Lebanese armed forces as they deploy throughout the South, including along the Blue Line, as Israel withdraws its armed forces from Lebanon as provided in paragraph 2;

(c) Coordinate its activities related to paragraph 11 (b) with the Government of Lebanon and the Government of Israel;

(d) Extend its assistance to help ensure humanitarian access to civilian populations and the voluntary and safe return of displaced persons;

(e) Assist the Lebanese armed forces in taking steps towards the establishment of the area as referred to in paragraph 8;

(f) Assist the Government of Lebanon, at its request, to implement paragraph 14;

"12. Acting in support of a request from the Government of Lebanon to deploy an international force to assist it to exercise its authority throughout the territory, *authorizes* UNIFIL to take all necessary action in areas of deployment of its forces and as it deems within its capabilities, to ensure that its area of operations is not utilized for hostile activities of any kind, to resist attempts by forceful means to prevent it from discharging its duties under the mandate of the Security Council, and to protect United Nations personnel, facilities, installations and equipment, ensure the security and freedom of movement of United Nations personnel, humanitarian workers and, without prejudice to the responsibility of the Government of Lebanon, to protect civilians under imminent threat of physical violence;

"13. *Requests* the Secretary-General urgently to put in place measures to ensure UNIFIL is able to carry out the functions envisaged in this resolution, urges Member States to consider making appropriate contributions to UNIFIL and to respond positively to requests for assistance from the Force, and *expresses* its strong appreciation to those who have contributed to UNIFIL in the past;

"14. *Calls upon* the Government of Lebanon to secure its borders and other entry points to prevent the entry in Lebanon without its consent of arms or related materiel and *requests* UNIFIL as authorized in paragraph 11 to assist the Government of Lebanon at its request;

"15. *Decides* further that all States shall take the necessary measures to prevent, by their nationals or from their territories or using their flag vessels or aircraft:

"(a) The sale or supply to any entity or individual in Lebanon of arms and related materiel of all types, including weapons and ammunition, military vehicles and equipment, paramilitary equipment, and spare parts for the aforementioned, whether or not originating in their territories; and

"(b) The provision to any entity or individual in Lebanon of any technical training or assistance related to the provision, manufacture, maintenance or use of the items listed in subparagraph (a) above;

except that these prohibitions shall not apply to arms, related material, training or assistance authorized by the Government of Lebanon or by UNIFIL as authorized in paragraph 11;

"16. *Decides* to extend the mandate of UNIFIL until 31 August 2007, and *expresses its intention* to consider in a later resolution further enhancements to the mandate and other steps to contribute to the implementation of a permanent ceasefire and a long-term solution;

"17. *Requests* the Secretary-General to report to the Council within one week on the implementation of this resolution and subsequently on a regular basis;

"18. *Stresses* the importance of, and the need to achieve, a comprehensive, just and lasting peace in the Middle East, based on all its relevant resolutions including its resolutions 242 (1967) of 22 November 1967, 338 (1973) of 22 October 1973 and 1515 (2003) of 18 November 2003;

"19. *Decides* to remain actively seized of the matter."

Appendix F

Political parties in Lebanon

Name (English)	Name (Arabic)	Acronym	Leader or Chairman	Political Position	Sect or ethnic group
Parties Associated with March 14 Coalition (2009)					
Lebanese Forces	al-Quwat al-Lubnāniyya القوات اللبنانية	LF	Samir Geagea	Lebanese nationalism	Maronite
Future Movement	Tayyar Al Mustaqbal تيار المستقبل	FM	Saad Hariri	Capitalism / Nationalism	Mainly Sunni Muslim
Progressive Socialist Party	Hizb al-Taqadummi al-Ishtiraki الحزب التقدمي الإشتراكي	PSP	Walid Jumblatt	Officially Socialism	Mainly Druze
Phalangist or Kataab Party	al-Kataab al-Lubnāniyya حزب الكتائب اللبنانية	Kataab	Amin Jemayel	Right wing, Lebanese nationalism	Maronite Christian
National Liberal Party	Hizb al-Wataniyyin al-Ahrar حزب الوطنيين الأحرار	NLP	Dory Chamoun	Liberalism	Maronite
Independence Movement	Harakat Al-Istiklal حركة الإستقلال	Al Haraka	Nayla Moawad	Lebanese Nationalism	Maronite
Tripoli Bloc (National agreement bloc)	Al-takatol al-trabolsi التكتل الطرابلسي	-	Mohamed Safadi	Localism, moderatism	Sunni
Democratic Renewal	Harakat al-tajaddod al-democraty حركة التجدد الدمقراطي	DRM	Misbah Ahdab	Reformism	Secular
Democratic Left	Harakat Al-Yassar Al-Democraty حركة اليسار الديمقراطي	DL	Elias Attallah	Left-wing	Secular
Armenian Democratic Liberal Party - Ramgavar	Hizb al-ramgavar حزب الرمغفار	ADL	Hagop Kassardjian	Liberalism	Armenian Secular
Social Democrat Hunchakian Party	Hizb al-henchag حزب الهنشق	Henchag	-	Socialist	Armenian Secular
Lebanese National Bloc	Hizb al-kitla al-wataniya حزب الكتلة الوطنية	NB	Carlos Eddé	Lebanese nationalism	Maronite
Islamic Group	Al-jamaa Al-Islamiya الجماعة الإسلامية	JI	Assaad Harmouch	Islamism	Sunni
Free Lebanese Armenian Movement	Harakit Al-Lubnaniyin Al-Arman Al-Ahrar حركة اللبنانيين الأرمن الأحرار	FLAM	-	Liberalism	Armenian Secular
Free Shia Movement	Tayyar el-Shii el-Horr التيار الشيعي الحر	TSH	Mohammad el Hajj Hassan	Islamism	Shia
Lebanese Peace Party	Hizb Assalam Al-Lubnany حزب السلام اللبناني	LPP	Roger Eddy	-	Secular
Shuraya Party	Hizb Al-Shuraya	-	-	Assyrianism	Assyrian

Parties Associated with March 8 Coalition (2009)					
Hezbollah	*Hezbollah* حزب الله	HA	Hassan Nassrallah	Islamism	Shia
El Marada	*Tayyar Al-Marada* تيار المردة	MM	Suleiman Frangieh, Jr.	Pesonalized/Liberal	Maronite
Amal Movement	*Harakat Amal* حركة أمل	AMAL	Nabih Berri	Moderate Islam	Shia
Free Patriotic Movement	*Tayyar Al-Watani Al-Horr* التيار الوطني الحر	FPM	Michel Aoun	Centrist	Mixed Christians
Syrian Social Nationalist Party	*al-Hizb al-Quami al-Ijtima'i al-Suri* الحزب القومي السوري الإجتماعي	SSNP	Asaad Hardan	Syrian Nationalism	Secular
Ba'ath Arab Socialist Party	*Hizb al-baas al-arabi al-'ishtiraki* حزب البعث العربي الإشتراكي	BAATH	Assem Qanso	Socialism; Arab Nationalism	secular
التكتل الشعبي	–	Elias Skaff	Elias Skaff	Personal/Liberal	Greek Catholic
Armenian Revolutionary Federation	*Tashnag* حزب الطشنق	ARF	Hovig Mkhitarian	Socialism-Democracy-Nationalism	Armenian-Secular
Lebanese Democratic Party	*Hizb al-lubnany al-democraty* الحزب اللبناني الديمقراطي	LDP	Talal Arslan	Personal/Liberal	Druze
Popular Nasserite Organization	*Al-Tanzim Al-shaabi al-nassiri* التنظيم الشعبي الناصري	NPO	Ossama Saad	Nasserism; Socialism; Arab nationalism	sunni
Lebanese Communist Party	*Al-Hizb al-shooyoo'i al-lubnany* الحزب الشيوعي اللبناني	LCP	Khaled Hadadi	Communism	Secular
Arab Liberation Party	*Hizb Al-Taharor Al-Arabi* حزب التحرر العربي	ALP	Omar Karami	Personal/Liberal	Sunni
Worker's League	*Rabitat Al-Shaghila* رابطة الشغيلة	WL	Zaher Khatib	Communist; Arab Nationalism	Secular
People's Movement	*Harakat Al-Shaab* حركة الشعب	SHAAB	Najah Wakim	Nasserism; Socialism; Arab Nationalism	Secular
Islamic Labor Front	*Jebhat Al-Aamal Al-islamy*	–	Fathi Yakan	Islamism	Sunni
Lebanese Unification Movement	*Tayyar Al-Tawhid Al-Lubnany* تيار التوحيد اللبناني	UC	Wiam Wahhab	Arab Nationalism	Druze
Lebanese Popular Congress	*Mo'tamar Al-Shaabi Al-Lubnany* المؤتمر الشعبي اللبناني	LPC	Kamal Chatila	Nasserism	Sunni
Arab Democratic Party	*Al-Hizb Al-Aarabi Al-Democraty* الحزب العربي الدمقراطي	ADP	Ali Eid	Personal/Syrian	Alawite
Islamic Charitable Projects Association	*Jam'iyat Al-mashari' Al-Khayriya Al-Islamiya Al-Ahbash* الأحباش	ICPA	Abdallah al-Harari	Islamism	Sunni
Union Party	*Hizb al-Ittihad* حزب الإتحاد	UP	Abelrahim Mrad	Nasserism	Sunni
Union of Muslim Ulama	*Tajamo' Al-ulama Al-Muslimun* تجمع العلماء المسلمون	UMU	–	Islamism	Mostly Sunni
Islamic Unification Movement	*Harakat Al-Tawhid Al-Islamy* حركة التوحيد الإسلامي	IUM	Said Shaaban	Islamism	Sunni
National Dialogue Party	*Hizb Al-Hiwar Al-Watani* حزب الحوار الوطني	NDP	Fuad Makhzoumi	Capitalism	Sunni

Glossary of key terms and concepts

1960 Electoral Law   The parties agreed to base the 2009 parliamentary elections on the Lebanon's 1960 electoral law, which takes into account smaller voting constituencies as the finest way to guarantee democratic representation in parliament, including the division of Beirut into three electoral constituencies.

al Assad, Hafez (1930–2000)   President of Syria from 1971 to 2000.

al-Hariri, Rafik   Prime Minister of Lebanon from 1992 to 1998 and again from 2000 until his resignation on October 20, 2004. He headed five cabinets during his tenure. Hariri was assassinated on February 14, 2005.

al-Hoss, Selim   A Prime Minister of Lebanon and a long-time Member of Parliament representing his hometown, Beirut.

Amal Movement   Founded in 1975 as the militia wing of the Movement of the Disinherited, a Shi'a political movement founded by Musa al-Sadr and Hussein el-Husseini a year earlier. It became one of the most important Shi'a Muslim militias during the Lebanese civil war.

Amnesty Law   An amnesty law for crimes perpetrated before March 28, 1991, was enacted in 1991 after which the militias (with the important exception of Hezbollah) were dissolved, and the Lebanese Armed Forces began to slowly rebuild themselves as Lebanon's only major non-sectarian institution.

Aoun, Michel   A Lebanese politician and former military commander. From September 22, 1988, to October 13, 1990, he served as Prime Minister and acting President of one of two rival governments that contended for power. He was defeated by Syria in the war of liberation and forced into exile. He returned to Lebanon on May 7, 2005.

Arab Deterrent Force   An intervention force composed almost entirely of Syrian forces, with token contributions from other Arab states, including Saudi Arabia and Libya.

Arab League   A regional organization of Arab states in North and Northeast Africa, and Southwest Asia. It was formed in Cairo on March 22, 1945, with six members: Egypt, Iraq, Jordan, Lebanon, Saudi Arabia, and Syria. Yemen joined in 1945. It currently has 22 members and four observers.

Arab Spring   The term used to describe the various revolutions and protest movements that erupted in several Arab countries against autocracy and corruption in 2011–2012.

Arafat, Yasser (1929–2004)   Chairman of the Palestine Liberation Organization, President of the Palestinian National Authority, and leader of the Fatah political party, which he founded in 1959. Many believe his death was the result of an Israeli covert operation, which led to his poisoning.

auspices   Patronage or guidance.

autocratic leadership   A system in which a single absolute figure is placed as a head of state without being subject to a transparent election or oversight. The entire state becomes subject to his decisions.

autonomous rights   Power decentralized to grant different groups ability to have self-rights that cannot be infringed upon by others.

autonomy politics   Politics is centered about groups struggling to self-rule and decentralized power.

Ayatollah Khomeini   The founder and supreme leader of the Islamic Republic of Iran. In 1979, he proclaimed political and religious authority as a head of state.

Ba'ath Party   A secularist Arab nationalism/Pan-Arabism political party opposed to Western imperialism and calling for the "renaissance" or "resurrection" of the Arab World and its unity as one united state.

Baghdad Pact   Defense pact involving Middle Eastern countries, from 1954 until 1979. It is also known as the Central Treaty Organization, and involved cooperation for security and defense and refraining from any form of interference in internal affairs.

balance of power   A balance of power exists when there is parity or stability between competing forces.

bar association   A professional body of lawyers. Some bar associations are responsible for the regulation of the legal profession in their jurisdiction; others are professional organizations dedicated to serving their members – in many cases, they are both.

bicameralism   The division of the legislative branch into two chambers, usually one based on popular election and the other based on regional or local election.

bloc vote   A voting system used in multi-member constituencies where voters can elect more than one representative in each constituency.

bipolar world system   A distribution of power in which two states have the majority of economic, military, and cultural influence internationally or regionally.

body politic   The people of a politically organized nation or state considered as a group.

census   The procedure of systematically acquiring and recording information about the members of a given population. It is a regularly occurring and official count of a particular population.

centrifugal party politics   Party competition is primarily about winning centrist-leaning population.

Chamber of Deputies   The name given to a legislative body such as the lower house of a bicameral legislature, or can refer to a unicameral legislature.

Chamoun, Camille   President of Lebanon from 1952 to 1958 and one of the country's main Christian leaders during most of the Lebanese Civil War (1975–1990).

Chehab, Fuad   President of the Lebanese Republic from 1958 to 1964. His mandate was one of the most distinguished in Lebanon's history, owing to the important reforms and large-scale social development projects that he introduced and initiated, bringing harmony and prosperity to the country.

Civil Campaign for Electoral Reform   A coalition of 66 Lebanese civil society organizations and two coalitions of non-governmental organizations that was launched in 2006 to advocate for the reform of electoral systems in Lebanon, particularly the parliamentary and municipal elections.

cleavage   The different traits that can be attributed to the same population.

clientelistic   The exchange of votes for favors, over a long period of time, among actors with asymmetric power, the clients having little power. Politicians would reward a portion of their supporters with public resources in return for electoral support.

collective security   The cooperation between various groups to achieve common security against external or domestic threat.

communal solidarism   A shared attitude to outsiders.

confessionalism   A system of government that distributes political and institutional power proportionally among religious communities.

consensus president   President agreed upon by all Lebanese parties. The Doha Agreement designated the appointment of Michel Suleiman as the candidate to be elected for the seat of Lebanon's consensus president.

conspiracy   A plot made between a group of people, organizations, or countries to achieve a particular purpose of committing an illegal act.

corporatism   A system of economic, political, or social organization that views a community as a body based upon organic social solidarity and functional distinction and roles amongst individuals.

Damour massacre   Took place on January 20, 1976, during the Lebanese Civil War. The Christian town on the main highway south of Beirut was attacked by Palestine Liberation Organization units. Part of its population was killed in the battle or massacred afterwards, and the remainder forced to flee.

decree   A regulation like law that is passed by higher assembly or head of state.

Doha Agreement   Reached by rival Lebanese factions on Wednesday, May 21, 2008. It marked the end of an 18-month political crisis. After battles broke out in Lebanon because of the ongoing political crisis, Qatar's prince Sheikh Hamad bin Khalifa Al Thani invited all Lebanese political parties to Doha to seek an agreement to end the ongoing political crisis and avoid an eventual civil war.

Eastern Question   Encompasses the diplomatic and political problems posed by the disintegration of the Ottoman Empire in the eighteenth, nineteenth, and twentieth centuries.

Egyptian–Israeli Peace Treaty (1979)   The main features of the treaty were the mutual recognition of each country by the other, the cessation of the state of war that had existed since the 1948 Arab-Israeli War, and the complete withdrawal by Israel of its armed forces and civilians from the rest of the Sinai Peninsula, which Israel had captured during the Six-day War in 1967. Signed in Washington, DC on March 26, 1979, following the 1978 Camp David Accords, by Egyptian President Anwar El Sadat, and Israeli Prime Minister Menachem Begin, and witnessed by US President Jimmy Carter.

electoral system   A method by which voters make a choice between options, often in an election or on a policy referendum.

elite cartels   Elite groups coordinate together ways and means to preserve their power.

exceptionalism   Generally used to refer to absent socialist political tradition in the United States of America. It has then been used to describe political phenomenon that have not been explainable by traditional theories, such as the absence of democratic transformations in the Arab world.

executive branch   The government bureaucracy responsible over the implementation of the laws.

Fifth Republic of France   A semi-presidential system introduced in France in 1958. Both the president and the prime minister share significant powers in this system.

financial autonomy   The ability to have the power to make local decisions regarding financial income and expenditures.

first-past-the-post   A system for choosing members of parliament or other representatives in which the candidate who gets the most votes wins.

Francophone   French-speaking individuals, groups, places, or countries directly or indirectly subjugated to French rule.

Free Patriotic Movement   A political party, led by Michel Aoun, former commander of the Lebanese army, who served as a transitory Prime Minister of one of two governments that contended for power in the final years of the Lebanese civil war (1988–1990). The movement was officially declared a political party on September 18, 2005.

French Mandate   The territories of modern Lebanon and Syria were mandated to French rule by the League of Nations following the end of World War I.

gentlemen's agreement   An unwritten agreement or transaction backed only by the integrity of the counterparty to actually abide by the terms of the agreement. It is not legally binding and could have a negative effect on business relationships if one party decides to default on their promise.

gerrymandering   A form of boundary delimitation (redistricting) in which electoral district or constituency boundaries are deliberately modified for electoral purposes, thereby producing secured electoral outcomes in favor of one party. Also, the division of a state or a country into election districts so as to give one political party a majority in many districts while concentrating the voting strength of the other party into as few districts as possible.

grade-one public employees   These include the president, ministers, all members of parliament, ministerial directors, ambassadors, higher judges, head of army, and other high post public administrations, such as the president of the public university and national councils.

Greater Lebanon   The political territory that constitutes modern Lebanon.

Greater Middle East   A political term coined by the Bush administration to group together various countries pertaining to the Muslim world, specifically Iran, Turkey, Afghanistan, and Pakistan. Various Central Asian countries and the lower Caucasus (Azerbaijan, Armenia, and Georgia), and Cyprus are sometimes also included.

Green Line   A line of demarcation in Beirut during the Lebanese civil war from 1975 to 1990. It separated the mainly Muslim factions in West Beirut from the Christian Lebanese Front in East Beirut.

Gulf Crisis (1990)   The final conflict, which was initiated with United Nations authorization by a coalition force from 34 nations against Iraq, with the expressed purpose of expelling Iraqi forces from Kuwait after its invasion and annexation on August 2, 1990.

hegemony   The political, economic, ideological, or cultural power exerted by a dominant group over other groups, regardless of the explicit consent of the latter.

Hezbollah   A Shi'a Islamist political and paramilitary organization based in Lebanon. It is now also a major provider of social services, operating schools, hospitals, and agricultural services for thousands of Lebanese Shias, and playing a significant force in Lebanese politics. It is regarded as a resistance movement throughout much of the Arab and Muslim world.

history of inter-sectarian grievances   Persistent shared feeling among the group of deprivation from having equal justice, rights, opportunities, proper respect, safety, or some other form of social good.

homogeneous society   A society where most of the people share the same type of cultural values, language, ethnicity and religious system.

ideological platforms   A set of policy objectives that a political group seeks to achieve.

Inaugurated   Elected president is formally declared head of state after an official ceremony.

interlocutors   Groups that informally explain the views of the government and can also relay messages back to the government.

institutionalization   To be institutionalized is to be embedded within an organization, social system, or society, as an established norm within that system.

Israeli Defense Force   The overall unified armed forces of Israel, consisting of the ground forces, airforce and navy.

Jemayel, Pierre   Founder of the Kataab Party (also known as the Phalangist Party), as a parliamentary powerbroker, and as the father of Bashir Jemayel and Amine Jemayel, both of whom were elected to the Presidency of the Republic in his lifetime.

judiciary   The court system in a country that preserves the legal foundation and application of the law.

jurisdiction   Authority granted to a legal body or to a political leader to deal with and make pronouncements on legal matters and, by implication, to administer justice within a defined area of responsibility.

Kanaan, Ghazi (1942–12 October 2005)   Also known as Abu Yo'roub. Syria's Interior Minister 2004–2005, and long-time head of Syria's security apparatus in Lebanon. His violent death during an investigation into the assassination of Rafik Hariri drew international attention.

Karami, Omar   Prime Minister of Lebanon on two separate occasions. He was Prime Minister for the first time from 24 December 1990 until 13 May 1992 and again in 1994–1995.

Karami, Rashid   A Lebanese statesman. He was one of the most important political figures in Lebanon for more than 30 years, including during much of Lebanese Civil War (1975–1990), and he served as Prime Minister eight times.

League of Nations   The international organization of post-World War I states, established for the furtherance of cooperation among nations, the settlement of international disputes, and the preservation of the peace.

Lebanese–Israeli Agreement   A failed US-backed attempt to create peace between Lebanon and Israel during the Lebanese Civil War, after Israel invaded Lebanon and besieged Beirut in 1982.

legislative branch   The government assembly that makes laws and set policies.

levies   Imposed or collected taxes.

Likud   The major center-right political party in Israel. It was founded in 1973 by Menachem Begin in an alliance with several right-wing and liberal parties.

majoritarian electoral system   A system which is based on a "winner takes all" principle. This is in contrast to the proportional representation family of electoral systems, which split the mandates in rough proportion with votes gained by each party.

March 8 Alliance   A coalition of various political parties in Lebanon. The Alliance formed the opposition to the Saniora's majority March 14 government. The Alliance has been generally regarded as a pro-Syrian Hezbollah-led group.

March 14 Alliance   Named after the date of the Cedar Revolution, a coalition of political parties and independents in Lebanon that called for sovereignty over all Lebanese territories, led by Member of Paliament Saad Hariri, son of the slain Rafik Hariri, as well as other figures such as Samir Geagea, head of the Lebanese Forces.

Moawad, Rene   President of Lebanon for 17 days in 1989, from November 5 to 22, when he was assassinated by unknown persons.

Mubarak, Hosni   A former Egyptian politician, dictator and military commander. He served as the fourth President of Egypt from 1981 to 2011. He was overthrown after a popular rebellion that swept many Arab countries and came to be widely known as the Arab Spring.

multi-polar system   A distribution of power in which more than two nation-states have nearly equal amounts of military, cultural, and economic influence.

Muslim Brotherhood A Sunni transnational movement and the largest political opposition organization in many Arab states. The world's oldest and largest Islamic political group, it was founded in 1928 in Egypt by school teacher Hassan al-Banna. The group won election in Egypt after its Arab Spring Revolution and took on the Presidency.

Nasser, Jamal Abdel (1918–1970) Elected Egyptian President in 1954, he was a pivotal figure in the recent history of the Middle East, and played a highly prominent role in the 1956 Suez crisis. Nasser has been described as the first leader of an Arab nation who challenged what was perceived as the Western dominance of the Middle East.

national identity The cultural and political traits by which a national group distinguishes itself from others.

National Pact An unwritten agreement that laid the foundation of Lebanon as a multi-confessional state. Following negotiations between the Shia, Sunni, and Maronite leaderships, the 1943 National Pact allowed the various sects to share power of key political posts.

nationhood The essence of which a group of people seeks to live together on a territory with shared and common bonds.

National Pact An unwritten agreement which laid the foundation of Lebanon as a multi-confessional state, and has shaped the country to this day. Following negotiations between the Shi'ite, Sunni, and Maronite leaderships, the National Pact was born in the summer of 1943, allowing Lebanon to be independent.

national unity cabinet An oversized government coalition which includes most political parliamentary political blocs, including both the minority and majorities. Such cabinets are typically formed in time of national crises, where the country is confronting common threats, which could be either external, internal, or both.

naturalization of Palestinians To grant full citizenship to the Palestinians.

nepotistic networks A group of close associates who provides its members an exchange system of benefits and favors.

obstructional/guaranteeing third Share of seats granted to the March 8 coalition in the Doha Agreement, which gave the opposition "veto power" in cabinet decisions.

Official Gazette A public journal that publishes all approved government announcements.

Operation Blue Bat US military operation with the purpose to bolster the pro-Western Lebanese government of President Chamoun against internal opposition and threats from Syria and the United Arab Republic.

Operation Litany An invasion in Lebanon up to the Litany River carried out by the Israel Defense Forces in 1978. It was a military success for the Israeli Defense Forces, as the Palestine Liberation Organization forces were pushed north of the river.

Organic Laws for Lebanon (1861) Forced by the interference of the major European powers, the Ottoman Empire granted autonomy to Mount Lebanon in these laws.

Ottoman feudal system   A production system with land rent, by means of which most of those who take part in production, such as peasants, are exploited. The feudal classes, those who possess the right to dispose of arable land, lease a plot of land to the peasant and claim in return a share of the gain.

Palestine Liberation Organization   Umbrella political organization claiming to represent the world's Palestinians. It was formed in 1964 to centralize the leadership of various Palestinian groups that previously had operated as clandestine resistance movements.

Palestinian Intifada (First, 1987–1993)   Palestinian uprising against Israeli occupation in the Palestinian Territories. Actions primarily included nonviolent civil disobedience and resistance movement, in addition to violent actions.

Pan-Arabism   The concept that all Arabs form one nation and should be politically united in one Arab state. Espouses Arab unification and advocates close cooperation and solidarity against perceived enemies of the Arabs.

pardon   Forgiveness of a crime and the cancellation of the relevant penalty granted by the President.

patrimonial relationship   Associated with the relations that govern the behaviors between a person in a position of power who provides benefits for another in return for loyalty.

patriotism   A devotion to one's country.

Phalangists   The Lebanese Social Democratic Party – better known in English as the Phalange – is a right-wing Lebanese political party. The party played a major role in the Lebanese War (1975–1990). In decline in the late 1980s and 1990s, the party slowly re-emerged in the early 2000s.

policy agenda   A list of subjects or problems to which people inside and outside government are paying serious attention to at any given time.

policy guidelines   Government policy goals that intends to achieve during its term in office. Some times referred to policy statements which must be approved by parliament during a vote of confidence.

political feudalism   An analogy used to describe the relationship between political leaders and subject loyalists in close similarity to that of landlords and peasants.

political Zionism   Political Zionism stressed the importance of political action, and deemed the attainment of political rights in Palestine a prerequisite for the fulfilment of the Zionist enterprise. Political Zionism is linked to Theodor Herzl, who considered the Jewish problem to be a political one that should be solved by overt action in the international arena.

Popular Front for the Liberation of Palestine   A secular, nationalist Palestinian political and paramilitary organization, founded in 1967. It has consistently been the second largest of the groups forming the Palestine Liberation Organization, the largest being Fatah.

power sharing   The way in which power is allocated and distributed among different groups within a government.

presidential system   A system of government where the president is usually elected directly by popular vote and presides over a cabinet of his choosing with extended power and authority.

Progressive Socialist Party   Founded in 1949 by members of various sects who were proponents of social reform and progressive change, the party flourished under the leadership of Kamal Jumblatt, a charismatic, albeit somewhat enigmatic, character. By the early 1950s, the party began taking on a confessional cast. By the 1970s, this tendency was unmistakably Druze.

protection racket   An extortion scheme whereby a criminal group or individual coerces other less-powerful entities to pay money, allegedly for protection services against external threats (usually violence or property damage, and sometimes perpetrated by the racketeers themselves).

proportional representation   A family of electoral systems which split the mandates in rough proportion with votes gained by each party.

Quornat Shehwan Gathering   A loose coalition of political organizations, comprising politicians, independent politicians, intellectuals, and businessmen, mostly Christians. The most important participating political parties were the Lebanese Forces and the Free Patriotic Movement.

Rejectionist Front   A hardline coalition formed in 1974 by radical Palestinian factions who rejected the Ten-point Program adopted by the Palestine Liberation Organization in its 12th Palestinian National Congress session. It opposed any concessions that would have prepared for negotiation with Israel on the grounds of a two-state solution.

rogue state   A controversial term applied by some international theorists to states they consider threatening to the world's peace. This means meeting certain criteria, such as being ruled by authoritarian regimes that severely restrict human rights, sponsor terrorism, and seek to proliferate weapons of mass destruction.

Saddam Hussein   The fifth President of Iraq, serving in this capacity from July 16, 1979 until April 9, 2003. He was overthrown by international forces led by the United States during what came to be known as the Second Gulf War (2003).

San Remo Conference (1920)   An international meeting of the post-World War I Allied Supreme Council, held in San Remo, Italy, April 9–26, 1920. It was attended by the four principal Allied Powers of World War I: Britain, France, Italy, and Japan. It determined the allocation of "class-A" League of Nations mandates for administration of the former Ottoman-ruled lands of the Middle East.

secular   Of or pertaining to worldly things or to things that are not regarded as religious, spiritual, or sacred; temporal: secular interests.

Senate   A senate is a deliberative assembly, often the upper house or chamber of a legislature or parliament.

single-party government   Government or cabinet or council of ministers that is formed and controlled by a single political party.

Six-day War   War fought June 5–10, 1967, between Israel and the neighboring states of Egypt, Jordan, and Syria. Israel emerged victorious and gained control of the Sinai Peninsula, the Gaza Strip, the West Bank, East Jerusalem, and the Golan Heights.

state-centric   An international relations approach that considers that politics revolves around the interests and power aspirations of the nation state.

statute   A formal written enactment of a legislative authority that governs a state, city or county. Typically, statutes command or prohibit something, or declare policy. As a source of law, statutes are considered primary authority (as opposed to secondary authority).

Suez crisis   A war fought by Britain, France, and Israel against Egypt beginning on October 29, 1956. The attack followed Egypt's decision of July 26, 1956, to nationalize the Suez Canal, and resulted in an Israeli military victory and occupation of the Sinai until 1957, but a political victory for Egypt because the British and French had to relinquish their control of the Suez Canal.

Sykes-Picot Agreement (1916)   A secret agreement between the governments of the UK and France, with the assent of Imperial Russia, defining their respective spheres of influence and control in Western Asia after the expected downfall of the Ottoman Empire during World War I.

Technocratic   Technocracy is a form of government in which experts in specialists in their own ministerial portfolios would be in control of all decision making.

Third Republic of France   A republican parliamentary democracy created on September 4, 1870, following the collapse of the Empire of Napoleon III in the Franco-Prussian War. It survived until the invasion of France by the German Third Reich in 1940.

trifecta   A system of betting in which the bettor must pick the first three winners in the correct sequence.

Tripartite Agreement (1985)   Provided for an immediate ceasefire and an official proclamation of the end of the state of civil war within one year. The militias would be disarmed and then disbanded, and sole responsibility for security would be relegated to the reconstituted and religiously integrated Lebanese Army, supported by Syrian forces.

troika   Any group of three persons, communities, nations, etc., acting equally in union to exert influence, control, or the like.

unicameral assembly   A one legislative or parliamentary chamber.

unipolar international system   Unipolarity in international politics is a distribution of power in which one state exercises most of the cultural, economic, and military influence.

United Arab Republic   A union between Egypt and Syria. The union began in 1958, and existed until 1961 when Syria seceded from the union. Egypt continued to be known officially as the "United Arab Republic" until 1971.

United Nations Interim Force in Lebanon   Created by the United Nations, with the adoption of Security Council Resolutions 425 and 426 on March 19, 1978, to confirm Israeli withdrawal from Lebanon, restore international peace and security, and help the government of Lebanon to restore its effective authority in the area.

universal suffrage   Consists of the extension of the right to vote to all adult citizens.

urbanization   Refers to a process in which an increasing proportion of an entire population lives in cities and the suburbs of cities.

veto power   The power or right vested in a group or a branch of government to cancel or postpone the political decisions.

Vichy Government   The right-wing government of unoccupied France after the country's defeat by the Germans in June 1940, named after the spa town of Vichy, France, where the national assembly was based under Prime Minister Pétain until the country's liberation in 1944.

War of Attrition   A military strategy in which a belligerent side attempts to win a war by wearing down its enemy to the point of collapse through continuous losses in personnel and equipment.

War of Liberation   On March 14, 1989, after a Syrian attack on the Baabda presidential palace and on the Lebanese Ministry of Defense in Yarze, Aoun declared a liberation war against the Syrian army, which was better armed than the Lebanese Forces.

Zine El Abidine Ben Ali   A Tunisian political figure who was the second President of Tunisia from 1987 to 2011. He was overthrown after a popular rebellion that swept many Arab countries and came to be widely known as the Arab Spring.

Zuama **clientelism**   (*zuama*) A *zaim* is a political leader, and rather than being exclusively an officeholder, he may be a power broker with the ability to manipulate elections and the officials he helps elect. Accordingly, *wastah* – the ability to attain access to a power broker – is widely sought, but only achieved at some price.

Further reading

Chapter 1

Diamond, L. (1999) *Developing Democracy*. Baltimore: Johns Hopkins University Press.
Duverger, M. (1954) *Political Parties*. New York: Wiley.
Horowitz, D. (1993) 'Democracy in Divided Societies', *Journal of Democracy*, 4 (4): 221–43.
Lijphart, A. (1985) 'Non-Majoritarian Democracy: A Comparison of Federal and Consociational Theories', *Journal of Federalism*, 15(2), pp. 3–15.
Lijphart, A. (2004) 'Constitutional Design for Divided Societies', *Journal of Democracy*, 15 (2): 96–109.
Lijphart, A. (2008) *Thinking about Democracy: Power Sharing and Majority Rule in Theory and Practice*. Abingdon: Routledge.
O'Leary, B. (2005) 'Debating Consociational Politics: Normative and Explanatory Arguments' in Noel, S. (ed.) *From Power Sharing to Democracy: Post-Conflict Institutions in Ethnically Divided Societies*. Montreal: McGill-Queen's Press, pp. 1–43.

Helpful websites

Democracy Building: www.democracy-building.info/index.html
International Foundation for Election Systems: http://www.ifes.org/
Lijphart's Election Archive (UC San Diego): http://libraries.ucsd.edu/locations/sshl/data-gov-info-gis/ssds/guides/lij/
Parliamentary democracy data archive: www.erdda.se/

Chapter 2

Boueiz Kanaan, C. (2005) *Lebanon 1860–1960*. London: Saqi.
Hemsley Longrigg, S. (1972) *Syria and Lebanon Under French Mandate*. New York: Octagon Books.
Hitti, P. K. (1957) *Lebanon in History: From the Earliest Times to the Present*. London: Macmillan.
Salibi, K. (2003) *House of Many Mansions: The History of Lebanon Reconsidered*. London: Tauris.
Shehadi, N. and Haffar Mills, D. (1988) *Lebanon: A History of Conflict and Consensus*. London: Tauris.

Spagnolo, J. P. (1971) 'Constitutional Change in Mount Lebanon: 1861–1864', *Middle Eastern Studies*, 7 (1): 25–48.
Spagnolo, J. P. (1971) 'Mount Lebanon, France and Daud Pasha. A Study of Some Aspects of Political Habituation', *International Journal of Middle East Studies*, 2 (2): 148–67.

Helpful websites

International Boundary Study – US Department of State: http://www.law.fsu.edu/library/collection/LimitsinSeas/IBS094.pdf
Proportional Representation Voting Systems: www.mtholyoke.edu/acad/polit/damy/BeginnningReading/PRsystems.htm
The League of Nations, Russia News Network: www.russiannewsnetwork.com/leaguenations.html
The Library of Congress Federal Research Division. Country Studies. A Country Study: Lebanon: http://lcweb2.loc.gov/frd/cs/lbtoc.html

Chapter 3

Farha, M. (2008) 'Demography and Democracy in Lebanon', *Mideast Monitor*, 3 (1). Available online at www.globalpolitician.com/24382-lebanon
Messara, A. N. (1988) 'Partage du Pouvoir: Le Cas de Liban' in *Lebanon: A History of Conflict and Consensus*, in N. Shehadi and D. H. Mills, eds. London: I. B. Tauris, pp. 240–57.

Helpful websites

Images of Greater Lebanon (Google image search): https://www.google.com/search?q=Greater+Lebanon&hl=en&tbo=u&rls=com.microsoft:en-us&rlz=1I7SKPT_enLB432&tbm=isch&source=univ&sa=X&ei=ORilULjYLsmc0QXtq4CoAg&ved=0CFMQsAQ&biw=1067&bih=511
Lebanon – Religious Sects. Global Security: www.globalsecurity.org/military/world/lebanon/religious-sects.htm
Lebanon's History, ed. T. Costello (1987). Ayman Ghazi: www.ghazi.de/french.html
The Lebanese Constitution, Republic of Lebanon Ministry of Information: www.ministryinfo.gov.lb/en/sub/Lebanon/LebaneseConstitution.aspx

Chapter 4

Agwani, M. (1965) *The Lebanese Crisis, 1958: A Documentary Study*. London: Asia Publishing House.
Douglas, L. (1996) 'His Finest Hour? Eisenhower, Lebanon, and the 1958 Middle East Crisis', *Diplomatic History*, 20 (1): 27–54.
Fisk, R. (2001) *Pity the Nation: Lebanon at War*. Oxford: Oxford University Press.
O'Ballance, E. (1998) *Civil War in Lebanon, 1975–92*. London: Palgrave Macmillan.
Rabinovich, I. (1984) *The War for Lebanon, 1970–1985*. New York: Cornell University Press, pp. 233–50.
Salameh, G. (1993) 'Independence: Fifty Years Later, How "National" is Independence?', *Beirut Review*, (6): 1–5.

Theodor, H. (1993) *Coexistence in Wartime Lebanon: Decline of a State and Rise of a Nation*. Translated from German by J. Richardson. London: The Center for Lebanese Studies, in association with Tauris, p. 728.

Winslow, C. (1996) *Lebanon: War and Politics in a Fragmented Society*. Abingdon: Routledge.

Helpful websites

Lebanon (Civil War 1975–1991), Global Security: www.globalsecurity.org/military/world/war/lebanon.htm

Lebanon's History: Civil War, Ayman Ghazi: www.ghazi.de/civwar.html

Krayem, H. The Lebanese Civil War and the Taef Agreement, Digital Documentation Center at AUB in collaboration with Al Mashriq of Høgskolen i Østfold, Norway: http://ddc.aub.edu.lb/projects/pspa/conflict-resolution.html

Eclipsed Lebanon, Pity the Nation – Charles Glass's Lebanon, Part 01 (video by Charles Glass): www.youtube.com/watch?v=V4HC6Fss8PM&feature=relmfu

Chapter 5

Ghosn, F. and Khoury, A. (2011) 'Lebanon After the Civil War: Peace or the Illusion of Peace?', *Middle East Journal*, 65(3): 381–97.

Pakradoni, K. (2009) *Sadma wa Sumud: 'Ahd Emile Lahoud, 1998–2007* [Shock and Endurance: The Era of Emile Lahoud, 1998–2007]. Beirut: Sharika al-Matbou'at lil Tawzee' wa al-Nashr [Arabic].

Salam, N. (2004) *Options for Lebanon*. Beirut: Al-Nahar Publishing [Arabic].

Takieddine, R. (2009) 'The International Tribunal and the Fourth Anniversary of the Hariri Assassination', *Al Arabiya News*, February 11. Available online at www.alarabiya.net/views/2009/02/11/66270.html (accessed March 28, 2013).

Useful websites

Tristam, P. (2005) 'Timeline: Events Surrounding Lebanon's Rafik Hariri's Assassination', About.com Middle East Issues: http://middleeast.about.com/od/lebanon/a/me090203a.htm

The Ta'if Accord (2009): www.al-bab.com/arab/docs/lebanon/taif.htm

Chapter 6

Christoff, S. (2008) 'Karim Makdisi Discusses the Doha Agreement and Lebanon's Economic Crisis', *The Electronic Intifada*. Available online at http://electronicintifada.net/content/karim-makdisi-discusses-doha-agreement-and-lebanons-economic-crisis/7554 (accessed March 28, 2013).

Daaboul, C. (2008) *The Doha Agreement, Lebanon and the Near Future of the Near East*. Paris: European Union Institute for Security Studies. Available online at www.iss.europa.eu/publications/detail/article/the-doha-agreement-lebanon-and-the-near-future-of-the-near-east/ (accessed March 28, 2013).

Lebanese Foundation for Civil Peace (2009) *Doha Agreement: Building a Culture of Pacts in Lebanon for Effective Citizenship*. Beirut: Librarie Orientale.

Schenker, D. (2008) *Lebanese Crisis Ends: Hizballah Victory or Temporary Truce?* Policy Watch 1375. Washington DC: Washington Institute for Near East Policy. Available online at www.washingtoninstitute.org/policy-analysis/view/lebanese-crisis-ends-hizballah-victory-or-temporary-truce (accessed March 28, 2013).

Stel, N. M. (2009) *Forcing the Lebanese Back to Dialogue.* Master's thesis, Faculty of Humanities, Utrecht University. Available online at http://igitur-archive.library.uu.nl/student-theses/2009-1022-200117/UUindex.html (accessed March 28, 2013).

Helpful website

Full text of Doha agreement, May 23, 2008: www.bloggingbeirut.com/archives/1359-Full-Text-of-Doha-Agreement.html

Chapter 7

Haddad, S. (2000) 'The Palestinian Predicament in Lebanon', *Middle East Quarterly*, 7 (3): 29–40. Available online at www.meforum.org/68/the-palestinian-predicament-in-lebanon (accessed March 28, 2013).

Kerr, M. (2005) *Imposing Power-sharing: Conflict and Coexistence in Northern Ireland and Lebanon.* Dublin; Irish Academic Press.

Krayem, H. (1997) 'The Lebanese Civil War and the Taef Agreement' in P. Salem, *Conflict Resolution in the Arab World: Selected Essays.* Beirut: American University of Beirut.

Helpful websites

Krayem, H. The Lebanese Civil War and the Taef Agreement, Digital Documentation Center at AUB in collaboration with Al Mashriq of Høgskolen i Østfold, Norway: http://ddc.aub.edu.lb/projects/pspa/conflict-resolution.html

Tristam, P. (2005) 'Timeline: Events Surrounding Lebanon's Rafik Hariri's Assassination', About.com Middle East Issues: http://middleeast.about.com/od/lebanon/a/me090203a.htm

Middle East Monitor: www.middleeastmonitor.com/

Chapter 8

Addis, C. L. (2009) *Lebanon: Background and US Relations.* Washington, DC: Congressional Research Service. Available online at http://fpc.state.gov/documents/organization/155577.pdf (accessed March 28, 2013).

Agwani, M. (1965) *The Lebanese Crisis, 1958: A Documentary Study.* London: Asia Publishing House.

Alin, E. G. (1994) *The United States and the 1958 Lebanon Crisis: American Intervention in the Middle East.* Lanham: University Press of America.

Collelo, T. (ed.) (1987) *Lebanon: A Country Study.* Washington: GPO for the Library of Congress. Available online at http://countrystudies.us/lebanon/104.htm (accessed March 28, 2013).

Gerges, F. A. (1993) 'The Lebanese Crisis of 1958: The Risks of Inflated Self-Importance', *Beirut Review*, 5: 83–113.

Lesch, D. (1996) 'Prelude to the 1958 American Intervention in Lebanon', *Mediterranean Quarterly*, 7 (3): 87–108.

Ovendale, R. (1994) 'Great Britain and the Anglo-American Invasion of Jordan and Lebanon in 1958', *International History Review*,16 (2): 284–304.

UN Security Council (2010) *Eleventh Semi-annual Report of the Secretary-General on the Implementation of Security Council Resolution 1559 (2004)*, Document S/2010/193. Geneva: UN, April 19. Available online at www.un.org/ga/search/view_doc.asp?symbol=S/2010/193 (accessed March 28, 2013).

Helpful websites

US Department of State, Bureau of Near Eastern Affairs. *US Relations with Lebanon: Fact Sheet*. www.state.gov/r/pa/ei/bgn/35833.htm

BBC News Middle East (2013) Lebanon Profile: http://news.bbc.co.uk/2/hi/middle_east/country_profiles/819200.stm

United States Army Center of Military History, Contingency Operations. *The Lebanon Operation (15 July – 25 October 1958)*. Historical Manuscript Collection Airborne Operations 2-3.7 AC.F Tab D: www.history.army.mil/documents/AbnOps/TABD.htm.

Chapter 9

El Khazen, F. (2003) 'Political Parties in Postwar Lebanon: Parties in Search of Partisans', *Middle East Journalism*, 57 (4): 605–24.

Salamey, I. (2009) 'Failing Consociationalism in Lebanon and Integrative Options', *International Journal of Peace Studies*, 14 (2): 83–105.

Salamey, I., and Tabar, P. (2012) 'Democratic Transition and Sectarian Populism: The Case of Lebanon', *Contemporary Arab Affairs*, 5 (4): 37–41.

Helpful websites

Civil Campaign for Electoral Reform: www.ccerlebanon.org/

European Union Observation Mission – Lebanon: www.eueomlebanon.org/

International Foundation for Electoral Systems: www.ifes.org

Lebanese Association for Democratic Elections: www.ladeleb.org

Lebanese Association for Electoral Reform: www.lade.org.lb [Arabic]

Lebanese Ministry of Interior and Municipalities: www.moim.gov.lb/ [Arabic]

Lebanese Parliamentary Monitor: www.lpmonitor.org [Arabic]

Chapter 10

Chambers, R. (2008) *Electoral Reform Needs in Lebanon in the light of the Recommendations of the 2005 EU Election Observation Mission*. Paper to the Foreign Affairs Committee of the European Parliament. Available online at www.europarl.europa.eu/meetdocs/2004_2009/documents/dv/270/270620/27062008_policypaper1EN.pdf (accessed April 29, 2013).

Christopher, M. B. (2012) *Lebanon: Background and US Policy*. Report for Congress. Washington, DC: Congressional Research Services. Available online at http://assets.opencrs.com/rpts/R42816_20121106.pdf (accessed April 29, 2013).

Hudson, M. (1976) 'The Lebanese Crisis: The Limits of Consociational Democracy', *Journal of Palestine Studies*, 5 (3/4): 109–22.

Helpful websites

Center for International Development: www.cid.suny.edu/
International Foundation for Electoral Systems: www.ifes.org/countries/Lebanon.aspx
Lebanese Center for Policy Studies: www.lcps-lebanon.org/
Lebanese Parliament official website: www.lp.gov.lb/
Lebanese National Youth Parliament: www.lnyp.org/
Yacoubian, M. (2009) Lebanon's Parliamentary Elections: www.usip.org/publications/the-issues-lebanon
United Nations Development Programme (2009) *Strengthening the Structures of the Lebanese Parliament*: www.undp.org.lb/ProjectFactsheet/projectDetail.cfm?projectId=44

Chapter 11

El-Mikawy, N. and Melim-McLeod, C. (2010) *Lebanon: Local Governance in Complex Environments Project Assessment*. Cairo: UNDP Available online at www.undp.org/content/dam/aplaws/publication/en/publications/democratic-governance/dgttf-/lebanon-promotion-of-decentralization-and-local-governance-an-assessment/DGTTF%20Lebanon.pdf
Lijphart, A. (1992) *Parliamentary Versus Presidential Government*. Oxford: Oxford University Press.

Useful websites

Transparency International: www.transparency.org
Presidency of the Republic of Lebanon. Office of the President: www.presidency.gov.lb/English/ContactPresidentOffice/Pages/default.aspx
Office of the Prime Minister: www.pcm.gov.lb/Cultures/ar-LB/Pages/default.aspx [Arabic]
Link to Ministries: www.informs.gov.lb/informs_ar/Government%20Forms/Ministries/Pages/Home.aspx [Arabic]
Gender Quotas and Parliamentary Representation, El-Helou, ed., *Al-raida*, Summer/Fall (126–127): http://inhouse.lau.edu.lb/iwsaw/raida126-127/EN/p001-105.pdf

Chapter 12

El Samad, F. (2008) 'The Lebanese Legal System and Research', *GlobaLex*. New York: Hauser Global Law School Program. Available online at www.nyulawglobal.org/Globalex/Lebanon.htm (accessed April 29, 2012).
Library of Congress (2012) *Legal Research Guide: Lebanon*. Washington, DC: Library of Congress. Available online at www.loc.gov/law/help/lebanon.php (accessed April 29, 2012).
World Bank (2005) *Lebanon Legal and Judicial Sector Assessment*. Washington, DC: World Bank. Available online at http://documents.worldbank.org/curated/en/2005/01/5749031/lebanon-legal-judicial-sector-assessment

Helpful websites

Directorate General of the Internal Security Forces: www.isf.gov.lb
Lebanese University: www.ul.edu.lb
Lebanon. Answers Corporation: www.answers.com/topic/lebanon
Lebanon Ministry of Justice: www.justice.gov.lb
Lebanon's Government. Travel Blog: www.travelblog.org/Middle-East/Lebanon/fact-gov-lebanon.html
Mattar Law Firm, Judicial Foundation and Legal Codification: www.mattarlaw.com/lebanon-law-lebanon-legal-system.htm
The ICRC in Lebanon: www.icrc.org/eng/where-we-work/middle-east/lebanon/overview-lebanon.htm
The Judicial Branch and Marbury v Madison. Social Studies Help Centre: www.socialstudieshelp.com/USRA_Judiciary.htm
General Security: www.general-security.gov.lb

Chapter 13

Arditi, B. (2005) 'Populism as an Internal Periphery of Democratic Politics' in Panizza, F. *Populism and the Mirror of Democracy*. London: Verso, pp. 72–98.

Brichs, F. I. (2011) *Political Regimes in the Arab World: Society and the Exercise of Power*. Abingdon: Routledge.

Diamond, L. (2010) 'Why Are There No Arab Democracies?' *Journal of Democracy*, 21 (1): 93–104.

Elbadawi, I. and Makdis, S. (2011) *Democracy in the Arab World: Explaining the Deficit*. Abingdon: Routledge.

Hudson, M. C. (1988) 'The Problem of Authoritative Power in Lebanese Politics: Why Consociationalism Failed' in Shehadi, N. and Haffar-Mills, D., eds, *Lebanon: A History of Conflict and Consensus*. London: Centre for Lebanese Studies in assoc. Tauris, pp. 224–39.

Panizza, F. (2005) Introduction: Populism and the Mirror of Democracy in Panizza, F., ed., *Populism and the Mirror of Democracy*. London: Verso , pp.1–31.

Posusney, M. and Angrist, M. (2005) *Authoritarianism in the Middle East: Regimes and Resistance*. Boulder, CO: Lynne Rienner Publishers.

Salamey, I. (2009) 'Failing Consociationalism in Lebanon and Integrative Options', *International Journal of Peace Studies*, 14 (2): 83–105.

Salamey, I. and Pearson, F. (2007) 'Hezbollah: A Proletarian Party with an Islamic Manifesto – A Sociopolitical Analysis of Islamist Populism in Lebanon and the Middle East', *Small Wars and Insurgencies*, 18 (3): 416–38.

Salamey, I. and Tabar, P. (2008) 'Consociational Democracy and Urban Sustainability: Bridging the Confessional Divides in Beirut', *Journal of Ethnopolitics*, 7 (2): 239–63.

Useful websites

Information International: www.information-international.com/info/index.php

Index